Translated Texts for

This series is designed to meet the need: ...medieval history and others who wish to br ....s source material, but whose knowledge ～. ᴜaun or Greek is not sufficient to allow them to do so in the original language. Many important Late Imperial and Dark Age texts are currently unavailable in translation and it is hoped that TTH will help to fill this gap and to complement the secondary literature in English which already exists. The series relates principally to the period 300-800 AD and includes Late Imperial, Greek, Byzantine and Syriac texts as well as source books illustrating a particular period or theme. Each volume is a self-contained scholarly translation with an introductory essay on the text and its author and notes on the text indicating major problems of interpretation, including textual difficulties.

Front cover drawing: A miniature from the Gospels of Beth Zabdai (12th c.)

A full list of published titles in the Translated Texts for Historians series is printed at the end of this book.

The Plate of Perm (6th c.), now in The Hermitage, St Petersburg

Translated Texts for Historians
Volume 22

Pseudo-Dionysius of Tel-Mahre
Chronicle
(known also as the Chronicle of Zuqnin)
Part III

Translated with notes and introduction by
WITOLD WITAKOWSKI

Liverpool
University
Press

First published 1996 by
Liverpool University Press
Senate House, Abercromby Square,
Liverpool, L69 3BX

British Library Cataloguing-in-Publication Data
A British Library CIP Record is available
ISBN 0-85323-760-3

Printed in the European Union by
Redwood Books, Trowbridge, England

CONTENTS

*[Headings in brackets do not appear in the text]

vi

ACKNOWLEDGEMENTS

The present work owes much to Dr Sebastian P. Brock, who first suggested that I might undertake an English translation of the *Chronicle* of Ps.-Dionysius. His generous help, extending to both the translation and the commentary, exceeded by far what may be regarded as the duty of the Syriac specialist of *Translated Texts for Historians*.

To Dr Mary Whitby (Royal Holloway, London) and Professor Michael Whitby (University of Warwick) I am grateful for many suggestions towards the expansion of the commentary. Although I found myself unable to achieve the high standard established by their own contribution to the present series, I am sure the readers of the translation will benefit from these additions as the translator did himself.

My thanks and warm memories go to the late *Malfono* Asmar el-Khouri whose advice and suggestions at an earlier stage of my work with the text of the *Chronicle* helped to solve many textual problems and saved me from some pitfalls, especially where the Syriac text itself needed emendation.

For similar help I am also indebted to FK Aziz Tezel, Uppsala, who kindly responded to all my questions connected with the Syriac text.

I have benefited as well from remarks and suggestions by Dr Jan van Ginkel, Groningen, who has made a Dutch translation of this text for his own research.

Also my thanks go to Mr Stephen Coombs, Stockholm, who spared no pains to correct my English, necessarily influenced by Ps.-Dionysius' style, making the *Chronicle* more palatable to an English reader.

Dr Mary Whitby in her capacity of editor of the TTH series was most helpful in dealing with all editorial and practical problems. I am indebted to Robin Bloxsidge and his staff at LUP for patiently solving many technical problems and producing camera ready copy.

I gratefully acknowledge the financial help of the Swedish Council of Research in Humanities and Social Sciences (HSFR), which made this project of translation possible.

BIBLIOGRAPHY AND ABBREVIATIONS

AANLR - Atti della Accademia Nazionale dei Lincei, Classe di scienze morali, storiche e filologiche: Rendiconti, Rome.

Agathias - *Agathiae Myrinaei Historiarum libri quinque*, ed. R. Keydell, Berlin 1967 (Corpus Fontium Historiae Byzantinae 2); Engl. transl. Agathias, *The Histories*, tr. J. D Frendo, (CFHB 2A), Berlin 1975.

AOCh - Institut français d'études byzantines: Archives de l'Orient chrétien, Paris.

ARALM - Atti della R[eale] Accademia dei Lincei: Classe di scienze morali, storiche e filologiche: Memorie, Rome.

Avi-Yonah, *Jews* - M. Avi-Yonah, *The Jews under Roman and Byzantine Rule: a political history of Palestine from the Bar Kokhba war to the Arab conquest*, Jerusalem 1984 (= Oxford 1976).

BAH - Institut français d'archéologie de Beyrouth: Bibliothèque archéologique et historique, Paris.

Barker, *Justinian* - J. W. Barker, *Justinian and the Later Roman Empire*, Madison, Wis. 1966.

BBA - Deutsche Akademie der Wissenschaften zu Berlin, Institut für griechisch-römische Altertumskunde: Berliner byzantinistische Arbeiten.

BMGS - Byzantine and Modern Greek Studies, Birmingham.

Brock, 'Thrice-holy hymn' - S. Brock, 'The thrice-holy hymn in the liturgy', *Sobornost/Eastern Churches Review* 7:2 (1985), p. 24-34.

Bury, *Later Empire* - J. B. Bury, *History of the Later Roman Empire: from the death of Theodosius I to the death of Justinian (A.D. 395 to A.D. 565)*, I-II, London 1923.

Byz - Byzantion: Revue internationale des études byzantines, Bruxelles.

BZ - Byzantinische Zeitschrift, Leipzig, Munich.

Cameron, *Circus Factions* - Alan Cameron, *Circus Factions: Blues and Greens at Rome and Byzantium*, Oxford 1976.

Capizzi, *Anastasio* - C. Capizzi, *L'imperatore Anastasio I (491-518): studio sulla sua vita, la sua opera e la sua personalità* (OChA 184), Roma 1969.

Charanis, *Church and State* - P. Charanis, *Church and State in the Later Roman Empire: the religious policy of Anastasius the First, 491-518* (University of Wisconsin Studies in the Social Sciences and History 26), Madison, Wis. 1939.

Chr. Ed. - Chronicum Edessenum, ed. I. Guidi, *Chr. Min.*, 1903, p. 1-13; an Engl. transl. by B. H. C.[owper], 'The Chronicle of Edessa',

Journal of Sacred Literature and Biblical Record, new [= 4th] ser., 9 (1864) p. 28-45.

Chr. Min. - *Chronica Minora*, ed. (& tr.) I. Guidi, E.-W. Brooks, J.-B. Chabot, (CSCO [1-6], SS 3:4 [= 1-6]), Paris 1903–05, tr. 1903–07.

Chr. Pasch. - *Chronicon Paschale*, ed. L. Dindorf, Bonn 1832; Engl. transl. of the relevant part: *Chronicon Paschale 284–628* AD, tr. with notes and intr. by Michael Whitby & Mary Whitby (Translated Texts for Historians 7), Liverpool 1989.

Chr. 1234 - *Anonymi auctoris Chronicon ad annum Christi 1234 pertinens*, ed. J.-B. Chabot, Paris, t. I: 1920, t. II: 1916 (CSCO SS 3:14 & 15); transl.: *Chronicon anonymum ad annum Christi 1234 pertinens*, t. I: (Latin) I.-B. Chabot (CSCO SS 3:14, Versio) Louvain 1937; t. II: (French) A. Abouna (CSCO 354, SS 154), Louvain 1974.

Clauss, *Magister officiorum* - M. Clauss, *Magister officiorum in der Spätantike (4.-6. Jahrhundert): das Amt und sein Einfluß auf die kaiserliche Politik* (Vestigia: Beitrage zur alten Geschichte 32), Munich 1980.

CSCO - Corpus Scriptorum Christianorum Orientalium, Paris, Rome, Louvain.

DACL - *Dictionnaire d'archéologie chrétienne et de liturgie*, Paris 1907–1953.

DHGE - *Dictionnaire d'histoire et de géographie ecclésiastiques*, Paris 1912-.

Dillemann, *Haute Mésopotamie* - L. Dillemann, *Haute Mésopotamie orientale et pays adjacentes: contribution à la géographie historique de la région du Ve s. avant l'ère chrétienne au VIe s. de cette ère*, (BAH 72), Paris 1962.

Downey, *Antioch* - G. Downey, *A History of Antioch in Syria: from Seleucus to the Arab Conquest*, Princeton, N. J. 1961.

Downey, Earthquakes - G. Downey, 'Earthquakes at Constantinople and Vicinity, A.D. 342–1454', *Speculum* 30 (1955), p. 596-600.

DTC - *Dictionnaire de théologie catholique*, Paris 1909-1950.

D'yakonov, *Ioann Yefesskiy* - A. D'yakonov, *Ioann Yefesskiy i yego tserkovno-istoricheskiye trudï*, St Petersburg 1908.

Eastern Frontier - *The Eastern Frontier of the Roman Empire: Proceedings of a colloquium held at Ankara in September 1988*, I-II, ed. by D. H. French & C. S. Lightfoot (British Institute of Archaeology at Ankara Monograph 11: BAR International Series 553, i-ii), Oxford 1989.

Evagrius - Evagrius, *Ecclesiastical History*, ed. J. Bidez & L. Parmentier, Amsterdam 1964 (= London 1898); a French transl.: Évagre, *Histoire ecclésiastique*, trad. par A.-J. Festugière, *Byz* 45 (1975), p. 187-488.

Frend, *Rise* - W. H. C. Frend, *The Rise of the Monophysite Movement: chapters in the history of the Church in the fifth and sixth centuries*, Cambridge 1972.

Frye, *Ancient Iran* - R. N. Frye, *The History of Ancient Iran* (Handbuch der Altertumswissenschaft 3:7), Munich 1984.

Gray, *Defense* - P. T. R. Gray, *The Defense of Chalcedon in the East (451–553)* (Studies in the History of Christian Thought 20), Leiden 1979.

Grumel, *Chronologie* - V. Grumel, *La Chronologie* (Traité d'études byzantines 1), Paris 1958.

Guilland, *Institutions* - R. Guilland, *Recherches sur les institutions byzantines,* I-II (BBA 35), Berlin 1967.

Hamilton-Brooks, see: Ps.-Zachariah

Harvey, *Asceticism* - S. Ashbrook Harvey, *Asceticism and Society in Crisis: John of Ephesus and the Lives of the Eastern Saints* (The Transformation of the Classical Heritage 18), Berkeley 1990.

Honigmann, *Évêques* - E. Honigmann, *Évêques et évêchés monophysites d'Asie antérieure au VIe siècle* (CSCO 127, Subs 2), Louvain 1951.

HTR - *The Harvard Theological Review*, Cambridge, Mass.

Janin, *Constantinople* - R. Janin, *Constantinople byzantine: développement urbain et répertoire topographique* (AOCh 4), Paris 1950.

Janin, *Églises* - R. Janin, *Les églises et les monastères* (La géographie ecclésiastique de l'Empire byzantin, I: Le siège de Constantinople et le Patriarcat Oecuménique, t. 3), Paris 1953.

Jansma, 'Jacques' - T. Jansma, 'Encore le credo de Jacques de Saroug: nouvelles recherches sur l'argument historique concernant son orthodoxie', *OS* 10 (1965), p. 75-88, 193-236, 331-370, 475-510.

JNES - *Journal of Near Eastern Studies*, Chicago.

John of Ephesus, *Lives* - John of Ephesus, *Lives of the Eastern Saints*, Syriac text ed. & tr. by E. W. Brooks, *PO* 17:1 [= 82] (1923), p. 1-307; 18:4 [= 89] (1924), p. 511-698; 19:2 [= 92] (1925), p. 151-285.

John of Ephesus, *Third Part* - Johannis Ephesini, *Historiae Ecclesiasticae pars tertia*, ed. E. W. Brooks (CSCO [105] SS 3:3 [=

54]), Paris 1935; Engl. transl.: *The Third Part of the Ecclesiastical History of John Bishop of Ephesus*, tr. by R. Payne Smith, Oxford 1860.

Joshua the Stylite - the Syriac text of his *Chronicle* is quoted according to PD I (see below); the translation: W. Wright (ed. & tr.), *The Chronicle of Joshua the Stylite: composed in Syriac A.D. 507, with a translation into English and notes*, Amsterdam 1968 [= Cambridge 1882].

JTS - *The Journal of Theological Studies*, Oxford.

Konzil von Chalkedon - *Das Konzil von Chalkedon: Geschichte und Gegenwart*, I-II, ed. A. Grillmeier & H. Bacht, Würzburg 1951–53.

Land - *Joannis episcopi Ephesi Monophysitae Scripta historica quotquot adhuc inedita supererant*, syriace edidit J. P. N. Land (= idem, *Anecdota Syriaca*, t. II), Lugduni Batavorum, 1868 (text); Latin tr.: W. J. Van Douwen & J. P. N. Land, 'Joannis episcopi Ephesi Syri Monophysitae Commentarii de beatis Orientalibus et Historiae ecclesiasticae fragmenta', *Verhandelingen der Koninklijke Akademie van Wetenschappen: Afdeeling Letterkunde* 18 (1889), 1-258.

Maas, *Lydus* - M. Maas, *John Lydus and the Roman Past: antiquarianism and politics in the age of Justinian*, London 1992.

Malalas - Malalas, *Chronographia*, ed. L. Dindorf, Bonn 1831; Engl. tr.: *The Chronicle of John Malalas*: a translation by E. Jeffreys et al. (Byzantina Australiensia 4), Melbourne 1986.

Michael the Syrian - *Chronique de Michel le Syrien patriarche jacobite d'Antioche (1166-1199)*, éd. et trad. en français par J.-B. Chabot, I-IV, Paris 1899–1924; (columns quoted: a - central, b - innermost, c - outermost; in tr.: a - fullpage, b - left, c - right).

Mus - *Le Muséon*, Louvain, Louvain-la-Neuve.

OCh - *Oriens Christianus*, Leipzig, Wiesbaden.

OChA - Orientalia Christiana Analecta, Rome.

OChP - *Orientalia Christiana Periodica*, Rome.

ODB - *The Oxford Dictionary of Byzantium*, I-III, ed. A. P. Kazhdan & al., New York 1991.

OLP - *Orientalia Lovaniensia Periodica*, Leuven.

OS - *L'Orient Syrien*, Paris 1956–1967.

OSue - *Orientalia Suecana*, Uppsala.

Palmer, 'Who wrote' - A. Palmer, 'Who wrote the Chronicle of Joshua the Stylite', in *Lingua restituta Orientalis: Festschrift J. Aßfalg*, ed. R. Degen & R. Schulz (Ägypten und Altes Testament 20), Wiesbaden 1990, p. 272-284.

PD - Pseudo-Dionysius.

PD I - *Incerti auctoris Chronicon Pseudo-Dionysianum vulgo dictum,* I, ed. (& tr.) I.-B. Chabot (CSCO [91], SS 3:1, Textus [= 43]), Paris 1927; Latin transl. (CSCO 121, SS 3:1, Versio [= 66]), Louvain 1949.

PD II - *Incerti auctoris Chronicon Pseudo-Dionysianum vulgo dictum,* II, ed. I.-B. Chabot (CSCO [104], SS 3:2 Textus [= 53]), Paris 1933; French tr.: *Chronicon anonymum Pseudo-Dionysianum vulgo dictum, II,* gallice vertit Robert Hespel (CSCO 507, SS 213), Louvain 1989.

PG - *Patrologiae Graecae cursus completus,* ed. J.-P. Migne, Paris 1857–1866.

Plassard, 'Crise séismique' - J. Plassard, 'Crise séismique au Liban du IVe au VIe siècle', *Mélanges de l'Université Saint-Joseph* 44 (1968), p. 9-20.

PLRE II - *The Prosopography of the Later Roman Empire, vol. II A.D. 395–527,* ed. J. R. Martindale, Cambridge 1980.

PLRE III - *The Prosopography of the Later Roman Empire, vol. III A.D. 527–641,* ed. J. R. Martindale, Cambridge 1992.

PO - *Patrologia Orientalis,* Paris, Turnhout.

Procopius, *Buildings* - Procopius, *Buildings,* with an English transl. by H. B. Dewing (The Loeb Classical Library: Procopius 7), London & Cambridge, Mass. 1940.

Procopius, *Wars* - Procopius, *History of the Wars, Books I-II,* with an English transl. by H. B. Dewing, (The Loeb Classical Library 48: Procopius 1), Cambridge, Mass., 1992 [= 1914].

Ps.-Zachariah - *Historia ecclesiastica Zachariae Rhetori vulgo adscripta,* t. I-II, ed. E. W. Brooks (CSCO [83-84], SS 3:5-6, Textus [= 38-39]), Paris 1919-1921; English transl.: *The Syriac Chronicle known as that of Zachariah of Mitylene,* tr. by F.J. Hamilton & E. W. Brooks, London 1899.

RECA - *Pauly's Realencyclopädie der classischen Altertumswissenschaft,* neue Bearbeitung begonnen v. G. Wissowa ... hrsg. v. W. Kroll, Stuttgart, München 1894–1972.

ROCh - *Revue de l'Orient Chrétien,* Paris 1896-1946.

Schove, *Eclipses* - D. J. Schove (in collaboration with A. Fletcher), *Chronology of Eclipses and Comets AD 1 to 1000,* Woodbridge 1984.

Segal, *Edessa* - J. B. Segal, *Edessa, 'The Blessed City',* Oxford 1970.

Shahid, *Martyrs* - Irfan Shahîd, *The Martyrs of Najrân: new documents* (Subsidia hagiographica 49), Bruxelles 1971.

Sharf, *Byzantine Jewry* - A. Sharf, *Byzantine Jewry from Justinian to the Fourth Crusade* (The Littman Library of Jewish Civilization), London 1971.

SS - (CSCO) Scriptores Syri.

Stein, *Bas-Empire* - E. Stein, *Histoire du Bas-Empire, II: de la disparition de l'Empire d'Occident à la mort de Justinien (476–565)*, Paris 1949.

Subs - (CSCO) Subsidia.

Trimingham, *Christianity among Arabs* - J. S. Trimingham, *Christianity among the Arabs in Pre-Islamic Times*, Beirut 1990 [= London 1979].

Vasiliev, *Justin* - A.A. Vasiliev, *Justin the First: an introduction to the epoch of Justinian the Great* (Dumbarton Oaks Studies 1), Cambridge, Mass. 1950.

Vööbus, *Asceticism I, II, III* - A. Vööbus, *History of Asceticism in the Syrian Orient: a contribution to the history of culture in the Near East*, I-III, (CSCO 184, 197, 500, Subs 14, 17, 81), Louvain 1958, 1960, 1988.

Witakowski, 'Chr. of Edessa' - W. Witakowski, 'Chronicles of Edessa', *OSue* 33-35 (1984–86), p. 487-498.

Witakowski, 'Malalas' - W. Witakowski, 'Malalas in Syriac', in *Studies in John Malalas,* ed. E. Jeffreys & al. (Byzantina Australiensia 6), Sydney 1990, p. 299-310.

Witakowski, *Syriac Chronicle* - W. Witakowski, *The Syriac Chronicle of Pseudo-Dionysius of Tel-Mahrē: a study in the history of historiography* (Studia Semitica Upsaliensia 9), Uppsala 1987.

Witakowski, 'Third part' - W. Witakowski, 'Sources of Pseudo-Dionysius for the Third Part of his *Chronicle*', *OSue* 40 (1991), p. 252-275.

Wright, *Chr. of Joshua* - see Joshua the Stylite.

Wright, *Literature* - W. Wright, *A Short History of Syriac Literature*, Amsterdam 1966 [= London 1894].

ZDMG - *Zeitschrift der Deutschen Morgenländischen Gesellschaft*, Leipzig, Wiesbaden.

INTRODUCTION

The Syriac historiographical work, of which the third part is presented here in translation, is a universal chronicle which came into being in Northern Mesopotamia at the end of the eighth century A.D. Its author is unknown, perhaps simply because of the poor state of preservation of the unique manuscript of the work. Due to an early attribution (see I, 2 below), later proved false, he is usually referred to as Pseudo-Dionysius. This conventional name has been perpetuated by the title of the standard edition of the Syriac text[1] (not likely to be replaced in the near future), and will consequently be retained here. As the place where the chronicler lived has proved to be the monastery of Zuqnin, the other conventional title by which the work is sometimes referred to is the *Chronicle of Zuqnin.*

Presenting to the public an English translation of only the third part (see section II below) of Pseudo-Dionysius' *Chronicle* may seem somewhat arbitrary, but the decision to do so was made when this part was still the only one for which no full translation into any European language existed.

The third part, moreover, has a value of its own, quite independently of the rest of the chronicle, due to its being based on an original, historiographical work contemporary with the events recounted, as well as to its distinctive point of view—that of the representative of a dissident religious community at a crucial period of its development. It thus constitutes an important source for the history of Byzantium in the sixth century, covering roughly the reigns of Anastasius, Justin I, and Justinian.

The contemporary historiographical work in question is the otherwise lost second part of the *Church History* of John of Ephesus, a Syrian of Monophysite conviction (see II, 1 below). A monk, later to become a bishop, he had often participated in the events he described. He lived during a difficult period in the history of the Monophysite movement, for a time sharing the afflictions of the persecution together with other non-conformist monks of the same persuasion. As an eye-witness he provides a vivid picture of the persecution, depicting the events from the perspective of the underdog, a perspective seldom supplied by the Greek historiography of the epoch.

---

[1] *Incerti auctoris Chronicon Pseudo-Dionysianum vulgo dictum*, ed. I.-B. Chabot, I-II, (CSCO [91, 104] SS ser. 3:1-2 [= 43, 53]), Paris 1927–33.

John's work is even more valuable as, in addition to an account of events in the eastern provinces, it also provides an insight into Constantinopolitan affairs. For in time John moved to the capital, even gaining access to Justinian's court. One of the emperor's aims was the religious unification of the empire, and John covered episodes of the campaign (against Manichaeans and pagans) in his narrative. Though still a religious dissident he had no objections to taking an active part in Justinian's plans and, in a passage often referred to, he proudly informs us of his missionary successes among the pagans in Asia Minor.

He is more reticent about Justinian's continued efforts to bring unity to the Church by means of discussions between representatives of the Chalcedonian and the Monophysite forms of Christianity. Perhaps our author cherished hopes that the Chalcedonian (imperial) side would be won over for Monophysitism, and when things did not turn out that way he may have felt less anxious to give a fuller account of the matter.

John also gave us an original account of the great Justinianic plague, far longer than those provided by other Byzantine historians. Penned in an emotional style, with the help of numerous quotations from Old Testament prophets, it contrasts with the calmer account of, say, Procopius. Yet it is worth reading since it has caught and transmitted to us the atmosphere of a bitterly tormented Constantinople which lost hundreds of thousands of its inhabitants during that plague.

For the reigns of Anastasius and Justin I, covered in the earlier sections of the part translated here, John must of course have used written sources. Notwithstanding the fact that much of this material may be known from elsewhere, even so these sections remain important for two reasons. The first is that his main source, the *Chronicle* of Malalas, appears in John of Ephesus (i.e. Ps.-Dionysius) in its original form, longer than that which is known to us from the independent transmission. The other reason is again the way in which our historian's point of view colours his narrative: he treats most of the events and persons with which he deals from the point of view of a dissident who is passionate about his cause, thus providing us with a perspective on these events and persons different from that of Orthodox Byzantine historiography.

I. The Chronicle as a whole

I.1. The manuscript and editions

The manuscript, preserved today in the Vatican Library (Syr. 162; 173 fols),[2] was brought there in 1715 from the Monastery of Saint Mary of the Syrians (Deir es-Suryānī) in the Nitrian Desert in Egypt by J.S. Assemani, who through his purchases laid the foundation for the Vatican Library Syriac manuscript collection. By a happy coincidence some of the missing folios of the manuscript were brought to England from the same monastery by H. Tattam in 1842 and are preserved today in the British Library (Add. 14, 665, fols 1-7).[3] The manuscript is a palimpsest (123 Vatican fols and all the London fols), the overwritten text being Greek (Old Testament excerpts) of the seventh/eighth century.[4]

The Syriac text dates from the (? early) ninth century and must have been written in Zuqnin. We infer this from the colophon on fol. 66v which was copied to replace what was probably a lost original folio. The scribe of the folio left a note which reads:

"Pray for the wretched Elisha of the monastery of Zuqnin who copied (Syr. ktab*) this leaf, that he might obtain mercy like the robber on the right hand (of Jesus). Amen and amen."* (PD I, 241, n. 6).

He may be identical with the scribe Elisha of Zuqnin who, according to a colophon of the year 903 in another manuscript of the British Library (Or. 5021), lived as an anchorite in Egypt.[5] If this is the same person, then he must have copied fol. 66 of PD's text while still in Zuqnin. As the chronicle was composed in that monastery (see I, 2 below) and one of its folios was replaced there at the end of the ninth century, then our manuscript almost certainly came into being there too. Later, it is

---

[2] S.E. & J.S. Assemanus, *Bibliothecae Apostolicae Vaticanae codicum manuscriptorum catalogus, I:3, complectens reliquos codices Chaldaicos sive Syriacos,* Paris 1926 [= Rome 1759], p. 328f.

[3] W. Wright, *Catalogue of Syriac manuscripts in the British Museum acquired since the year 1838, III,* London 1872, p. 1118f.

[4] Published by E. Tisserant, *Codex Zuqninensis rescriptus Veteris Testamenti: texte grecque des manuscrits Vatican Syriaque 162 et Mus. Brit. Additionnel 14665 édité avec introduction et notes,* (Studi e Testi 23) Rome 1911.

[5] F. Nau, in his review of E. Tisserant's work (see previous note), *ROCh 16* (1911), p. 137f.

generally believed, the manuscript was brought to Deir es-Suryānī by Archimandrite Moses of Nisibis who in the years 926–932 collected 250 manuscripts from Syrian and Mesopotamian monastic libraries and transported them to Egypt.[6]

There also exists a copy—today in the Bibliothèque Nationale, Paris (Syr. 284, 285)—made by Paulin Martin in 1867 from the Vatican manuscript (fols 44-152). Although marred by faults, the copy proved important for the establishment of the text for the critical edition: the Vatican manuscript has deteriorated since Martin's time and the editor used this copy to restore many illegible passages.

J. S. Assemani estimated the value of the text as a historical source very highly. Accordingly he adopted a number of excerpts from it in his monumental collection of Syriac writings, known generally as the *Bibliotheca Orientalis*, which he published in four *octavo* volumes.[7] In the nineteenth century two partial editions of the *Chronicle* appeared. That of the first part (up to fol. 43) was prepared by O. F. Tullberg[8] and that of the fourth (and last) part (fol. 121 to the end of the Vatican ms.) by J.-B. Chabot, the latter being provided with a French translation.[9]

The standard edition of the full text of the work was produced in the years 1927–33 by the same Jean-Baptiste Chabot for the Syriac series of the *Corpus Scriptorum Christianorum Orientalium* in two volumes (henceforth: PD I & PD II; see abbrev.). Before his death in 1949 Chabot managed to publish only the translation (into Latin) of the first half of the text (PD I), and thus until 1990, when R. Hespel's French translation of the second half (PD II)[10] appeared, apart from some

---

[6] J. Leroy, 'Moïse de Nisibe', in *Symposium Syriacum 1972*, (OChA 197) Rome 1974 p. 465.

[7] J. S. Assemanus, *Bibliotheca Orientalis Clementino-Vaticana in qua manuscriptos codices Syriacos...*, I-IV, Rome 1719–1728.

[8] *Dionysii Telmahharensis Chronici liber primus: textum e codice ms. Syriaco Bibliothecae Vaticanae* transscripsit, notisque illustravit O. F. Tullberg, Uppsala 1850.

[9] *Chronique de Denys de Tell-Mahré; quatrième partie*, publ. et trad. par J.-B. Chabot, (Bibliothèque de l'École des Hautes Études: sciences philologiques et historiques 112) Paris 1895.

[10] *Chronicon anonymum Pseudo-Dionysianum vulgo dictum, II*, gallice vertit R. Hespel, (CSCO 507, SS 213), Louvain 1989.

fragments, only the third part[11] remained inaccessible to those unable to read Syriac.

1.2 The author

J. S. Assemani thought that the chronicle he had in his hands was the work of the Syrian Orthodox (Jacobite) patriarch Dionysius of Tel-Mahrē (818–845), whom he knew to have written a chronicle. Consequently the fragments published in the *Bibliotheca Orientalis*, as well as the two nineteenth century partial editions, bear the patriarch's name as that of the author. The view that Dionysius of Tel-Mahrē was the author of the *Chronicle* survived until 1896 when two scholars—François Nau and Theodor Nöldeke—proved independently of each other that it could not have been the work of the patriarch.[12] Since however no positive identification of the author could be provided (see below), the name of the patriarch, though with the addition of 'Pseudo-', which features on the title page of J.-B. Chabot's edition of the Syriac text as well as on those of both CSCO translation volumes, is still used as the conventional name of the author (henceforth: PD).

All we know about him is what can be deduced from the text itself. He lived in the eighth century, as can be inferred from autobiographical details (he knew some ecclesiastics of the age, he met a "false prophet" in 770/71, etc.)[13] and from the date of his working on the *Chronicle*. Its last dated lemma is 1085 of the Seleucid era (773/4 A.D.), but it might very well have been 1086 Sel. had the last folios not been lost. Though we do not know when he started writing the *Chronicle* we do know that

[11] A German translation of the section dealing with the Najran events was published by N. Pigulewskaja, in her *Byzanz auf den Wegen nach Indien*, Berlin 1969 (BBA 36), p. 325-335; excerpts (from the Paris manuscript) in French by F. Nau, 'Études sur les parties inédites de la chronique ecclésiastique attribuée à Denys de Tellmahré (845)', *ROCh* 2 (1897), p. 54-68.

[12] F. Nau, 'Note sur la chronique attribuée par Assémani à Denys de Tell-Mahré, patriarche d'Antioche', *Journal Asiatique* 9:8 (1896), p. 346-358; Th. Nöldeke, in his review of Chabot's edition of PD's part 4 in *Wiener Zeitschrift für die Kunde des Morgenlandes* 10 (1896), p. 160-170. They argued that other Syriac historians (Michael the Syrian, Bar Hebraeus) who quoted patriarch Dionysius' work knew nothing about the *Chronicle* of Joshua the Stylite which is preserved nowhere but in PD, whereas the quotations from the patriarch could not be found in the text of PD. Moreover the latter wrote in 775 (see below), whereas Dionysius was patriarch 818–845 and wrote his work towards the end of his life.

[13] For other details see: Witakowski, *Syriac Chronicle* p. 93.

he was at work in 775, as is revealed by the dates provided in the introduction to the fourth part (PD II, 146, 5-7/108f): the year 1086 of the Seleucid era (Oct. 774 – Sept. 775 A.D.), and 158 of the Hejira (11 Nov. 774 – 30 Oct. 775). But, as he informs us in another preface, that to the whole work (very badly preserved, PD II, 419, 27-31), apparently added after the completion of the work, he finished it in "the year 1087 of Alexander the Macedonian [775/6 A.D.], in which Mahdi son of Abdallah comes to power over ... the Arabs [775 A.D.] and Leo son of Constantine begins to rule over the Greeks [24 September 775]."

On the basis of some expressions of the type "our monastery of Zuqnin" which occur in the text of the fourth part (eg. PD II, 206, 1/159), as well as from the dedication of the work to some persons of the Zuqnin monastery (PD II, 420, 8-12), it can be established that the chronicler was a resident of that monastic house, located just north of Amid (modern Diyarbakır in south-eastern Turkey).

Some scholars have attempted to identify the author as a stylite of Zuqnin by the name of Joshua. The basis of this supposition was a second note of the scribe Elisha, found (after the one already quoted) on folio 66v:

> *"May the grace of the great God and our Saviour Jesus Christ be upon the priest Mar Joshua the stylite of the monastic house of Zuqnin who wrote (or: copied, Syr.* ktab) *this book of record of the evil times which passed, and of the horrors and terrors which this tyrant did to the people."*

It was again F. Nau who in 1897 asserted that this colophon provided the name of the actual author of the whole chronicle of PD.[14] On the authority of F. Nau the identification of Pseudo-Dionysius as Joshua the Stylite was adopted by a number of renowned syrologists. It is true that

---

[14] 'Les auteurs des chroniques attribuées à Denys de Tellmahré et à Josué le Stylite', *Bulletin critique* 18 (1897), p. 54-58, repeated in 'Études sur les parties inédites de la chronique ecclésiastique attribuée à Denys de TellMahré (†845)', *ROCh* 2 (1897), p. 41-54.

F. Haase refuted this opinion in 1916[15] but it has recently been revived by A. Palmer.[16]

Folio 66 is placed in the middle of the historiographical work known as the *Chronicle of Joshua the Stylite*[17] which PD incorporated in full into his *Chronicle* (PD I, 235-317). Nau pointed out that the author of this incorporated chronicle, must, in view of his acquaintance with Edessene affairs, have been an Edessene, whereas Joshua, as is stated in Elisha's note, was a monk of Zuqnin. Thus Joshua the Stylite, being a Zuqninian, could not be the author of the chronicle hitherto attributed to him, and in this case, (apparently because he had to be the author of something) Nau concluded that he was the author of the whole Ps.-Dionysian chronicle.

However, neither Nau's premise nor his conclusion, endorsed by A. Palmer in *Abr-Nahrain*, is necessarily true. Firstly, it can be pointed out that Joshua's knowledge of Edessa's vicissitudes and his being a stylite in Zuqnin are not mutually exclusive since he might have lived both in Edessa and in Zuqnin at different times. He is well informed not only about Edessene affairs but also about events in Amid.[18] Recording the vicissitudes of the latter city, in the vicinity of which Zuqnin was situated, was evidently as important to him as recording those of Edessa, as can be inferred from the fact that he put the names of *both* cities in the title of his chronicle (cited below). If he was a native of Edessa, which would account for his acquaintance with events there, he might have written his book *after* he had moved from that city to Zuqnin, a move which would explain the Amidene sections of his work.[19]

---

[15] 'Untersuchungen zur Chronik des Pseudo-Dionysios von Tell-Mahrê, *OCh* 2:6 (1916), p. 268-70; and 'Die Chronik des Josua Stylites', *OCh* 2:9 (1920), p. 69f.

[16] In his review of Witakowski, *Syriac Chronicle* in *Abr-Nahrain* 28 (1990), p. 144f: "Since I find Nau's argument convincing, I shall call the author of the Zūqnīn Chronicle Yēshū', the Syriac form of Joshua." However, in an article published in the same year ('Who wrote', p. 274) A. Palmer takes another stand and writes: "The compiler of the chronicle ending in AD 775 was a monk of Zuqnin. So was Joshua but this does not entail that Joshua was the compiler, as was suggested by Nau."·

[17] It was also published separately with an English translation by W. Wright, *The Chronicle of Joshua the Stylite*, Cambridge 1882 [= Amsterdam 1968].

[18] This was noted by F. Haase, 'Die Chronik des Josua Stylites', *OCh* 2:9 (1920), p. 69f; also by A. Palmer, 'Who wrote', p. 275.

[19] Thus we may be confronted with *two* chronicles of Zuqnin, one embedded in the other, a possibility which calls for caution in multiplying titles of historiographical works on the basis of hypotheses concerning their origin.

Nevertheless, wherever Joshua lived, his authorship of the chronicle attributed to him depends on the interpretation of the verb *ktab* employed by Elisha in his colophons; it certainly means 'copied' in the first note and may have the same meaning in the second as well, although we cannot be absolutely sure.

However, whether Joshua was the author or only a scribe of the chronicle known under his name is of lesser importance here, the main issue being whether he can be identified as PD. And this, as we shall see, is quite unlikely, because the colophon does not refer to PD's *Chronicle* but to (Ps.-)Joshua's.

Firstly a certain parallelism can be observed between the title of (Ps.-)Joshua's chronicle and Elisha's note. The former was:

"A history (maktbānūtā d-taš'ītā) *of the time of affliction which took place in Edessa and Amid and all Mesopotamia"*

and according to Elisha Joshua wrote (or copied):

"...this book of record (ktābā hānā d-'uhdānā hānā)[20] *of the evil times which passed, and of the horrors and terrors which this tyrant did to the people."*

This parallelism makes it probable that Elisha had nothing but Ps.-Joshua's chronicle in mind.

However, a more cogent argument seems to be that such a description of the contents of a historiographical work as Elisha provides *cannot* refer to a universal chronicle, a genre based on the idea of the history of salvation. Even if the expression 'this tyrant' in the note be understood as the Devil and not as the Persian king,[21] the whole universal chronicle of Pseudo-Dionysius was not a mere record of "evil times... and of horrors and terrors" as Nau's and Palmer's interpretation of Elisha's note implies. A historiographical work, which naturally contains the narrative of the Creation of the world (see I.3 below), the

---

[20] I fail to see why the repetition of *hānā* ('this') makes *ktābā* ('book') and *'uhdānā* ('record') refer to PD's and (Ps.-)Joshua's chronicles respectively, as suggested by A. Palmer, 'Who wrote', p. 274.

[21] So was it interpreted by W. Wright who translated: "... which the (Persian) tyrant wrought among men" (*Chr.* of Joshua the Stylite, p. X), and so it is understood by A. Palmer, 'Who wrote', p. 273, n. 12.

nativity of Jesus, the homage of the Magi, the spread of Christianity, and so on, can hardly be referred to in this way.

It seems quite possible that PD was, or had been before setting about writing the *Chronicle*, a steward of his monastery, as may be inferred from his interest in the price of food, often attested in the *Chronicle*[22] and from his mention of journeys in search of books.[23] In any case an interest in the price of food is more understandable in a steward than in a stylite or any other ascetic.[24]

PD's motive for writing history was of a moral nature. He wished to admonish people not to sin. To this end he decided to show posterity how their predecessors had fared, using as a deterrent examples of calamities—in the description of which he delights—known to him both from written sources and from his own experience. His view of history is strictly Christian, with God and Satan being the real protagonists of history, ultimately responsible for good and evil deeds or events respectively. Natural catastrophes are explained as God's punishments for people's sins—in fact they are usually called '(God's) wrath' (Syr. *rugzā*).[25] PD notices however that despite all the plagues mankind does not show much improvement (cp. PD II, 133, 8-10/below p. 119).

---

[22] E.g. PD II, 178, 29-179, 1/135; for further references see Witakowski, *Syriac Chronicle*, p. 93, n. 26; A. Palmer does not regard this interest as sufficient for accepting that PD was a steward (the review [n. 16], p. 145), yet in the article ('Who wrote', p. 276) he uses exactly the same argument for his hypothesis that (Ps.-)Joshua was a steward; Palmer may have realized the inconsistency and asserts that PD's interest in food-prices is only a literary device in which he follows (Ps.-)Joshua. However, knowledge of the price changes is not really a literary *topos* simply to be copied from one text to another (as for example his quoting from Jeremiah or Isaiah, a habit in which he may have followed the rhetorical pattern of one of his sources, John of Ephesus), but something which is gained from genuine experience of the market.

[23] PD II, 146, 27-147, 2/109.

[24] A. Palmer (review [n. 16], p. 144f) rejects our assumption because there was already one *sā'ōrā* in Zuqnin, mentioned in PD II, 420. I cannot see why there could not be more than one steward in a monastery which quite probably housed over one hundred monks. This can be inferred from the report of 42 monks of Zuqnin dead in an epidemic (PD II, 205, 26-206, 2/159), which, again despite A. Palmer's criticism, seems to me informative even as it stands; if the monastery had housed, say, just 50-60 monks of whom 42 died, we may be pretty sure that PD would have presented this information in much more dramatic language than the matter-of-fact wording we find.

Whether a steward in a monastery was called *sā'ōrā* or *parnāsā* is of lesser importance. If A. Palmer is right about the steward being called *parnāsā* rather than *sā'ōrā*, then his argument (review, p. 144f) that there was already one *sā'ōrā* in Zuqnin has no bearing on PD's being a steward.

[25] It was probably his interest in catastrophes which caused him to keep in full John of Ephesus' accounts of them (in contrast to Michael the Syrian who abbreviated them).

1.3 The genre of the Chronicle and its place in Syriac historiography

PD's work belongs to the genre of universal (or world) chronicles, a term implying that the historiographical narrative, starting with the Creation of the world and Adam and continuing to the epoch contemporary with the author, runs through the whole, universal, span of history, at least as it was conceived by the Christian historiographical tradition. It covers—also at least in theory—the whole of mankind; in reality, however, this latter dimension of the universality of the chronicle is limited to what is provided by the sources available to the chronicler or, in the part which is his original contribution, the horizon of his own experience.

In PD's case the geographical scope of the work only very seldom stretches beyond the East Mediterranean area,[26] varying somewhat in accordance with changes of outlook in his sources. Finally, in the part which is the chronicler's original contribution, his perspective is limited to Northern Mesopotamia.

Universal chronicle writing in Syriac did not begin with the work of PD. This specifically Christian genre of historiography was implanted in Syriac literature by the translation of the classic work of the genre, the *Chronicle* of Eusebius of Caesarea. This translation has not been preserved, but the Eusebian material is recognizable in a number of Syriac chronicles (on both sides of the confessional divide, i.e. in the works of both Monophysite and Nestorian historians) which excerpted, reproduced more or less in full and/or extended the archetype.[27]

The basic element of the universal chronicle built on this pattern is the dated lemma. This is usually short, again in accordance with the Eusebian archetype which was in tabular form with relatively little space for lemmata. Some of the Syriac representatives of the genre preserved this tabular form (Jacob of Edessa, Elias Bar Shinaya); others abandoned it, but still kept the short lemmata (the *Chronicle to the year 724*, the *Chronicle to the year 846*), and the two groups can be classified together as the so-called 'short chronicles' (or 'short lemma chronicles'). In this respect PD was innovative, for while keeping the

---

[26] One such exception is the lemma on the Byzantine conquest of Africa and Italy, below p. 82.

[27] On the reception of Eusebius' *Chronicle* in Syriac historiography see P. Keseling, 'Die Chronik des Eusebius in der syrischen Überlieferung', *OCh* 23 (1926–27), p. 23-48, 223-241; 24 (1927), p. 33-56, and Witakowski, *Syriac Chronicle*, p. 76-89.

dated lemma skeleton of the short chronicle he felt free to fill the
lemmata with material originating from other genres of historiography,
for instance Church history, hagiography etc., thus creating the genre
which we have called the 'developed chronicle'.[28] In this he was
followed by later Syriac chroniclers, for instance Michael the Syrian.[29]

I.4 The sources

PD's innovation is important to us from another point of view too:
it meant that he copied his narrative sources in long excerpts, and
sometimes, it appears, in their entirety, instead of summarizing them. He
has thus preserved for us some sources which would otherwise be lost.

PD's usual procedure is to use one main source for a given period,
organizing the material from it in the form of dated lemmata,
irrespective of whether the source in question was itself a chronicle or
not. Thus, according to his own statement in the introduction to the
fourth part of the *Chronicle* (PD II, 145, 17-146, 8/108), he used the
Chronicle of Eusebius,[30] the *Church History* of Socrates Scholasticus
and the *Church History* of John of Ephesus. These are supplemented
with additional material from compositions such as the *Cave of
Treasures*, the *Story of the Magi*, Eusebius' *Church History*, the
Chronicle of Edessa, the *Story of the Seven Sleepers*,[31] John Rufus'
Plerophoria, the *Henoticon* of Zeno and the *Chronicle* of (Ps.-)Joshua
the Stylite.[32] PD must also have used written sources, so far
unidentified, for the initial lemmata of the fourth part, though he
presents it as being totally original.

II. The Third Part

The *Chronicle* itself does not divide into any sections, and the idea
that the historiographical material may be composed of four parts is

---

[28] Witakowski, *Syriac Chronicle*, p. 83.
[29] It does not follow, however, that Michael knew PD's *Chronicle*; in fact none of the
extant Syriac chronicles knows of PD's work.
[30] In fact the first main source is the *Old Testament*, but PD does not name it.
[31] In PD's version of this story the number of the sleeping young men is eight.
[32] For more information on PD's sources see Witakowski, *Syriac Chronicle*, p. 124-136.

conveyed only in the introduction to the fourth part, mentioned above. Thus the chronicler may have regarded the part based on John of Ephesus' *Church History* as the third part. However, the division which we conventionally apply here is a rather mechanical one and follows the scheme of the editor of the whole chronicle, J.-B. Chabot. He did, it is true, publish the whole text in two volumes (PD I & PD II), but since the second of these contains both new text and text which he had previously published as the "fourth part" (PD II, 145, 17-381),[33] it has become natural to refer to the new text in the volume (PD II, 2, 1-145, 16) as the "third part".

This "third part" covers the time span from the last three years of the emperor Zeno to the fourth year of the reign of Justin II, i.e. the years 489–569.

Although the material taken from John of Ephesus starts in what should be taken as the second part (according to the modern division), there is no doubt that John's work also served as a source for the third part translated here, and in fact as the main one.

II.1. John of Ephesus' Church History *as the main source of the third part*

John was born *c.* 507 in the region of Amid. As a four-year old boy he was left by his parents in the monastery of 'Arʿā Rabbethā to lead an ascetic life. At the age of 15 he moved to the monastery of John Urtāyā in Amid. Devoted to the Monophysite cause he shared the bitter experience of persecution together with other monks of the monasteries of Amid. In 529 he was ordained deacon by John of Tella, another champion of Monophysitism. After a period of travelling, during which he visited Constantinople, Antioch, Palestine and Alexandria, he settled in the capital, enjoying there, together with other Monophysites, the protection of the empress Theodora. Notwithstanding his confessional allegiance he had quite close contacts with the emperor Justinian who, *inter alia*, entrusted him in 542 with a mission to convert to Christianity the peoples of Asia Minor, apparently still pagan at that time. The mission was a success: 70, 000 people were baptized (see below p. 72). Also John became known as a stern inquisitor of pagans and heretics

---

[33] See above, n. 9.

and his zeal extended to digging up and burning the bones of the
Montanists (see below p. 71 & 112). In 558 he was ordained titular
bishop of Ephesus by Jacob Baradaeus but he never settled there. For
his intransigent and extreme anti-Chalcedonian attitude he was
imprisoned in 571 and released only after Tiberius II's accession (574).
In his last years he must have felt embittered to see the internal strife
within the Monophysite party, the informal head of which he became
after the death of the patriarch Theodosius of Alexandria in 566. After
another period of imprisonment (in Chalcedon) and banishment from the
capital, he died soon after 588.[34]

John is known to be the author of two works: the *Lives of the Eastern
Saints*, a collection of biographies of Monophysite ascetics,[35] and the
Church History. Of this only the third and final part has survived in
independent manuscript tradition;[36] this, however, was unknown to PD.
The first part is completely lost and neither PD nor any other Syriac
historian seems to know it.

The state of preservation of the second part of John's *History* is
complicated. PD reproduced much of it in the third part of his *Chronicle*
which makes the latter one of the major witnesses to John's text.
Another important witness is the *Chronicle* of Michael the Syrian.[37]
Two other sources, the *Chronicle to the year 846*[38] and the *Chronicle to
the year 1234*,[39] preserve John's text to a much lesser degree.

The separate manuscript tradition of John's second part is limited—so
far as is known—to excerpts in two manuscripts published by J. P. N.
Land.[40] The excerpts in one of them (Add. 14, 647) do not give John's

[34] P. Allen, 'A new date for the last recorded events in John of Ephesus' *Historia
ecclesiastica*', *OLP* 10 (1979), p. 251-254; Michael Whitby, *The Emperor Maurice and
his Historian: Theophylact Simocatta on Persian and Balkan Warfare*, Oxford 1988, p.
110-112; on John's life see D'yakonov, *Ioann Yefesskiy*, p. 4-165; Honigmann, *Évêques*,
p. 207-215. A thesis on John has recently been prepared by Jan van Ginkel at the
University of Groningen, '*John of Ephesus: A Monophysite historian in sixth-century
Byzantium*', 1995.
[35] John of Ephesus, *Lives*. An important recent study of the *Lives* is Harvey, *Asceticism*.
[36] John of Ephesus, *Third Part*, see Abbreviations.
[37] Michael the Syrian, see Abbreviations.
[38] *Chronicon ad annum Domini 846 pertinens*, ed. E.W. Brooks, *Chr. Min.*, p. 157-238
(text), 121-180 (tr.).
[39] *Chr. 1234*, see Abbreviations.
[40] Land (see Abbreviations): the Syriac text, p. 289-329, 385-391; the Latin tr. (W. J. Van
Douwen & J. P. N. Land), p. 216-249.

name, but his authorship is clear from the parallel text in PD, which attributes it to John of Asia (= John of Ephesus).[41]

In the same collection J.P.N. Land also published extracts from another manuscript[42] which are attributed to John by the title ("By the same holy Mar John of Asia, from his book of *Church History* on the persecution ...", Land 289, 1f) and by the colophon ("The stories which we have gathered from John of Asia are finished", Land 329, 21f). It is more probable, however, that these latter extracts are drawn from another copy of the *Chronicle* of PD, since they have the same system of dated lemmata as PD, whereas John of Ephesus, to judge from the third part of his *History*, did not use such a system.[43]

As we know from Michael the Syrian the second part of John of Ephesus' *Church History* began with Constantine the Great,[44] and as we know from John's surviving third part, it followed the course of events up to the sixth year of Justin II.[45]

John himself used a number of sources which can be identified. First in order of appearance in PD is the *Chronicle* of (Ps.-)Joshua the Stylite. This, as was mentioned above, has been reproduced by PD in full in his second part,[46] but again in the third part there are some lemmata based on that source. These seem to have been extracted by John, and PD when copying the material from him did not omit them. He may have done so inadvertently but at least in some cases he was conscious of repeating himself and added a remark: "... as we have recorded above..." (e.g. lemmata 810 Sel. & 811, below p. 3 & 4).

Another of John's sources was the Byzantine *Chronicle* of John Malalas. A comparison with the extant version of Malalas[47] shows some differences, i.e. John of Ephesus usually has more material to hand. This can be explained by the fact that he excerpted the original *Chronicle* of

---

[41] Land 387, 5-388, 13; the attribution in PD II, 140, 5; below p. 124.

[42] Land 289, 1-329, 22.

[43] For discussion of the dependence of this manuscript on PD (as well as other source problems), see Witakowski, 'Third part'.

[44] "John of Asia says in the *beginning* of his book that when Constantine...", Michael the Syrian 121a, 16-22/I, 239.

[45] John of Ephesus, *Third part*, 4, 11-14/3.

[46] See above p. xxi & n. 17.

[47] Malalas, see Abbreviations.

Malalas,[48] whereas what is preserved in the unique manuscript of the (nearly) complete work is an abbreviated version.

John also used the *Church History* of Pseudo-Zachariah of Mitylene,[49] taking from it, for instance, Simeon of Beth Arsham's *Letter on the Himyarite martyrs* (p. 53-62).

Some lemmata were written by John on the basis of his own experience, as for instance those, already mentioned, on the mission to the pagans of Asia Minor, and on the Great Plague (p. 72 & 74-98 respectively). The latter, rather a long account, as well as that on the persecution of the Eastern monks (p. 22-41),[50] had originally been composed as separate books (the narrative of the plague has even kept the original division into chapters) and were later incorporated by John into his *Church History*.

PD does not seem to have much altered, or edited, the sources he copied, as may quite often be seen in the lemmata where he kept John's utterances in the first person (e.g. p. 33; 41; 76; 98). He copied some fragments of John's work without any adjustment to the demands of his own work. He even forgot to omit John's cross-references to his own text, as for instance in the story of the Great Plague where John compares the behaviour of people during the plague in Constantinople to that in Alexandria (p. 102), whereas the fragment on the plague in the latter city, which would have made such a comparison intelligible, was omitted by him.

Along with John of Ephesus' work PD also used other sources, as for instance the *Chronicle of Edessa*, but again in its original form of which the extant chronicle[51] is an abbreviation.[52]

Lists of patriarchs and bishops came from an unknown source which was also used by Ps.-Zachariah and Michael the Syrian. Whether its origin had the nature of church diptychs or some other semi-official *fasti episcopales* cannot be determined here.

---

[48] See Witakowski, 'Malalas'.

[49] Ps.-Zachariah, see Abbreviations.

[50] Witakowski, 'Third part', p. 260.

[51] *Chr. Ed.*, see Abbreviations.

[52] On the original *Chronicle of Edessa*, see Witakowski, 'Chr. of Edessa'.

II.2. Dates

PD had no formal problem with adapting the material of, say, the *Chronicle of Edessa* into his own work since the two were both composed of the same elements, dated lemmata. In this regard he had, however, problems with the work of John of Ephesus because only a few dates could be found in it. Consequently PD had to provide most of them himself, that is, to invent them. That this procedure was seldom successful, at least from the point of view of modern criticism, goes without saying.

It cannot be totally ruled out that there is some rationale behind some of these dates, as for instance a dependence on a source of chronicle type which provided the dates according to the era of Philip Arrhidacus, Alexander the Great's brother,[53] yet the majority of the dates still seem to be the result of PD's attempt to turn his material into a chronicle.[54]

To account for the faulty dates A. D'yakonov suggested that PD used an annalistic source, which had combined three further sources: the *Chronicle of Edessa* and two other chronicle-like sources of which one was inaccurate by 3-4 years in both directions and the other basically by 8 years plus 1-3 by additional error in both directions, i.e. altogether by 5-11 years.[55] Although such a source is otherwise completely unknown, the hypothesis would account for double or triple entries, such as those on the earthquakes in Phoenicia (lemmata 864, 870, 876, p. 115, 119-121, 125 respectively).

III. The present translation

The present translation tries, as far as possible, to be literal. The language of the author (or of his main source, John of Ephesus) does not manifest any high literary value, whether from the stylistic or from the logical point of view, a fact which makes the enterprise of translation an arduous task. The author much too often uses words such

---

[53] See Michael Whitby, 'The Era of Philip and the Chronicle of Zuqnin', *Classica et Mediaevalia: revue danoise de philologie et d'histoire* 43 (1992), p. 179-185.

[54] For instance in part 2 we find the material from John Rufus' *Plerophoria* (known from independent manuscript transmission, as well as from Michael the Syrian's *Chronicle*) divided up and attributed to successive dated lemmata.

[55] D'yakonov, *Ioann Yefesskiy*, p. 219-227.

as *d-* ('which', 'of'), *kad* ('when' 'while'), *tūb* ('behold', 'again'), *'āp* ('also'), not to mention *w-* ('and'), *gēr* ('for', 'indeed'), *dēn* ('but'), etc. which, as mere verbiage, have had sometimes to be omitted. Moreover there occur repetitions which have also been omitted.

The semantic structure of Syriac as used by John of Ephesus and PD is not that of a modern language; for instance, inherently imprecise words such as *saggi'ē -* ('many'), *šarkā -* ('the rest', 'the others'), and so on, are used very often. Translating such a text involves rather more interpretation on the part of the translator than may be the case with texts by authors with linguistic discipline closer to our own. The wording often requires complementary information in order that the whole sentence may be understood by a modern reader. We supply this additional information in parentheses, trying to represent the author's intended meaning.

Beside many probable faults in the text which must have come into being in the process of copying, the author himself, or his sources, may be blamed for some of the confusions. This is the case where the logical subject is first introduced in the plural but subsequently in the same (usually very long) sentence it is changed to the singular (or *vice versa*).

Another source of ambiguity is the frequent use of pronouns instead of substantives. This may often be acceptable as sufficiently informative in Syriac because of differences of gender which cannot always be rendered in English. Yet quite often this usage blurs the meaning of the sentence in the original itself. To remedy this we have again resorted to the practice of giving in parentheses the substantives to be understood.

We have not noted small differences between variant readings in Chabot's and Land's texts, but larger discrepancies (a different fragment of text, material not found in Chabot's text) are indicated in the footnotes.

In cases in which the translation is based on a different reading of the Syriac text, our suggestions for the improvement of the manuscript reading are provided in footnotes. These are also given whenever a simple scribal error has been detected.

The quotations from the Bible have been adjusted, as far as possible, to the wording of the *Revised Standard Version*. However, in cases where either the *Peshitta*, the semi-official Syriac translation of the Bible, differs from that, or PD (or his source) gives another, though recognizable, text of a Biblical passage different from the standard, the wording has not been adjusted to the *RSV* and the text has been translated as it stands.

The peculiarities of Ps.-Dionysius' terminology have been kept. For instance, we always retain PD's "Romans", even where we would today rather say "Byzantines".

The technical Greek and Latin terms of an administrative, economic or military nature have been left untranslated (though explained in the notes) since just as they seem unfamiliar to the "general reader" today, so they must have appeared to most Syriac readers in the Middle Ages.

The spelling of proper names, apart from familiar ones, has been adjusted to the forms given in *The Prosopography of the Later Roman Empire II & III*, ed. J. R. Martindale, Cambridge 1980–92, or to *The Oxford Dictionary of Byzantium*, ed. A. P. Kazhdan, Oxford 1991, and in other cases to W. H. C. Frend, *The Rise of the Monophysite Movement*, Oxford 1972.

We have not been able to identify all the toponyms which occur in the text (especially the names of monasteries). Most place names are shown on the maps at the end of the volume.

The dates of the emperors, patriarchs etc. are given in accordance with V. Grumel, *La chronologie* (Traité d'études byzantines 1), Paris 1958.

For the convenience of the reader all the dates given in the *Chronicle* according to the Seleucid era (which started on 1 October 312 B.C.) have been converted into dates of the Christian era. This conversion is, however, purely mechanical and the dates thus obtained do not imply any accordance with the dates generally accepted by contemporary historians for the events in question. On the contrary, most of PD's dates seem to be faulty, and in any case they should be subjected to the customary historical checks before any conclusion is reached on the basis of them (see also above II.3).

The red headings of the manuscript, as well as some other titles of similar status not written in red, are printed in italics.

The bold numbers in square brackets refer to the pages of the Syriac text in Chabot's edition. All references given in the notes are, however, to the pages of this volume, as are those of the index.

In references to texts other than PD, first numbers indicate the Syriac (pages, columns, lines) or Greek (pages only) texts in the standard editions (the titles of which are provided in the list of abbreviations), and numbers after the oblique stroke denote the respective English translations, if such exist, and if not, the standard translations into any other European language.

PSEUDO-DIONYSIUS OF TEL-MAḤRĒ
THE CHRONICLE, part III

[p. 2] The year 800[1] (A.D. 488/9): the School of the Persians in Edessa[2] was destroyed.[3]

The hierarchs who became famous in succession:[4]

In Rome: Hilary assumed (the episcopacy) after Leo.[5]

In Alexandria: after the wicked Proterius was killed, the holy Timothy, the disciple of Dioscorus,[6] assumed (the episcopacy), and after him another Timothy, who was called the Trembling Cap.[7]

In Constantinople: Anatolius, and after him Gennadius, and then Acacius.[8]

---

[1] According to the Seleucid era (beginning on 1 October 312 B. C.), used throughout the part of the chronicle which is translated here.

[2] The School of the Persians in Edessa was so called because from its origin in the fourth century many of its pupils and teachers came from Persian territory. It was the mainstay of Antiochene theology (connected with such names as Diodore of Tarsus, Theodore of Mopsuestia and Nestorius, from whom it took the name Nestorian) in the Syriac-speaking area even after the Council of Ephesus anathematized it in 431. After the destruction of the School by the bishop Cyrus II it was re-established in Nisibis (under Persian rule, and thus out of the control of the Byzantine authorities), to which most of the teachers moved; see A. Vööbus, *History of the School of Nisibis* (CSCO 256, Subs 26), Louvain 1965, p. 7-32.

[3] The lemma comes from the *Chronicle of Edessa* 8, 18f/35.

[4] This and further lists of patriarchs, bishops etc. come from some kind of *fasti episcopales*, not preserved in separate transmission. They were also used by Ps.-Zachariah of Mitylene (cp. I, 205, 3 3-206, 14/99f; II, 15, 15-16, 3/143f) and Michael the Syrian (cp. 248c, the new chapter, 1-249, 25/II, 141f; 256, 10-20/II, 153c).

[5] Leo the Great: 440–461; Hilary: 461–468.

[6] Dioscorus, patriarch of Alexandria 444–451; d. 454, a staunch Monophysite; he presided at the second Council of Ephesus in 449 (better known as *Latrocinium Ephesinum*, or Robber Council), which was a victory for Monophysite theology. Two years later he was deposed, a result of the acceptance by the Council of Chalcedon (451) of dyophysite theology as orthodox.

[7] Proterius: 451-457 (a Chalcedonian, which is why PD calls him 'wicked'—he was lynched by Monophysite mob, Frend, *Rise*, p. 155); Timothy Aelurus: 457-460, 475-477; Timothy Salofaciolus: 460-475, and 477-482; Trembling Cap: the Syriac is a translation of the Greek nickname Σαλοφακίολος; as φακιόλον is the turban worn by the Eastern archbishops, the nickname ('one whose turban does not fit') may refer to a person who does not fit his office, K. Ahrens & G. Krüger, *Die sogenannte Kirchengeschichte des Zacharias Rhetor in deutscher Übersetzung*, Leipzig 1899, p. 310.

[8] Anatolius: 449–458; Gennadius: 458–471; Acacius: 472–489.

In Ephesus: John, and after him Paul, who was deposed because he did not accept the Council of Chalcedon.[9]

In Antioch: Domnus, after him Maximus and after (him) Martyrius who was expelled, (then) Peter who came back from exile.[10]

In Jerusalem: Anastasius, who took over (the see) after Juvenal; after him Martyrius, and after him Sallustius, who is famous at this time.[11]

Again in Antioch: after Peter the believer[12] there was Calendion, who was deposed, after him there was Palladius, and after him Flavian.[13]

In Constantinople: after Acacius there was Fravitta,[14] and after him Euphemius, who was deposed in the days of (the emperor) Anastasius.[15]

In Alexandria: after Timothy, John, who was expelled, after him Peter, and after him Athanasius.[16]

In Rome: after Hilary, Simplicius, and after him Felix, who is famous at this time.[17]

All these hierarchs followed one another up to the death of the emperor Zeno.[18]

Also at this time the faction of the Greens[19] set fire to and burned the synagogue of the Jews.[20] They dug up [p. 3] all the bones of the dead

---

[9] R. Janin (Éphèse, in: *DHGE* vol. 15 (1963), col. 558) lists for the period in question two bishops of Ephesus called John: John II (*c.* 457) and John 'the heretic' known from Evagrius, *Hist. eccl.*, III, 6; Janin does not mention Paul (475–476/7), on whom see Honigmann, *Évêques*, p. 119.

[10] Domnus: 441/2–450; Maximus: 451-455; Martyrius: 459–470; the chronicler omits Basil (457-8) and Acacius (458-9); Peter the Fuller: 470, for the second time 475–477, and again 485–489; Honigmann, *Évêques*, p. 3.

[11] Juvenal: 422-458; Anastasius: 458-478; Martyrius: 478–486; Sallustius: 480–494.

[12] The author uses this term of the Monophysites.

[13] Calendion: 479–484; Palladius: 490–498; Flavian II: 498–512.

[14] Ms.: *pw'nts*; corruption of *pr'wyts* (?).

[15] Fravitta: 489–490; Euphemius: 490–496.

[16] John I Talaia: 482; Peter II Mongus: 482–489; Athanasius II Keletes: 489–496.

[17] Simplicius: 468–483; Felix III: 483–492.

[18] Zeno's reign: 474–491.

[19] The Syriac uses here the Greek term Πράσινοι. The Greens, and their main rivals, the Blues (Βένετοι), were circus factions, originally associations which organized games and other entertainments in larger Byzantine cities. The factions were often responsible for violent riots, sometimes with social and political overtones; see Cameron, *Circus Factions*.

[20] The *pogrom* took place in Antioch as is known from Malalas (389/218), from whom the lemma ultimately comes. According to other witnesses to the original Malalas, the Greens attacked the Jews because the latter were on the side of the Blues (Malalas, transl., p. 218, n. 15). The exact date of the event is unknown, but it must have taken place in the last years of Zeno's reign and thus the date PD assigned is approximately correct. See

who were (buried) around their synagogue and they burned them in the fire. When this became known to the emperor Zeno, he was angry with the Greens and said: "Why did they not burn all the Jews, living along with the dead?" And so ended this affair: no investigation was made.

In the year 808 (A.D. 496/7) the emperor Zeno died, and after him Anastasius, a Christian and a believer, who came from Dyrrachium,[21] acceded to the throne.[22]

The year 809 (A.D. 497/8): Euphemius, (the patriarch) of Constantinople, went into exile because he was found to be a Nestorian. In his place came Macedonius.[23]

The year 810 (A.D. 498/9): many locusts came on the country and destroyed everything. This was as we have recorded above.[24]

In the same year there was a violent and mighty earthquake. Nicopolis[25] was destroyed by it, except for the church and the bishop's house, and it buried all its inhabitants.

In the same year a sign like darkness[26] appeared in the sky.

---

also Stein, *Bas-Empire*, p. 32; Avi-Yonah, *Jews*, p. 246; Downey, *Antioch*, p. 499; Sharf, *Byzantine Jewry*, p. 28; Cameron, *Circus Factions*, p. 149f.

[21] Modern Durrës in Albania.

[22] The correct date is 491; Anastasius (491–518) assumed the throne by marrying the empress Ariadne, Zeno's widow.

[23] Euphemius was deposed by a synod in Constantinople (495) which found him to be a Nestorian. His removal seems to have been caused by his opposition (based on his Chalcedonian views) to *Henoticon* (see n. 96), which was then generally accepted by the Church (except in Rome) and by the emperor; cp. Ps.-Zachariah, VII, 1, transl. p. 139, 150 (who treats him as a Nestorian); Evagrius, III, 32; Theodore Lector, *PG* 86, col. 188f; Frend, *Rise*, p. 200; Gray, *Defense*, p. 35; Macedonius II: 496–511.

[24] In the *Chronicle* of Ps.-Joshua the Stylite incorporated into Ps.-Dionysius' work, PD I, 235-317; English translation: W. Wright, *The Chronicle of Joshua the Stylite*, Amsterdam 1968 [= Cambridge 1882]. Most of the events mentioned in this and the following lemma are an abbreviated version of Ps.-Joshua's lemmata for 810 and 811; PD I, 259-262/23-26.

[25] The fact that the earthquake struck Abarne and Arsamosata (see below) suggests that the reference is to Nicopolis, an episcopal see in Armenia I, not Nicopolis-Emmaus in Palestine, as W. Wright thought, *Joshua*, p. 24, n.; J. Sturm, Nicopolis (8), *RECA* 17 (1936), col. 536–538; Grumel, *Chronologie*, p. 478 (year 499).

[26] Syr.: *heššōkā*; perhaps to be corrected to 'spear' (*nayzkā*), as in the *Chr. Ed.* (8, 30/36, item 76) from which this information is probably derived.

And again on the very same day of (the appearance of) the sign and of the earthquake, the warm springs of Abarne[27] stopped flowing for three days, and then returned (to flow) as previously. Also the river Euphrates stopped its flow on the same day. Also the great temple of Arsamosata, on the day of a gathering there, fell as a result of the earthquake and caused many people to perish inside it.

In the year 811 (A.D. 499/500) on the 23rd of the month of October, on Saturday, the sun darkened [**p. 4**] for eight hours.[28] The earth was covered by dust as if ash or brimstone were scattered over it.[29] And on the same day another sign appeared—in the wall of Edessa: there was a breach in the wall south of the Great Gate, the stones from that place being scattered to a considerable distance from it.

Also in the same year in November, three signs appeared in the sky in the middle of the day, as it were a rainbow appearing in the clouds, their curve(s) being turned downward and their end(s) upward. One of them (was seen) on the southern side, in the middle of the sky, the second to the east of it, and the third to the west, (all) pointing towards the sky.

Also in the same year, in the month of January,[30] another sign appeared in the sky, in the south-western corner, resembling a spear, which some people called the "Broom of Perdition", while others called it the "Spear of War". But this matter has been recorded by us above.[31]

The year 812 (A.D. 500/501): there was famine, (an attack of) locusts and a severe plague.[32]

---

[27] Modern Çermik, north-east of Edessa; E. Honigmann, *Die Ostgrenze des byzantinischen Reiches von 363 bis 1071 nach griechischen, arabischen, syrischen und armenischen Quellen*, (Corpus Bruxellense Historiae Byzantinae 3), Bruxelles 1935, p. 35; Dillemann, *Haute Mésopotamie*, p. 93f.

[28] None of the dates given for the year in question in Grumel's list of eclipses (*Chronologie*, p. 460), or that of Schove, *Eclipses*, corresponds to the date provided by PD.

[29] The so-called Great Chronographer, an otherwise unknown source from which some excerpts were copied into one of the manuscripts of the *Chronicon Paschale* (see L. M. Whitby, 'The Great Chronographer and Theophanes', *BMGS* 8 (1982–83), p. 1-20), also mentions ash (στάκτη instead of στακτή, 'balsam', as C. Mango emends), see extract 3 in *Chr. Pasch.*, transl. p. 195, & n. 3.

[30] The Syriac text has only *kānūn* and no further qualification, and thus both December (*Kanun I*) and January (*Kanun II*) are possible. This is, however, again a repetition of Ps.-Joshua's information (PD I, 263, 22/26), where the latter occurs.

[31] In the *Chronicle* of Ps.-Joshua the Stylite, PD I, 263, 22-26/27; Grumel, *Chronologie*, p. 470; Schove, *Eclipses*, p. 291.

[32] Ps.-Joshua: PD I, 270, 28f/34.

The year 813 (A.D. 501/2): there was a great earthquake and Ptolemais, Tyre and Sidon were overthrown.[33] Also the synagogue of the Jews[34] was ruined and fell. And in the same night of the earthquake, which took place on the 22nd in the month of August, at the dawn on Friday, a sign like a burning fire appeared in the northern quarter (of the sky).

The year 814 (A.D. 502/3): Kavad conquered Amid[35] and Theodosiopolis,[36] killing and taking into captivity their inhabitants. [p. 5] In Amid 85, 000 corpses were carried out through the Northern Gate, not to mention those carried through other gates. They were cast into pits and ditches, and buried there.[37]

In the school called "of the Urtaye"[38] while all the monks of the Monastery of John of the Urtaye[39] were attending a service, two *speculatores*[40] attacked them, slaughtered 90 men and took the rest of them captive.

---

[33] Plassard, 'Crise séismique', p. 13; the epicentre was probably in the sea.

[34] In Berytus; the author's or a copyist's oversight; cp. Joshua the Stylite's chronicle, PD I, 274, 13/37.

[35] The chronicler thus reports the beginning of the Persian-Roman war (502–506). Kavad invaded Roman territory after Anastasius' refusal to pay him contributions towards the cost of defending the Caspian passes, which had been stipulated in the Persian-Roman treaty of 442. The most extensive account of this war seems to be provided by Ps.-Joshua the Stylite; for other accounts see: Procopius, *Wars* I, VII-IX, & Ps-Zachariah, VIII, 3-5; see too E. Merten, 'De bello persico ab Anastasio gesto', *Commentationes philologicae Ienenses* VII:2 (1906), p. 139-201; Bury, *Later Empire*, II, p. 10-15; Stein, *Bas-Empire*, p. 92-101; Frye, *Ancient Iran*, p. 323. On Kavad's siege of Amid, cp. Procopius, *Wars*, I, VII, 3f, 12. In the so-called *Narrationes variae*, annalistic excerpts concerning Amid (*Chr. Min.*, 331, 2-4/260), the capture of that city is dated to 813 Sel., i.e. one year earlier than in PD, but in accordance with Ps.-Joshua.

[36] In Armenia (modern Erzurum), as is clear from Ps.-Joshua, PD I, 274, 23, Wright 37; not Theodosiopolis/Reshaina, on the Khabur.

[37] Ps.-Joshua: PD I, 274, 18-275, 4/37 (Theodosiopolis) & PD I, 276, 6-280, 22/38-43 (Amid).

[38] Syr. *Urtāyē*; the inhabitants of the region of Anzitene (main city: Arsamosata) with a distinct language. They were the descendants of the ancient people of Urartu (Honigmann, *Évêques*, p. 236; H. Hübschmann, *Die altarmenischen Ortsnamen*, Strassburg 1904, p. 236f; A. Harrak, 'The Survival of the Urartian People', *Bulletin of the Canadian Society for Mesopotamian Studies* 25 (1993), p. 43-49), whose state, centred around the Lake Van, was a dangerous neighbour of Assyria on her northern flank, until in the eighth century B.C. it was conquered by the latter.

[39] In Amid, cp. John of Ephesus, *Lives*, PO 19:2 (1925), p. 219, which is the source of the present lemma.

[40] Latin: 'scouts, men on reconnaissance'.

In the same year the Romans and Persians made battle at Tel-Beshmay[41], and the Romans were defeated. Then (the Persians) also attacked Tella[42] and Edessa, and ravaged the region of Harran, as it has been recorded by us above.[43]

In the same year another sign, like darkness,[44] was (visible) in the sky.

At this time (the following) pastors were famous in the Church:

Jacob, the bishop and teacher of Batnae of Serugh,[45] Philoxenus of Mabbug,[46] Peter of Edessa, Antoninus of Aleppo, Constantine of Laodicea, Peter of Apamea, Thomas of Amid, John of Tella, John of Hierapolis, Paul, the patriarch of Alexandria, John of Harran, Nonnos of Circesion, Paul of Callinicos, Peter of Reshaina, Theosebeios of Ephesus, Aaron of Arsamosata, Entrechios[47] of Anazarbos, Felix of Rome, Sallustius of Jerusalem.[48]

The year 815 (A.D. 503/4): there was a great earthquake and the island of Rhodes was ruined in it. This was Rhodes' third collapse, and since it took place at night, it caused many people to perish and few survived. The merciful emperor sent much gold to those [p. 6] who were found (still) alive on (the island). They started to dig out and extract the bodies of those who had been squashed, as if in a deadly wine-press, in (this) great cataclysm.[49]

The year 816 (A.D. 504/5): the Romans went ravaging, killing, destroying, plundering and pillaging the whole Persian territory from Nisibis to the border of Beth Aramaye.[50] They killed every male from 12 years upward, and the rest they took off captive. They also laid waste Persian Armenia, plundering, pillaging and taking everybody captive.

---

[41] West of Mardin.

[42] I.e. Constantina.

[43] In PD I, 277, 7-278, 4; Wright, p. 39f; cp. Procopius, Wars, II, 13, 8-15.

[44] Cp. n. 26.

[45] See below n. 160.

[46] See below n. 97.

[47] Ms.: 'ytyrkyws; see also n. 123 below.

[48] On the hierarchs named here (most of whom are Monophysites) see Honigmann, Évêques, index; for the patriarchs of Rome and Jerusalem, see above nn. 17 & 11; the (Chalcedonian) patriarch of Alexandria is Paul the Tabennesiot: 537–540.

[49] Cp. Malalas 406/227f; Evagrius III, 43, p. 145f/359.

[50] (Central) Babylonia.

In the same year the saintly Nonnos became bishop of Amid. When he sent Thomas his archdeacon on certain errands to the capital, Thomas plotted treacherously against him together with people from Amid who were also in the capital. They snatched away the episcopal office from him, and thus Thomas became bishop of Amid instead of Nonnos.[51]

The year 817 (A.D. 505/6): at the order of the emperor Anastasius the city wall of Dara in Mesopotamia was built.[52]

In the same year Celer, the *magister*[53] came to make peace between the Romans and the Persians.

The year 818 (A.D. 506/7): there was a fight and a great riot against Anastasius, because, in accordance with the custom of the East[54], he wanted to add (to the Thrice-holy hymn), "Thou who wast crucified for us, have mercy upon us".[55] And because of this there were great riots and many killings and the plundering of many people in the capital.[56]

The emperor Anastasius, being a God-loving (person), wished to add to the (formula), "Holy art Thou, God, Holy art Thou, Mighty, [**p. 7**]

---

[51] Cp. C. Karalewsky, 'Amid', *DHGE* 2 (1914), col. 1239f.

[52] On the foundation of Dara: Procopius, *Wars* I, 10, 13-19; Ps.-Zachariah, VII, 6; see also P. Collinet, 'Une "ville neuve" byzantine en 507: la fondation de Dara (Anastasiopolis) en Mésopotamie', in *Mélanges offerts à M. G. Schlumberger*, Paris 1924, p. 55-60; W. Ensslin, 'Zur Gründungsgeschichte von Dara-Anastasiopolis', *Byzantinisch-neugriechische Jahrbücher* 5 (1926-27), p. 342-347; B. Croke & J. Crow, 'Procopius and Dara', *Journal of Roman Studies* 73 (1983), p. 143-159; M. Whitby, 'Procopius' description of Dara (*Buildings* II.1-3)', in *The Defence of the Roman and Byzantine East: Proceedings of a colloquium held at the University of Sheffield in April 1986*, ed. by Ph. Freeman & D. Kennedy, (BAR International Series 297:ii), Oxford 1986, p. 737-783, esp. 751f.

[53] I.e. the *magister officiorum*, one of the highest Byzantine officials, the chief of the central civil administration, a member of the imperial council (*consistorium*) in charge of the palace guards, diplomatic negotiations (as is clear from Celer's mission), armament factories and border defence; see Clauss, *Magister officiorum*; on the actual holder of the office, Celer (2), see *PLRE II*, p. 275-277, and Clauss, p. 150f.

[54] The *praefectura Orientis* is meant here.

[55] The formula ὁ σταυρωθεὶς δι'ἡμᾶς, Thou who wast crucified for us', was introduced first in Antioch by the patriarch Peter the Fuller (470, 485–489), and later under the influence of Syrians (e.g. *praefectus praetorio* Marinus, see below n. 63), an attempt to introduce it in the capital was made by the emperor Anastasius; see Frend, *Rise*, p. 168; Brock, 'Thrice-holy Hymn'.

[56] The riot in Constantinople against what was conceived as a Monophysite addition to the Trisagion took place in November 512 (on the authority of the *Chronicle* of Marcellinus Comes (*Chronica minora saec. IV. V. VI. VII*, vol. 2, ed. T. Mommsen (Monumenta Germaniae Historica: Auctores antiquissimi 11), Berlin 1894, p. 97); Charanis, *Church and State*, p. 48-50; Stein, *Bas-Empire*, p. 177f; Capizzi, *Anastasio*, p. 119-121; Frend, *Rise*, 220.

Holy art Thou, Immortal", the words, "Thou who wast crucified for us, have mercy upon us", as the regions of the East and many (other) people did. Now, the whole family of the noble Juliana,[57] including herself and the majority of the city, were Nestorians,[58] so when the emperor ordered this, all of Constantinople following the monks of the Akoimetai[59] and others, gathered against him amidst clamour, riot, threat and many protests (and said) 'This (formula), "Thou who wast crucified for us", which he wants to introduce to the faith of the Christians, is something new and alien.' Furthermore they named that robber who was crucified together with our Lord, Dumachos,[60] crying out to him, "Thou who wast crucified for us,[61] have mercy upon us", and other rubbish of that kind.

Then they ran and surrounded the palace shouting, "Another emperor for Rome!" The city prefect, whose name was Plato,[62] had to flee and hide himself from the wrath of the people. But they ran to the house of Marinus the Syrian,[63] the ex-prefect,[64] that is, the regent, to kill him. When (they) learned [that he had managed] to escape from them, they set fire to and burned his house, (having) plundered all his possessions.

---

[57] Anicia Juliana, a patrician of royal descent (her father Olybrius was the emperor of the West in 472, her mother was the daughter of Valentinian III, emperor 425–455), known for her attachment to Chalcedonianism; cp. *PLRE II*, p. 635f; C. Capizzi, 'Anicia Giuliana (462 ca–530 ca): ricerche sulla sua famiglia e la sua vita', *Rivista di Studi bizantini e neoellenici* 5 (1968), p. 191-226; M. Harrison, *A Temple for Byzantium*, London 1989, esp. chs. I & V.

[58] In the mouth of the Monophysite Ps.-Dionysius, as well as of his source John of Ephesus, this simply means 'Chalcedonians'.

[59] A monastery in Constantinople in which incessant services were held, hence the name "The monastery of the sleepless" Μονὴ τῶν 'Ακοιμήτων (Janin, *Églises*, p. 20); its monks were extremely pro-Chalcedonian.

[60] Ms.: *dwmks*; this name of the thief on Christ's right comes from the apocryphal *Acts of Pilate*, known also as the *Gospel of Nicodemus* (9, 5) of the fourth century, where it occurs in the form 'Dysmas'; (*The Apocryphal New Testament: being the apocryphal gospels, acts, epistles and apocalypses*, transl. by M.R. James, Oxford 1953, p. 103); Dysmas' unrepentant colleague is there called Gestas. In the Christian Oriental tradition (Syriac, Arabic, Ethiopic) the names of the thieves are Dumakos and Titos, but the roles are changed, Titos being the repentant one.

[61] The name Dumachos occurs sometimes in the form Demas, which is a pun on δι' ἡμᾶς ("for us") of the formula; Brock, 'Thrice-holy hymn', p. 29.

[62] Plato (3), *PLRE II*, p. 891f.

[63] Marinus (7), *praefectus praetorio* for the East (?512–515 & 519), *PLRE II*, p. 726-728. Praetorian prefect: one of the highest civilian dignitaries in the Byzantine empire, who in his prefecture acted as a vice-emperor, with responsibilities in taxation, justice, public construction etc.; *ODB* p. 1710.

[64] The Syriac uses here the Greek loan-term ἀπὸ ἐπάρχων.

They said that, being a Syrian, he had deceived the emperor into introducing the (formula), "Thou who wast crucified for us". So with axes they broke up his silver in the treasury and divided (it between themselves). Also, on finding in his house a poor Syrian monk, they killed him; cutting off his head and setting it upon a pole they carried it [**p. 8**] as they rushed around the city, shouting "Here is the conspirator who is the enemy of the Trinity".

Having come to the house of Juliana, the noble patrician, they called out to her husband Areobindus[65] to become the emperor of the Roman empire;[66] but Areobindus fled to the other side.[67]

On the horse-races arranged by the emperor's order, at which he appeared without his crown.

The emperor ordered horse-races (to be held). He ascended to his seat (in the hippodrome) in ordinary dress, without the crown. When the people of the city saw the emperor's humble appearance and found him appeasing them with kind words, their anger calmed down and they (then) began to praise him and to beg him to put on his imperial crown. He in his turn, urged them not to attack one another. They obeyed him, and for some days remained in peace and tranquillity in relation to him and to each other. (But) finally they were agitated by other causes and started another riot. Then he gave orders to punish them, thus very much strengthening his power as an emperor. He poured on their heads retribution for their previous cruelty. Many perished under torture and many were thrown into the sea. Thus a great fear beset all the populace and they remained in enforced tranquillity, not only in the capital but in all Roman cities.[68]

---

[65] Areobindus, a Roman commander in the war with the Persians (503–505), *PLRE II*, p. 143f.

[66] Lit. 'Romania'.

[67] 'The other side', i.e to Galata on the other side of the Golden Horn; John of Ephesus must have read πέραν ('to/on the other side or shore') in his source (= the original *Chronicle* of Malalas, confirmed by the *Chr. Pasch.* 610/102), whereas the Oxford Malalas (407/228) has ἐν περάματι, "(... fled and hid) in Perama".

[68] PD (via John of Ephesus) seems to have preserved the extensive original account of Malalas on the Trishagion riot. The extant Malalas (406–408/228), John of Nikiu (89, 58) *Chr. Pasch.*, (610/102, preserved fragmentarily), and Evagrius III, 4 have a shorter account of the riot; for other chronicles dependent on Malalas, see Malalas, transl. p. 228, n. 19.

On the expulsion and the exile to which Macedonius, the patriarch of Constantinople, was condemned.[69]

When many evils thus came about due to Macedonius, the heretic, God wished that his wickedness might be removed from the Church of the believers, and go (instead) to the synagogue of the Jews, his adherents. Then the emperor gave orders about his exile, and, as he wanted [**p. 9**] to put to shame (the patriarch's) like-minded friend, the *magister*,[70] he gave these (orders) to him, which broke him down and caused him much pain. The *magister*, however, hastened to execute the order which had been given to him. He went out and found (Macedonius) in a church, to which he had fled in order to hide, (sitting) with his head bowed between his knees. He said to him, "The lord of the world has doomed you to exile". He asked, "Whither?", and (the *magister*) answered, "To the place to which your former colleague went, to Euchaita".[71]

But the stewards entreated him saying, "Our lord, we entreat your honour to have mercy upon his old age and not to lead him forth in daytime, lest the city be incensed, but allow him to stay till the evening that he may leave under cover of darkness". They swore (by) the Gospel that they would [guard][72] him till the evening, and that he would not absent himself; and they left people to guard him.

So in the year 820, on the seventh of July (509 A.D.)[73] in the evening, the *magister* came with a numerous auxiliary force and they brought Macedonius out of God's church and delivered him to those who had been ordered to conduct him into exile. What happened to him

---

[69] On the deposition of Macedonius, who was accused of having falsified Scripture in favour of the Nestorian cause, and on the role played in his removal by Severus, the future patriarch of Antioch, see W. H. C. Frend, 'The fall of Macedonius—a suggestion', in *Kerygma und Logos: Festschrift für C. Andresen*, ed. A. M. Ritter, Göttingen 1979, p. 183-195.

[70] *Magister officiorum*, Celer; see above, n. 53.

[71] Macedonius' predecessor, Euphemius, was also exiled in 496 to Euchaita (τὰ Εὐχάιτα) in Pontus, modern Avkhat, R. Janin, 'Euchaïtes', *DHGE* 15 (1963), col. 1311.

[72] This and further lacunae are filled by J.B. Chabot on the basis of the *Church History* of Pseudo-Zachariah of Mitylene.

[73] In fact, Macedonius was deposed on 11 August 511.

he deserved, (for) [he caused] great [turbulence][74] in the whole Church of the Orthodox. Thus calm and quiet ensued in [the Church...][75]

After him another monk, whose name was [Timothy][76] ascended the (patriarch's) throne in the capital.

The year 821 (A.D. 509/10): the holy Simeon, bishop of Beth Arsham, called Simeon the Persian Disputer, became famous.[77] At one time [p. 10] he instructed in the faith and baptized three noble and famous men from among the Magians. When their companions heard that they had turned away from the Magian religion and become Christians, they informed the king about them. The (converts) received this edict: if they had really turned away and would not renounce Christianity, they should die. But those (converts), who had become worthy of the crown of life, on learning of the king's threat of the sword, neither feared nor trembled, all the more so as the blessed (Simeon) himself had armed them with an ardent desire to bear witness (as martyrs) in exchange for eternal life. And they stood up to the sentence of the sword meted out against them, saying, "Woe to us if we renounce the living God who created the heaven and the earth, and His Son, our Lord Jesus Christ, who called us, and in His grace brought us close to Himself. (Woe to us) if we renounce Him and worship a thing created by Him instead of Himself." Then these blessed men, ten days after their spiritual birth, departed to God in admirable martyrdom through swift death by the sword.

At this time in the region of Perrhe[78] Satan inspired among some people the error of neither eating bread, nor drinking water. Some of the brethren of their monasteries are not known but others, archimandrites, drew upon themselves vain glory and futile infamy. They falsely declared that they did not eat bread, and did not drink water, and they claimed to be abstainers from wine. But the natural feelings of hunger and thirst they impiously satisfied with the Holy Mysteries. Most of

---

[74] *šāgūšūtā*, after Paulin Martin's copy (Paris, Bibliothèque Nationale, Ms. Syr. 284) quoted by Hamilton-Brooks, p. 176, n. 5, which makes better sense ("the Orthodox" being the Monophysites) than Chabot's reconstruction, *dehltā* ('fear'), PD 9, 20.

[75] Chabot suggests, "in the capital", PD 9, n. 7.

[76] Lacuna in the manuscript restored by Chabot; Timothy I: 511–518.

[77] On Simeon, Monophysite bishop of Beth Arsham in Persia, who was known as the 'Disputer' because of his frequent disputes with Nestorian hierarchs in Persia, see Shahîd, *Martyrs*, p. 159-169, and his life by John of Ephesus, *Lives, PO* 17:1 (1923), p. 137-158, from which (p. 141) PD's lemma is excerpted.

[78] Perrhe in Euphratesia, north of Samosata.

their nourishment consisted of the Eucharist, which is why they deliberately leaven the bread they make for the Host, and carefully season it to make it their food and not the Mystery [p. 11] of Christ's Body, which is prefigured by the unleavened bread. Moreover, whenever they feel constrained (by hunger) they offer up ordinary bread at each other's hands and eat it. When they go on a journey or travel a long way, then two or three times in a single day they would appease their natural hunger and thirst with the same Body and Blood of Christ our Lord. Having reached their destination, in the evening they would offer the oblation again, receiving it as if they were fasting. Even during Holy Lent they dared to act thus without fear of God or human shame. It was said about them that when they had prepared the Eucharist on a paten they ate from it freely as much as they wanted. Each one of them mixed warm water with the cup of the living Blood and drank as much as he wanted, then filled it again and gave to his companion.

Holy Rabbula of Edessa and holy Gemellinus bishop of Perrhe stood up against this error.[79]

The year 822 (A.D. 510/11): Vitalian revolted against Anastasius.[80]

The year 823 (A.D. 511/12): in Sidon of Phoenicia a synod gathered. The leading men of this synod were the following: Symmachus, patriarch [p. 12] of Rome, Timothy, patriarch of the capital, Flavian, patriarch of Antioch, John, patriarch of Alexandria, Elias of Jerusalem, John of Tella, Philoxenus of Mabbug.[81] (As) Flavian was found to be a

---

[79] The story of the monks of Perrhe is a summary of the so-called *Letter* of Rabbula, bishop of Edessa, to Gemellinus, bishop of Perrhe. In a fuller form it is preserved in the *Church History* of Ps.-Zachariah II, 178, 11-189, 26/301-310. If its real author was Rabbula (d. 435), who lived a century before the date under which the *Letter* is quoted by PD, then the story is chronologically out of place both in Ps.-Zachariah and in PD, and this is why some scholars thought that instead of Rabbula (spelt *rbwl'*) one should read Paul (*pwl'*), who was a bishop of Edessa from 510 to 526. A. Vööbus ('Solution du problème de l'auteur de la "Lettre à Gemellinos, évêque de Perrhé"', *OS* 7 (1962), p. 297-306) reinvested Rabbula with the authorship of the *Letter*; see also E. Honigmann, *Le Couvent de Barsaumā et le patriarcat jacobite d'Antioche et de Syrie*, (CSCO 146, Subs 7), p. 27-35, who suggested that the monks of Perrhe were archimandrite Bar Sauma (not to be confused with the Nestorian Bar Sauma of Nisibis) and his followers, known to have contributed to the victory of the Monophysites at the Robber Council in Ephesus (449).

[80] The rebellion of Vitalian (*PLRE II*, p. 1171-1176), the military commander in Thrace, started in May 513; Bury, *Later Empire*, I, p. 447-452; Capizzi, *Anastasio*, p. 123-127; Charanis, *Church and State*, p. 51-65.

[81] See below n. 97.

heretic,[82] the emperor Anastasius ordered (the participants of the synod) to gather again, in Antioch, to appoint a (new) patriarch instead of Flavian. When they gathered (again), they appointed there a monk by the name in Severus[83] of the Monastery of Theodore. He was the grandson of Severus, the bishop of Sozopolis in Pisidia,[84] one of the Two Hundred and Twenty (Fathers) who, together with the Teacher Cyril, carried out the deposition of Nestorius.[85]

If you find "it gathered in Sidon", and then you find it spelt as, "it gathered in Ṣaidon", do not be perplexed: both are the same although in language they are different.[86]

When this holy man (Severus) came over to the *bema*,[87] and ascended the throne of Saint Ignatius, then all the Antiochenes together with their wives and children proclaimed, shouting together, "For a long time we have wanted to partake of the Holy Mysteries. Set our city free from Council of Chalcedon! Anathematize now this (council) which has

---

[82] The Monophysite bishops, with Philoxenus of Mabbug as the main instigator, did not manage to depose Flavian (who in fact kept firmly to the *Henoticon* formula, on which see below n. 96) at the council of Sidon, but somewhat later in 512 at Laodicea. His removal put the whole patriarchate of Antioch into Monophysite hands; Honigmann, *Évêques*, p. 12-15; Frend, *Rise*, p. 216-219; Symmachus may have only been represented by legates.

[83] Severus (468–538), Monophysite patriarch of Antioch 512-518, was one of the most important figures in the development of Monophysite theology, the framer of its christology; see Honigmann, *Évêques*, p. 19-25; J. Lebon, 'La christologie du monophysisme syrien', in *Konzil von Chalkedon*, I, p. 425-580; Frend, *Rise*, p. 201-235; idem, 'Severus of Antioch and the origins of the Monophysite hierarchy', in *The Heritage of the Early Church: essays in honor of... G.V. Florovsky...*, ed. D. Neiman & M. Schatkin, (OChA 195), Rome 1973, p. 261-275; Chesnut, *Three Christologies*, p. 9-56; I. R. Torrance, *Christology after Chalcedon: Severus of Antioch and Sergius the Monophysite*, Norwich 1988.

[84] This is probably an early fiction which has pervaded all the Syriac sources on Severus; the Coptic version of his homily on Leontius, where there is evidence of his coming from a pagan family, is likely to be more reliable; see G. Garitte, 'Textes hagiographiques orientaux relatifs à saint Léonce de Tripoli, II: L'Homélie copte de Sévère d'Antioche', *Mus* 79 (1966) 335–386, esp. p. 339.

[85] At the Council in Ephesus, 431.

[86] The latter (ms. *Ṣydwn*) is the usual Semitic (Aramaic, Syriac, Hebrew, Phoenician) form of the toponym, (cp. Jud. 1, 31), whereas the former (ms. *Sydwn*) is the Syriac transcription of the Greek name (Σ(ε)ιδῶν). This remark was added by PD on the basic of a secondary marginal note which he must have found in a manuscript of his source, *The Life of Severus* by John of Beth Aphtonia. The two known manuscripts of this work have a similar note, "Sidon is 'Ṣaidon' (*Vie de Sévère par Jean supérieur du monastère de Beith-Aphthonia*, ed. with French transl. by M.-A. Kugener, *PO* 2:3 (1981 [=1904], p. 238 [=154], n. 1).

[87] *Bema* (βῆμα): in the eastern churches a slightly elevated part, either in the apse or, as in Syria, in the middle of the building, where the bishop's chair was placed; often separated from the rest of the church by a chancel screen.

Council of Chalcedon! Anathematize now this (council) which has turned the world (upside down)! Anathematize now the council of the distorters (of the faith)! The cursed Council of Chalcedon! The cursed *Tome* of Leo! Let all the bishops anathematize (it) now! Who will not do so is a wolf and not a shepherd."

If there was anybody who was believed to be a follower of Flavian, he would hear his own name (being called), "So and so, anathematize the synod!"—which was what happened. When the synod was anathematized by all, while (the people) cried out these and similar (words) and made acclamations, [**p. 13**] the Teacher Severus rejoiced all the more greatly at these things.

He composed a homily filled with teaching of complete theological soundness at that time, in which he confounded Nestorius' anthropolatry,[88] and exposed Eutyches'[89] dreamlike phantasy. Also, in many words he strongly attacked the Synod of Chalcedon and the Tome of Leo and admonished us to keep away from those two perilous rocks, equal in ungodliness. Instead we should go the royal way[90] and confess one nature out of two in God the incarnate Word.[91]

And after saying a few words on the right conduct of life, as time allowed, he sent off the tired people to their bodily rest. Thus it was a glorious day because of the accession of this glorious man.

When he directly thereafter arrived at his episcopal residence and found the kitchen servants and the cooks of the residence and all the equipment installed by them, he removed (it all) from the place. He also destroyed the bath which was there, just as Josiah and Hezekiah, the God-loving kings, did to the statues of Baal.[92] He reverted to the austere customs of monasticism, which were his habit previously. He practised lying down on the earth, refraining from washing, (performing) the

---

[88] Syr. *pālhūt barnāšā*, 'man-worship'; one of the standard Monophysite reproaches against Nestorianism which allegedly saw only a man in Jesus.

[89] Eutyches: the archimandrite of a monastery in Constantinople who held extreme Monophysite opinions denying that Christ's human nature was consubstantial with man's nature, a view which rendered void Christ's redemptory death on the Cross. Though accepted as orthodox by the Robber Council (449), he was anathematized two years later by the Council of Chalcedon. Mainstream Monophysites (Severans) opposed Eutychianism as much as the Chalcedonians did; see T. Camelot, 'De Nestorius à Eutyches: l'opposition de deux christologies', in *Konzil von Chalkedon*, I, p. 236-242.

[90] I.e. without deviating to the left or right, cp. Num. 20, 17.

[91] Cp. M.-A. Kugener (ed.), 'Allocution prononcée par Sévère après son élévation sur le trône patriarcale d'Antioche', *OCh* 2 (1902), p. 265-271.

[92] 2 Kings 23.4, 14, 19, 18.4 for Josiah and Hezekiah respectively.

offices with long psalmody, eating vegetables like the youths of Babylon.[93] He had brought from the market place bread which was very inferior and low quality.[94]

The year 826 (A.D. 514/5): a synod gathered in Tyre by the order of the emperor Anastasius. All the bishops of the East gathered there, from Apamea [**p. 14**], Euphratesia, Osrhoene, Mesopotamia, Arabia, and Phoenicia in Lebanon. The leading men of this synod were: Severus patriarch of Antioch, Timothy of the capital (being represented) by deputies, Elias of Jerusalem—by deputies, John patriarch of Alexandria, Symmachus patriarch of Rome, Philoxenus of Mabbug, John of Tella, and Paul[95] of Edessa. John Bar Aphtonia and Cosmas of the monastery of Mar Aqiba became famous. Severus made the truth shine out and expounded the edict (of) *Henoticon*, proclaimed by the emperor Zeno,[96] and demonstrated that it was (aimed) at annulling the (decisions) made at Chalcedon. They openly condemned it there and also the addition to the creed. The bishops who gathered together with Severus and Akhsenaya[97] proclaimed the complete truth.[98]

---

[93] Dan. 1. 12, 16.

[94] The whole account of Severus' accession (beginning, "When this holy man (Severus)...) is taken from Severus' *Vita* by John of Beth Aphtonia (*Vie de Sévère* [see above n. 86]).

[95] Chabot's correction; ms: Rabbula.

[96] *Henoticon*: the compromise Christological formula propounded by the emperor Zeno in 482 in order to bring unity to the Church split into the Chalcedonian and the Monophysite parties. The text of the formula is given by PD in the previous part of the chronicle, PD I, 231, 1-234, 24/172-174; for an English transl. from Syriac see Ps.-Zachariah, Hamilton-Brooks, p. 121-123; and from Greek (Evagrius, III:14), Frend, *Rise*, p. 360-362; on the vicissitudes of the formula ibid., p. 143-183.

[97] I.e. Philoxenus, the name (cp. 1 Tim. 3, 2) he took on becoming bishop of Mabbug/Hierapolis (485–519, †523); a staunch Monophysite churchman, instrumental in the choice of the Monophysite monk Severus as patriarch of Antioch, which meant a temporary victory for this theology in the patriarchate; known for his many writings and for sponsoring a revised translation of the New Testament. On his life: A. D. Vaschalde, *Three Letters of Philoxenus bishop of Mabbôgh*, Rome 1902, p. 1-23; on his theology: Chesnut, *Three Christologies*, p. 57-112; the most comprehensive monograph is A. de Halleux, *Philoxène de Mabbog: sa vie, ses écrits, sa théologie*, Louvain 1963.

[98] A more exhaustive account of the synod of Tyre is given by Ps.-Zachariah II, 54, 19-56, 22/183f, the source of the present lemma. The synod reconfirming the *Henoticon* marked perhaps the highest achievement of the Monophysite cause (within the imperial Church) to which all the four Eastern patriarchs subscribed; Elias of Jerusalem, who signed reluctantly, was replaced in 516 by a pro-Monophysite incumbent; Symmachus of Rome, who was represented by deputies, did not accept the synod; Frend, *Rise*, p. 227f.

The year 827 (A.D. 515/6): Ilmarqios[99]'in Rome revolted against the emperor Anastasius and acquired all the Western countries. He assumed royal power in Rome, for he was a stern man.[100]

The year 828 (A.D. 516/7): many people of (Upper) Egypt, Alexandria and Transjordania—Edomites and Arabs—gathered and came to the feast of the Encaenia,[101] of the setting up of the Cross in Jerusalem, which took place on the 14th September. Then demons entered into many (of them) and they barked at the Cross like dogs. Then (the demons) calmed down and left them.

This caused a lot of anxiety and distress to discerning people, but they could not understand exactly the cause until the event itself [p. 15] manifested the outcome: God had let people know beforehand about the strife concerning the faith which came thereafter, and the scandals which subsequently occurred.[102]

The hierarchs who were famous in the days of the emperor Anastasius:

In Rome there was Felix, and after him Symmachus, and after him Hormisdas;[103]

In Alexandria, among the believers: Athanasius and John; and John and Dioscorus;[104]

In Antioch: Flavian who was deposed,[105] and Severus the believer;[106]

---

[99] Syr.: *'ylmrqyws* from ὁ Οὐαλαμῆ ρου i.e. Valamer's son; Theodoric, king of the Ostrogoths (471–526), is meant (his father was Theodemer, and Valamer his uncle); *PLRE II*, p. 1077-1084; see also J. Moorhead, *Theoderic in Italy*, Oxford 1992.

[100] Probably the seizure of Italy by Theoderic is meant here; the correct date is 493; cp. Ps.-Zachariah II, 56, 12-22/184, which is the source of this lemma.

[101] Encaenia: the feast established to commemorate the dedication of the basilica of the Holy Sepulchre in Jerusalem (near Golgotha) built by the Emperor Constantine the Great in 335; soon an additional motif, that of the *Inventio Crucis* by Helena, the mother of Constantine, was associated with the feast which, because of frequent elevations of the Cross, has become known as the the Feast of the Exaltation of the Cross (ὕψωσις τοῦ σταυροῦ); A. Frolow, *La relique de la Vrai Croix* (AOCh 7), Paris 1961, p. 161-165; E. Dinkler & E. Dinkler-von Schubert, 'Kreuz', *Reallexikon zur byzantinischen Kunst*, vol. 5, (Stuttgart 1991), col. 19; see also, M. Black, 'The Festival of Encaenia Ecclesiae in the Ancient Church with special reference to Palestine and Syria', *The Journal of Ecclesiastical History* 5 (1954), p. 78-87.

[102] The account comes from Ps.-Zachariah II, 58, 10-20/186.

[103] See n. 17; Symmachus: 498–514; Hormisdas: 514–523.

[104] See n. 16; John I: 496–505; John II: 505–516; Dioscorus II: 516–517.

[105] On the deposition of Flavian (498–512), see n. 82.

[106] See n. 13; Severus: see n. 83.

In Constantinople: Euphemius and Macedonius the heretics, Timothy the believer, and John who accepted the Council of Chalcedon in the beginning of Justinian (the Elder's)[107] reign, but soon died; and Epiphanius became (patriarch) after him;[108]

In Jerusalem: Sallustius, Elias [who was expelled and Joh]n[109] who accepted the council in the days of Justinian the Elder, and after him Peter.[110]

The hierarchs who officiated in the days of Justinian the Elder, and who introduced (the decisions of) the Council of Chalcedon:

In Rome: Hormisdas;

In Alexandria: Timothy;[111]

In Jerusalem: Peter;

In Antioch: Paul the Jew, Euphrasius who was burned (alive) in a cauldron of pitch during the fall of Antioch,[112] and Ephrem of Amid;[113]

In Constantinople: Epiphanius.

These were (the hierarchs) in the days of Justinian the Elder, who reigned after Anastasius.

The year 829 (A.D. 517/8): the emperor Anastasius died; after him reigned Justinian the Elder. He was trained in warfare and Roman discipline, but was not acquainted with any teaching from the words of the holy prophets or teachers inspired by the Holy Spirit. Thus in the beginning of his reign those who confessed two [p. 16] Natures in Christ after the Union deceived him, and, as he was a simple man and was not educated in the divine dogmas, he was seduced with words into introducing the Council of Chalcedon into the Church, which had enjoyed some tranquillity since the time of the *Henoticon*[114] proclaimed by the emperor Zeno for the abolition of the Council. The believing

---

[107] I.e. Justin I, 518–527; he was called "Justinian the Elder" by Syriac historians in order to differentiate him from Justinian (the Great), his nephew and successor (527–565); the names of the two could easily be confused in Syriac script.

[108] See n. 15; Macedonius: 496–511; Timothy I: 511–518; John II: 518–520; Epiphanius: 520–535.

[109] Lacuna filled by Chabot on the basis of Ps.-Zachariah, II, 59, 23.

[110] Cp. n. 11; Elias I: 494–516; John III: 516–524; Peter: 524–552.

[111] Timothy III: 517–535.

[112] See below, p. 46f.

[113] Paul II (called "the Jew" by the Monophysites): 519–521; Euphrasius: 521–526; Ephrem: 527–545.

[114] *Henoticon*: see no. 96.

people had lived in peace without being disturbed in the entire Roman domain, (but) then (the emperor) ordered that the Council be subscribed to and that it be proclaimed in the Church, and that everybody who would not accept the Council should be sent into exile. After that many dissensions and disagreements sprang up in the Church.[115]

(The emperor) was cunningly advised by those who urged him into it that (the decisions of) the three valid Councils should also be subscribed to and proclaimed together with that of Chalcedon, in order that in this way they might be enabled to deceive the believers, who resisted that of Chalcedon, and thereby ensnare them into thinking that those valid ones belong together with that (of Chalcedon), lest they shun (the latter) and withdraw from (it). So the emperor quickly yielded to this (advice) too, and ordered that it be done in this way.[116]

But the bishop of the city, by the name of John, having realized that wrong things were about to happen in the Church, omitted to inscribe the Councils on the church (diptychs). When the day of a feast came, on which customarily the imperial couple would go to church, Justinian (the Elder)'s wife, whose name was Lupicina,[117] who was also zealous in this matter and urged others about it, sent a message to the bishop, "If you do not inscribe the Councils in the diptychs of the church, I will not come to church, and I will not receive communion from your hands." In this way he was compelled to inscribe and proclaim [p. 17] these four Councils on that feast. Then uproar, riot and tumult arose among all the believers. But when Amantius, the *praepositus*[118] and

---

[115] The real protagonist behind Justin's decision to give imperial support to Chalcedonian teaching (for which the majority of the inhabitants of Constantinople had opted) was his nephew Justinian. In his contacts with Pope Hormisdas in 518 (which eventually ended the so-called Acacian schism between Rome and Constantinople) Justinian wrote separate letters in addition to those by Justin and the patriarch John. Whereas the two latter asked the pope to send legates to Constantinople, Justinian demanded that the pope come to the capital in person; Vasiliev, *Justin*, p. 135, 164.

[116] John of Ephesus possibly has in mind the *Libellus Hormisdae*, which the pope's legates brought to Constantinople in 519 with the demand that all the bishops of the empire should subscribe to it as a condition of reunion with Rome. Eventually over 2000 bishops did so; Frend, *Rise*, p. 236-241.

[117] Her name as empress was Euphemia, *PLRE II*, p. 423.

[118] *Praepositus (sacri cubiculi)*: a high chamberlain in charge of court ceremonies and audiences; Guilland, *Institutions*, I, p. 333-380; on the holder of the office see *PLRE II*, p. 67f; Guilland, ibid., p. 178f, 277.

Andreas, the *cubicularius*[119] also resisted it, they were executed for this reason.[120]

Immediately after the introduction of the Council of Chalcedon, riot and great tumult at once arose in the capital. The people were in commotion, congregations were disturbed, male and female monasteries were in commotion and many dissensions appeared among the Christians. They divided into two parts, two sects and two factions.

While these things were happening, persecution reached the countries of the East. The holy Severus, the patriarch, left his see and his city on learning about the vehemence of the persecution, and went to Alexandria. Thereafter all the Orthodox[121] bishops were forced to leave their sees.

The names of the holy bishops who were chased out of their sees:[122]

From Cilicia: Entrechios[123] of Anazarbos, Julius of Aigai,[124] John of Mopsuestia, Paul of Epiphania, John of Irenopolis, Paul of Little Alexandria.

From Cappadocia: Proclus of Colonia, Musonius of Thermae, Nicephorus of Sebaste.

From Syria: the holy Severus patriarch of Antioch, Constantine of Laodicea, Antoninus of Aleppo, Philoxenus of Mabbug, Peter of Apamea, Nonnos of Seleucia who died in Amid, Isidore of Qenneshrin, Mara of Amid—these two died in Alexandria, Thomas of Damascus who died in Constantinople, Alexander of Abila who died in exile, Thomas of Yabrud who died [**p. 18**] in exile, John of Palmyra who died in exile, John of Hawarin,[125] died in exile, Sergius of Cyrrhus, died in

---

[119] *Cubicularius*: a chamberlain, a eunuch attendant of the imperial bedchamber; Guilland, *Institutions*, I, p. 269-282; on the holder of the office, Andreas (10) Lausiacus, see *PLRE II*, p. 88; Guilland, ibid., p. 179.

[120] The execution of Amantius and Andreas in fact had political causes—their attempt, just before Justin's accession, to put on the throne another candidate; Vasiliev, *Justin*, p. 102-108.

[121] I.e. Monophysite.

[122] The subsequent list has been preserved only by Syrian historians, i.e., in addition to PD, by the *Chronicle to the year 846* (*Chr. Min.* p. 225, 24-228, 8/171-173), and by Michael the Syrian (266b, new ch., 9-267, 28/II, 171-173); it was first published by H. G. Kleyn, 'Bijdrage tot de Kerkgeschiedenis van het Oosten gedurende de zesde eeuw', in *Feestbundel aan Prof. M. J. De Goeje*, Leiden 1891, p. 61-68; since the original was probably in Greek, E. Honigmann, (*Évêques*, p. 146-148) provided a Greek retroversion.

[123] Ms.: *'ytrkyws*; see also n. 47 above.

[124] Syr.: *Hgwn* (Hegon ?).

[125] Greek: Εὐάρεια or Εὔαρις ; Honigmann, *Évêques*, p. 98.

exile, Thomas of Germanicia, died in Samosata, Paul of Edessa, accepted the council and came back to his city, John of Harran, died in Antioch, John of Hemerion,[126] died in exile, Eustathius of Perrhe, died in exile, Peter of Reshaina, died in exile, Nonnos of Circesion, died in exile, Paul of Callinicos, died in exile, Marion of Shura,[127] died in exile, John of Tella, died as a martyr in Antioch at (the hands of) Ephrem of Amid, Thomas of Dara, died in exile, Aaron of Arsamosata, died in exile.

From Asia, Caria and Aphrodisias: Euphemius, the archbishop of Aphrodisias, died in the persecution, Menophanes of Antioch on the river Meander, Zeuxis of Alabanda, died in exile, Peter of Alinda, died in exile, Julian of Halicarnassus, became a phantasiast,[128] Theosebeios of Ephesus: he was required to come to the capital in order to accept the council; he arrived, threw himself down before an altar and on the third day died; Hilarianos of Neocaesarea,[129] Helpidios of Kestroi, Theodore of Olbia, Luke of Anemurion,[130] Eusebianos[131] of Hadriane, Peter of Melota,[132] Victor of Philadelphia, Peter of Mandane,[133] Agathodoros of Isba,[134] Pelagius of Kalenderis, Photinos of Arsinoe, Alexander of Khonokhora.

In all, 54 bishops.

[p. 19] The year 831 (A.D. 519/20): Paul the Jew became patriarch of Antioch. After the departure of the holy Severus, Antioch remained one year without a bishop. Thereafter, the instrument of perdition was chosen and sent there—Paul, (also) called Eutyches, that is a Jew, if it be allowed to say so. He had been a warden of the hospice (in the

---

[126] Syr. '*mwryn*; the name of the bishop should be corrected to Thomas, Honigmann, *Évêques*, p. 53.
[127] Michael the Syrian (267c, 8/II, 172) quoting also John of Ephesus: *Shūrā d-Rhūmāyē*; Gr.: Σοῦρα.
[128] Phantasiasts: see below n. 431.
[129] Read 'Diocaesarea' (as in the *Chronicle to the year 846*, in *Chr. Min.*, p. 228, 3/173); cp. Honigmann, *Évêques*, p. 90.
[130] Ms.: '*mwry*'; Honigmann, *Évêques*, p. 92.
[131] Ms.: '*wsbyn*'; The *Chronicle to 846*: '*wsbyws* (i.e. Eusebius); Michael the Syrian: '*sykwn*' from '*wsbwn*' (?).
[132] Probably a corruption of Meloe; Honigmann, *Évêques*, p. 95.
[133] As in the *Chronicle to 846*, p. 228, 6; PD: *mndy'*.
[134] Ms.: '*yswn*; see: Honigmann, *Évêques*, p. 134.

quarter of) Euboulos[135] in the capital. He fitted the Lord's words uttered in the Gospel, "Scandals will come (but) woe to the man by whom they come".[136] This suits very well this man who was heir to that 'woe' just mentioned, through whom tumult, schisms, scandals and dissensions came to God's Church all over the East. It was he who introduced (the doctrine) of the despicable Council of Chalcedon, and had it inscribed first in the church of Antioch and then in all the churches under the sway of Antioch. It was due to this that violent and cruel persecutions took place, and the expulsion of all the bishops named (above), as well as of (the inmates of) all the monastic houses who did not accept or consent to Paul the Jew's wickedness.[137]

The year 836 (A.D. 524/5): before that, however, at the beginning of the reign of the emperor Justin,[138] a star appeared [p. 20] in the East, similar to a huge spear. The point of the spear was turned downwards. It revolved in a frightening way and long rays were seen by everyone to come out of it. It was called, according to the Greeks, a "comet". Fear overwhelmed everybody who saw how awfully it arose, looked and shone, and how it revolved and altered in a threatening fashion, so that many people would talk about many things they thought to be imminent in the future—a chastisement, war and perdition, (all of it) because of the terrible appearance of the star.[139]

Nor was there any delay in these things: many afflictions followed quickly along with war causing much bloodshed. Also, what is most grievous and bitter, it soon brought about turmoil in the Church, (that is) dissensions, disagreements, persecutions, killings and (other) evils. The star looked like this.[140]

---

[135] Ms.: 'pksndwkwr' d-'sdnwkyn d-'wbls, which is most probably corrupted Greek: ὁ ἀπὸ ξενοδόχων τῶν Εὐβούλου, 'ex-warden of the hospice (in the quarter) of Euboulos', as in Malalas, 411/232, Chabot p. 19, n. 3; on the hospice, Janin, *Églises*, p. 571.

[136] Cp. Mt. 18, 7 and Lk. 17, 1.

[137] On Paul the Jew, see Vasiliev, *Justin*, p. 235f. Criticised for enforcing the Chalcedonian orthodoxy in his province too harshly, he resigned in 521, before two years of his episcopacy had elapsed; ibid., p. 206

[138] Here the manuscript has: ywstyn', whereas the excerpt in a London Ms., published by Land, has: ywstnyn', "Justinian".

[139] Cp. Malalas 411/231; *Chr. Pasch.* 612/104f; Grumel, *Chronologie*, p. 470 (year 519); Schove, *Eclipses*, p. 292 (year 520).

[140] There was a picture of the comet in the margin of the manuscript folio 91v, now lost. A similar (?) picture of a comet has been preserved on fol. 136v, reproduced in Witakowski, *Syriac Chronicle*, p. 2.

The year 837 (A.D. 525/6): there was a sudden fire all over Antioch.[141] Most of the city suddenly caught fire, as if as a result of God's wrath, after He had given warning by the sign about the collapse and the destruction which threatened. Thus in every locality in the city the fire kept breaking out all of a sudden for six months. A multitude of souls perished in it as well as many of its buildings. The people did not succeed in learning whence the fire came, as it started to burn from the highest—fifth and sixth—storeys and, thus kindled, it devastated all the people in its vicinity.[142] **[p. 21]**

On the persecution launched by Paul the Jew[143] against all the churches and monasteries and the rest of the Christians all over the East.[144]

Together with these, also the great and small monasteries of chaste monks were persecuted in all the districts of Antioch, Seleucia, Qenneshrin, Aleppo, Apamea and Mabbug, all over Arabia and Palestine and in all the cities of the South and North, in the desert of the hermits as far as the Persian border, as well as (in) other cities and regions all over the East. They (had to) leave (their monasteries), were robbed, captured, put in irons, locked up in prisons, (brought) before courts and (subjected) to various tortures. Also, many were mercilessly sent to their death through tortures and having their belongings seized. Moreover, Roman armed troops of barbarians attacked them, and *chorepiscopi,*[145] *periodeutae,*[146] as well as other persecutors, who oppressed them everywhere and mercilessly drove them from one place to another. Also (they treated them) with blows from sticks and swords in a barbarous and cruel way, with no restraint from the fear of God, sometimes treating[147] them mercilessly as they (would treat) pagans. And then (the

---

[141] October 525; cp. Malalas 417/236; Theophanes AM 6018; Downey, *Antioch*, p. 520f.

[142] Compare the account of the fires connected with the earthquake of A.D. 525/6, below p. 44f.

[143] The London excerpt adds in the margin, "who was the patriarch of the heretics in Antioch", Land, p. 289.

[144] On this persecution see Vööbus, *Asceticism* III, p. 206-214; Harvey, *Asceticism*, p. 67f.

[145] Non-urban bishops of lower standing than diocesans.

[146] Visiting priests.

[147] Read *methaššhīn*, as in the London manuscript.

oppressors) pillaged, scourged and tortured also the rest of the believers[148] who took in the persecuted and let them enter their villages or houses. From then on one mighty storm of violent persecution [p. 22] at the same time struck grievously and with violence all the countries, cities and villages. One succession of evils extended over all the churches, monasteries, cities and villages as far as the desert of the hermits, the inhabitants of the wilderness. In every city and village, (among) communities and regions, the greedy and barbarous plundering of possessions was unceasing, not only from "pilgrims",[149] monks and nuns, but also from young people[150] and women with babies. All kinds of people were persecuted, driven out, scoffed at, and sent into various exiles in various countries. They endured all kinds of torments, evils and tribulations (which) they suffered for the sake of the truth of the right and flawless faith.

Even if these things were to be described briefly, their accounts would surpass the limits of this narrative, since they should be described in many books and nobody can include them all because they surpass (the very possibilities of) any narrative.

Especially monastic houses, great and small all over Syria, male and female monasteries, western and eastern, suffered and endured in the time of Paul the Jew and again in that of Euphrasius and Ephrem.[151] (The monks) were constantly enduring and suffering all (kinds of) persecutions, tribulations and tortures, as well as severity of hunger and thirst, cold and nakedness. If some of them rested one day in a place, the next day they would be driven out from it. It happened that even at evening (they would be forced to go), since they were not even treated as (ordinary) travellers, [p. 23] or allowed to spend the night in any monastery where they might stay.

So now without any shelter, like animals, in fields and on mountains most of them would spend the nights under the (bare) sky. Sometimes during the hard days of winter, in rain and in snow and ice, due to the

---

[148] I.e. laity.

[149] Syr. ʿedyāyē, which seems to be a technical term for itinerant monks, similar in sense to 'aksnāyē' (ξένοι); Isaac of Antioch (*Homiliae Sancti Isaaci Antiocheni*, ed. P. Bedjan, Paris 1903, p. 90, 563) uses the word ʿedyāyē in this sense.

[150] Land's Ms.: ʿālmāyē ("the laity"), which according to Chabot (PD, 22, n. 3) may be the original reading, thus suggesting for the whole passage: "... not only from the Church people (Chabot would read ʿedtānāyē instead of ʿedyāyē), monks and nuns, but also from the laity and women with babies."

[151] The patriarchs of Antioch in the years 519–521, 521–526, 527–545 respectively.

harshness of bad weather and the severity of the hard winter and in winds, huddling together they stayed sitting on rocks all the night with nothing else beneath them, so that none of them could bend over and lie down on his side on the earth. The persecution went so far that they were expelled from their monasteries and (had to) descend from their columns and leave their hermitages. Also, they were dragged away from (their monastic) stations.

Similar things happened many times to many monasteries. When they had completed their canon of services and at evening were sitting for a meal consisting of what had been sent to them by God, then suddenly the persecutors would arrive and fall upon them with sticks, while their tables were set and dishes filled. And so (the oppressors) would drive them out and themselves sit down at the tables and eat the food prepared for (the monks). And so they had to leave hungry, tired and vexed in their souls. There were among them many old and disabled men and women advanced in years, (stylites) who had descended from columns, and those who had come out of the hermitages (having spent there) a long time. Such were the tortures, distresses and bitter tribulation which the whole monastic body, both men and women, suffered and endured more than anybody else during Paul's entire time of office. [**p. 24**]

From that time on one blow of persecution was unleashed on all the congregations, which did not agree to Chalcedonian communion, (also) in other regions, successively up to the Persian border.

When Paul's first year came to an end the emperor saw that because of his tyranny the (whole) world had severed itself from the Church, and having learned about many evil things which (Paul) did, he removed him and winnowed him out (like chaff) from the Church. (Thereafter) he also departed this life and went to render an account of these things before God's justice, and to obtain the retribution for his doings. That which was due for his error he would receive in his own person, as it is written.[152]

---

[152] Cp. Rom. 1, 27.

The story of Paul of Edessa and of the evil things which occurred because of his removal.[153]

When the thick smoke of tumult and persecution all over the East was rising up even more, it also reached as far as the city of Edessa. At that time its bishop was Paul, whose faith was suspected of being unsound: he was seized by the evil malady of the (doctrine of) the Two Natures. He did not show the falsity of his mind since he trembled before the keen ardour of the Edessenes. When he was summoned (by the patriarch) for the first, second and third times, but did not come, then a man by the name Patricius,[154] together with numerous Roman troops, was sent after him. He arrived in Edessa and wanted to catch Paul but he escaped and hid in the (sunken) font of the baptistery as if to show (to the locals) that he did not want to go. Then the inhabitants of the city and all the monks from its neighbourhood gathered, burning with lively ardour for the truth, and carrying stones, ran to the palace where Patricius was staying; (there) they hurled stones at him [**p. 25**] and all his men in order to drive them out of the city, so that they might be unable to carry Paul off. When he saw the large crowd which gathered against him, and their heavy stoning on all sides, he gave orders to slay them. So the Gothic troops,[155] came out with their bows and arrows and many people were struck and died, and (others) fled before them. (The troops) started to slay them with swords, especially those who wore monk's attire: they killed by the sword every one of them that they found. And many lost their lives in the slaughter—all who did not manage to escape or to hide somewhere to save themselves: (for) those who hid saved themselves from the slaughter. And there was great lamentation and sorrow in the whole Church. In this way they took Paul and left.

When Paul appeared before Paul the Jew, (patriarch) of Antioch, it seemed to many that the former was of the same opinion as the latter and secretly agreed with him. But in order to keep the matter secret from the Edessenes, to prevent them from shunning Paul and not accepting him, the two of them skilfully arranged the affair so that Paul was released and came back to his city, pretending that he was not in

[153] On Paul, see Jansma, 'Jacques', p. 193-236.

[154] Patricius (14), *magister militum* 500-518, *PLRE II*, p. 840-842.

[155] I.e. Byzantine soldiers recruited from among the Goths. The Edessenes had previous (505-506) unpleasant experience of the presence of Gothic mercenaries billeted in their city; cp. Ps.-Joshua, PD I, 310, 13-313, 28/70-73.

agreement with (Paul the Jew). The Edessenes came out to welcome him and the Orthodox accepted him as somebody who had fought and won.

After some time the bishop of Harran died and Paul intended to enthrone there a priest of the Edessene church by the name of Asclepius,[156] whose brother was *praefectus praetorio*[157] in the capital. Although (Paul) gave (Asclepius) to believe (he would appoint him), he went back on his word and appointed somebody else instead of him. In the end Asclepius departed to see his brother and told him that Paul did not accept the Council of Chalcedon. When the story reached the emperor, he sent Pharesmanes, who was **[p. 26]** a *stratelates*,[158] to remove Paul from Edessa. Thus he left (his see) and Asclepius became (the bishop) in his stead.

Paul the Jew died after one year (in office). In his place came Euphrasius.[159] It was he who ordained Asclepius in Edessa and at the same time incited him to persecutions and plunder. What he was encouraged to do, he did many times over and continued to do throughout his episcopacy.

Prior to that, however, before he was removed, Paul invited the blessed Mar Jacob, the bishop and teacher of Batnae of Serugh,[160] to visit him. He, however, excused himself from coming because he saw that (Paul) was not sound in his faith. When Paul put pressure on the blessed man to come, he entered the church and threw himself before the altar and prayed with grief, and with many tears. He said, "My Lord God, (who) knowest what is in the hearts of all (people), and who examinest kidneys and hearts:[161] if Thou knowest that the false teaching of the Two Natures is in Paul's heart, let me not see his face". And

---

[156] Asclepius Bar Mallāhē, bishop 522–525, *PLRE II*, p. 163; Jansma, 'Jacques', p. 210-226.

[157] Praetorian prefect (the Syriac uses two Greek terms, ὕπαρχος, instead of ἔπαρχος, of the πραιτωρίων); his name was Demosthenes (4), *PLRE II*, p. 353f; on his office, see n. 63.

[158] Στρατηλάτης: a general, the commander of an independent military unit; Guilland, *Institutions*, I, p. 385-392; on the incumbent see *PLRE II*, p. 872f.

[159] Patriarch 521–526.

[160] Jacob of Serugh: a prolific Syriac poet and writer (ca. 451–521), called "the Flute of the Holy Spirit", bishop 519-521; W. Hage, 'Jakob von Sarug', *Theologische Realenzyklopädie* 16 (1987), p. 470-474; on his theology see Chesnut, *Three Christologies*, p. 113-141; Jansma, 'Jacques'.

[161] Based on Jer. 11, 20; 17, 10; 20, 12; in the Old Testament kidneys are treated as the seat of man's thoughts, desires and affections.

when (Paul) repeatedly pressed him to come, he left the city of Batnae and went as far as the monastery called "of the Persians", which is at a distance of six miles from Edessa. He arrived and spent the night in that monastery. In the night it was revealed to him about his (own) departure, and he was ordered to return to his city. So he rose in (the middle of) the night, hastened to his attendants (to tell) them promptly to prepare the beasts of burden for the journey back to (their) city. He said, "In two days I shall depart this world," and to the astonishment and amazement of his attendants he returned and arrived in his city. He left orders concerning his congregation and his whole teaching, and two days later he departed this world. The power of this holy man's prayer, together with all his teachings, became famous in the whole Church of God and all over Syria: everybody was astounded [**p. 27**] and gave praise to God.

Having learnt about this Paul appointed in his place a man by the name of Moses.

On the persecution of the great Monastery of the Orientals in Edessa[162] and all other monasteries in the entire East and West.

In the days of Paul (the monks) of this great and famous Monastery of the Orientals in Edessa saw that he was unsound as far as the truth was concerned. They broke off and separated themselves from him, thus breaking the habit of receiving communion from the church in Edessa. So they broke (it) and from now on they made (the eucharistic) offering in the monastery and did not take communion from the church any more. Other Edessenes and Amidenes did so too. They demanded from everybody, from the great to the small, that he anathematize, in his own handwriting, the Council of Chalcedon, the *Tome* of Leo, and everybody who speaks of or confesses Two Natures in Christ after the Union. Thus all of them decided and wrote. Also the same text was written on the outside of the gates of all the monasteries. All the monasteries all over Syria did so.

However by the instigation of the wretched Asclepius,[163] Pharesmanes the *stratelates* expelled the monks of the Monastery of the Orientals in the inclement season. They were told and forced to leave, but they said, "How can you require us to leave in this inclement winter time? Not

---

[162] Outside the South Gate; Segal, *Edessa*, p. 190.
[163] The London ms. adds, "who was the bishop of Edessa".

even the barbarians, who have no mercy, would do so. There are old people among us and many infirm people [**p. 28**] who are confined to their beds and are not able to put their feet on the ground." Then Pharesmanes ordered Asclepius to give them beasts of burden and camels to carry their baggage, and so, two days before Christmas, they set out carrying their sick and elderly on litters.

As the city learned about their departure, all men and women, old and young, adolescents and children ran to see them and to be blessed by them. When they saw them leaving, being pushed and driven out, they wailed, raising their voices in bitter weeping, especially as they saw the old and infirm carried on litters. They wailed loudly and said amidst the weeping, "Woe to us, for in our days Christianity is perishing! Woe to us, what things have happened in our days! Woe to us, what do we see with our (own) eyes: in our generation the ruin of the Christian faith! From now on by what shall we conduct our life?"

Following that wretched and ungodly spectacle of the ruin of the faith, the persecution and retreat of God's servants, men and women hastened up weeping and wailing and grasped the legs of the blessed men to press them to their eyes. They wailed and wept bitterly and cried woe to themselves. Thus they all left carrying their crosses.[164] Many people remained with them for two or three days, while (monks) from other monasteries left and joined them: the monks of the monastery of Mar Zakkai,[165] the monks of the monastery of Mar Conon, the monks of (that of) Exedrae,[166] the monks [**p. 29**] of Naphshatha,[167] the monks

---

[164] Mt. 16, 24; Mk. 8, 34; Lc. 9, 33; 14, 27.

[165] Near Callinicus/Raqqa on the Euphrates; the monastery is known to have its own rules, set up by John Bar Qursos bishop of Tella (519–521), who was one of its inmates; Vööbus, *Asceticism, III*, p. 179-181.

[166] Probably identical with the Monastery of Exedra (ἐξέδρα: 'portico, gallery') near Edessa, on the hilltops (*Chr. 1234*, I, 181, 22/143), so called because it probably had a "gallery" of its dead archimandrites, Segal, *Edessa*, p. 191, n.

[167] Syr.: 'souls' but also 'funerary monuments, or towers' (cp. M. Gawlikowski, 'La notion de tombeau en Syrie romaine', *Berytus* 21 (1972), p. 5-15, esp. 11); the monastery is known from the *Chr. 1234*, p. I, 181, 24/143, which mentions "a great church of Mar Jacob of 'Naphshatha', (transl. as "stelae") between the mountains"; today Deyr Yakup, *ca.* 7 km south of Edessa (Segal, *Edessa*, p. 29), on the remains of which, see F. W. Deichmann & U. Peschlow, *Zwei spätantike Ruinenstätten in Nordmesopotamien*, (Bayerische Akad. der Wiss., phil.-hist. Klasse: Sitzungsberichte 1977:2), Munich 1977, p. 41-63.

of the monastery of Mar Samuel,[168] the monks of Hendibana, (of) the monastery of Eusebius of Abhna,[169] (of) the monastery of Mar Julian Saba on the River of the Medes, and (of) other monasteries.

That beloved and great group arrived at the monastery of Mar Solomon of Maqqelyatha[170] on Christmas Day. Then the blessed men burned in keen ardour and said to all the people (present), monks and laymen, "Since each of us has written and signed with his name a writ and anathematized the Council of Chalcedon, as well as the impious *Tome* of Leo and we are prepared to celebrate the (Holy) Sacrifice and make offering on this feast-day, know that we shall not give communion to him who will not do what we did and anathematize as we have anathematized". Thus all the people agreed and promptly pronounced the anathema. Then they received communion and gave thanks to our Lord. Then the monks dismissed the laymen and all the people, and departing by themselves they arrived at Tella de-Mauzelath.[171]

The whole city went out to meet them, and welcomed them with incense and lamps, but (also) with pain and great weeping. They stayed there for one day in the monastery called of Beth Arbaye.[172] From there they went straight to Tel Beshmay and stayed in the martyrium called after Mar Sari, but after they had been there a few days Bar Kaili, of evil memory, who was (bishop) of Amid, sent and had them expelled from there. Then they descended southward to the region of Marda[173] and stayed in the monastery called Ayn Haylaph.

---

[168] Near Ḥāh (*ca*. 40 km north-east of Nisibis); P. Krüger, 'Das syrisch-monophysitische Mönchtum im Ṭūr-'Ab(h)din von seinen Anfängen bis zur Mitte des 12. Jahrhunderts', *OChP* 4 (1938), p. 37.

[169] Syr.: 'stone'.

[170] Probably a Syriac plant name.

[171] Constantina, modern Viranşehir, *ca*. 80 km east of Edessa, beyond the Khabur.

[172] I.e. (originally) for monks coming from Beth 'Ar(ā)bāyē, the Mesopotamian province between Nisibis and Shiggar (Sinjar).

[173] Mardin.

After about six and a half years, thanks to the endeavours of the Empress Theodora,[174] Belisarius[175] received an order to allow them to come back to their monastery.

When they had stayed there for a little time—about eight [**p. 30**] years—by Satan's instigation there was a dispute among them. Some seventy men decided to leave. Many things happened between them and although many tried to persuade them to accept (each other) and be reconciled, they did not consent. When they became stirred up by Satan, one of (the disputers), whose name was Elisha, went in his madness together with (some) others to Ephrem, the patriarch of Antioch. In opposition to the whole monastery they became reconciled with him. He provided them with letters (of introduction) and sent them to the emperor. (Also), from fear of the empress, he changed their garments, dressing them in the clothes of *magistrianoi*[176] and so he sent them to the emperor.

Having arrived, they informed the emperor (about what had happened) and gave him the letters. Elisha with all his band received strict orders, whereupon they went back and expelled (the other monks) for the second time. They came and took possession of the monastery, they searched through its belongings and took everything from it. (Then) they again sent the blessed men away, having tortured them. Because of this the persecution was instigated again all over the East.

The story of Mara, the bishop of Amid; on how he and the Amidene monasteries were persecuted.

When Paul the Jew's persecution reached the blessed bishop of Seleucia in Syria, after the departure of the blessed Severus, he (also) left his see. This blessed man Nonnos [**p. 31**] went to stay quietly in the city of Amid; for he was from there.

---

[174] Theodora (empress 527–548, *PLRE* III, p. 1240f) was known for her pro-Monophysite sympathies, notwithstanding her husband's fight for Chalcedonian orthodoxy. She supported and protected many Monophysite hierarchs (even keeping them in her palace). See Frend, *Rise*, passim.

[175] Belisarius (*ca.* 500–565; *PLRE III*, p. 181-224): Justinian's renowned military commander, successful in battles and/or wars against Persians (530), Vandals (533–534) and Ostrogoths (535–540), see below n. 370; in the epoch concerned he was *dux* (see n. 182) *Mesopotamiae* (527–529), or *magister militum* (στρατηλάτης) of the East (529–531).

[176] Officials or messengers belonging to the office of the *magister officiorum*; known also as *agentes in rebus*; Clauss, *Magister officiorum*, p. 23–40.

When this happened, the bishop of Amid, the blessed Thomas, an ascetic monk, an honourable, spiritual, saintly and compassionate man, departed this world. Before the persecution he had prayed to God saying, "Oh Lord, almighty God who sittest above the cherubs and seraphs harnessed to Thy glorious chariot! If the persecution is going to reach this place, take my soul from me, that my eyes may not watch the tumult of Thy holy Church, which Thou hast redeemed and saved by the precious blood of Thy only (Son), our Lord Jesus Christ." Thus after his prayer, Thomas, this noble man of God, next day departed this life, went to his rest and was buried in peace. Everyone was astonished and praised God at the power of the prayer of the holy Thomas.[177]

However, after his decease they seized the blessed Nonnos, the bishop of Seleucia, who was living in peace in that city, and placed him in the see of the church of Amid by force, against his will. But before he had spent as much as three months in his episcopacy, he departed this world.

After him there was the blessed Mara, (who came) from (the family) of noble and famous people (which) was called the house of Constantine.[178] He distinguished himself greatly in the office of bishop, but after a few years of his (episcopacy) the persecution reached the regions of Mesopotamia and the blessed Mara was also seized. He was required either to acknowledge, accept and proclaim the Council of Chalcedon, or else he would be deposed and would have to leave his see. But the blessed Mara chose to be driven away together with the staunch (ones) and to leave his see, and not to succumb to loving the bishop's chair more than the truth of the immaculate orthodox faith. So he accepted exile for the sake of Christ's truth [p. 32] and was expelled to the city of Petra, which is in the desert of Arabia of Palestine, together with his two sisters, virgins of Christ and deaconesses, whose names were Shmuni and Nonna, and with the blessed Isidore, the bishop of Qenneshrin. When they had spent about seven years in exile, [the emperor Justin] died (and) the victorious Justinian [ascended the

---

[177] Cp. the content of the year-lemma 816 b, above, p. 7.

[178] Syr.: *mn rwŕb' w-īdī'ē d-metqrā d-bēt Qwstntn'* (PD 31, 20); according to Ps.-Zachariah VIII, 5, (II, 79, 12/208): "Mara [was] the son of Constantine, the prefect" (or governor, ἡγεμών; Syr.: *Mr' Br Qwstnt hgwmn'*), and he had been the steward (*rbyt'* from *rb-byt'*) of the church; see also Honigmann, *Évéques*, p. 101.

throne].[179] As a result of the endeavours of his wife Theodora, who was a believer, he agreed and gave orders that the blessed Isidore and Mara might leave this grievous and harsh exile in the city of Petra, and come to Alexandria the Great. This (also) took place and they in fact arrived there. They received some respite from the tribulations of the previous exile. Later they ended their lives in Alexandria, and only the holy Mara's bones were brought by his blessed sisters to Amid and laid in the temple Beth Sharla,[180] which he had built.

On Abraham Bar Kaili, on crucifixions and other killings and evildoings which he wrought, and on the holy martyr Cyrus, the priest of the village Ligin.

In Amid a man by the name of Abraham, a cleric of that church, became bishop. He was called Bar Kaili,[181] and (although) his family came from Tella he arrived in (Amid) from Antioch. Then Satan possessed him totally, and he devoted himself to violent persecution without mercy, to pillage and the destruction [**p. 33**] of people's souls more than his earlier and more recent predecessors. This villain used (all means) including the killing, crucifixion and burning of believers in a barbarous and cruel way, without mercy. Impudently he plotted by every means foul ruses for the destruction of people—tortures, cruel scourging and pernicious confinement in prison, both in the tribunal building and in the deepest pit which was in the prison, into which murderers and others sentenced to death were thrown and where they were executed, after which their bodies were secretly removed and cast in desolate graves, like those of dumb animals.

In order to deceive the Amidenes' keen ardour for the true faith he pretended to them that he would not preach (the doctrine of) the Council. But during the time of the *dux* Thomas, a Goth who was the

---

[179] The text is corrupt, most probably due to the fact that the names of both emperors were spelled alike. The restoration is J. S. Assemani's (*Bibliotheca Orientalis* II, Roma 1727, p. 48).

[180] Or rather martyrium Beth Shurla, as in John of Ephesus, *Lives, PO* 17:1, p. 197, 2; and Ps.-Zachariah II, 80, 7f/209 (Beth Shura), where it is the name of the village in which the church was.

[181] As is seen from the story of the persecution of the Monophysites instigated by the patriarch Ephrem (see below, p. 37) Abraham Bar Kaili was appointed in Amid after Ephrem's accession in 527. His episcopacy lasted for *ca.* 30 years; see also, C. Karalewsky, 'Amid', *DHGE* 2 (1914), col. 1240.

dux[182] at that time, he gave orders to bring and crucify four persons at every single gate. They hung on their crosses till the evening. As next day the commemoration of the blessed Mother of God was to be celebrated outside the northern gate of Amid, the wicked bishop rode out to celebrate it. When he saw the bodies hanging on the crosses he forbade them to be taken down until it was necessary because of the smell of corruption. (Only) then would he let them to be taken down and buried.

Also when he learned that there was an uprising (and the people) were shouting these words, "Behold! the new martyrs by the hand of the Christians have appeared! So why do the Christians blame any longer the pagan judges who did that, when now they themselves, like those, [p. 34] do (the same)", he tormented men and women because they had stood up against him when he demanded that they should accept the Council of Chalcedon.

And all these things (happened) in our presence and we saw it with our (own) eyes.[183]

First he expelled[184] and ousted (the monks from) all the holy monasteries in the vicinity of the city, and then from the whole country around it. Also he made a list of the quarters, mansions and houses of the city, of men and women, each one by his name. He demanded that they be entered on to the church register[185] and that they receive communion, even babes, and not only those which had been born but also those which had not yet been born. He demanded that the women should be registered so that when they had given birth, they should bring the (babes) to be baptized. If it happened that a new-born child died or (that a babe) was miscarried, unless clergy came to see it, the family of the dead babe which had not been brought to be baptized was in danger. And these evil deeds, that is pillaging and destruction, were done not only in this city but in all the country around it and in the (whole) diocese of Amid.

---

[182] A high military commander over the forces in a border province of the empire, here Mesopotamia; the actual incumbent is perhaps identical with Thomas named in Ps.-Zachariah II, 92, 23/223; *PLRE II*, p. 1114 (Thomas 11).

[183] John of Ephesus speaks here.

[184] Read *trad.*

[185] The Syriac uses here the Greek loanword ματρίκιον (G. W. H. Lampe, *Patristic Greek Lexicon*, Oxford 1961, p. 834).

On the holy martyr Cyrus.

Here is (something) most terrible, grievous and cruel: (the story of) a priest whose name was Cyrus, from the village of Ligin, who was seized and required to receive communion. When he refused, he was brought to the city before the bishop. He violently shouted at him in indignation saying:

"Why do you not receive communion?"

And he answered:

"You make your communion repugnant to me and I cannot partake of it, for communion given by force [**p. 35**] is not a communion."

Then (the bishop) swore:

"You will not leave here, but you will take communion."

(Cyrus also) swore:

"I will never accept the forced communion from you."

Then the bishop had the Eucharist brought and gave orders to hold the priest, to fill a spoon (with the Eucharist) and to put it into his mouth. (But) as he shut his mouth they could not insert the spoon into it. Then the bishop gave orders to bring a whip, to stick its handle into (the priest's) mouth and in this way to get the spoon (also) into his mouth. They held his teeth apart (so forcefully) that they were nearly pulled out. With the handle (of the whip) inserted in his mouth he mumbled, not being able to move his tongue nor to speak normally to them. He swore saying:

"By Christ's truth, if you put the Eucharist into my mouth, I will spit it out upon your faces."

Thus in bitter wrath and threatening (him) with death they inserted the spoon to one side of the whip and poured the Eucharist into his mouth. But he blew and ejected it from his mouth. Accordingly they called him "the Spitter".

When Bar Kaili saw what that priest did, he used it as a pretext to kill him which had been his intention (in the first place). As the others perished by his hand so he would cause also (the priest) to perish. Intoxicated with the ferocity and cruelty of Satan, who "was a murderer from the beginning",[186] he promptly gave orders to carry wood and fire

---

[186] Jn. 8, 44.

to the *tetrapylon*[187] in the city and (there) to burn the priest. It was the Wednesday of fasting in Holy Week. [**p. 36**] So he had the priest put in [the *tetrapylon*] and wood gathered there from the vicinity. They set him on fire and burned him. (The people of) the city wailed and wept at this horrible and heart-rending sight, as they watched a man burning and dense smoke rising as from dumb and irrational beasts (being burnt). This was a hideous and inhuman deed, which, with all its ferocity, stupidity and obduracy of heart, (only) dumb beasts can inflict on each other.[188] All (the people of) the city were so agitated and shocked at the evil deed of burning that priest in (such) iniquity and wickedness that they thought to burn Bar Kaili, doing to him the same thing that he had displayed by burning that priest. There were (however) some nobles of the city (who) out of fear of the emperor restrained them from doing so. Many people however separated themselves from (Bar Kaili) regarding him as a murderer and a Jew, and they ceased (to receive) communion from him.

(Bar Kaili) being afraid[189] lest the matter become known to the emperor and lest he sentence him to be burnt as he himself had burned (a man), in anticipation he wrote falsely and informed (the emperor) that a certain priest had trampled the Eucharist with his feet, and because of this had been burned. Thus he managed to deceive (the emperor) and to cause the murder to pass (without consequences).

That we have not deviated from the truth, nor misrepresented it in what we have described, the Lord is our witness and all the contemporaries of that wicked and ferocious deed. This evil became known all over the East and West, and everybody was horrified by what was done by people wearing the robes of priesthood but [**p. 37**] far removed from its virtues.

If we set about recording his other evildoings which "we saw with our own eyes, touched with our hands and heard with our ears",[190] we would need many volumes (to describe) how he formed strange thought(s), and again (how) "he devised plans", as is written.[191]

---

[187] A monumental gate-like construction with four entrances built in Roman cities on the cross of the main streets. The best example in the East is the Great Tetrapylon in Palmyra (3rd c. A.D.).

[188] Read *nethashūn* (after Chabot, p. 36, n. 4 and Martin).

[189] Read *dhel*.

[190] Cp. 1 Jn. 1, 1.

[191] Cp. Jer. 18, 11.

Everyday he passed various evil sentences against those who did not submit to the heresy of the two Natures, whereas himself he did not embrace it willingly but only out of obsequiousness.

Sometimes he sent the "shorn ones"[192] who were called there the "fugitives"[193] and lodged them in the houses of the believers who would not surrender to him. They did such things as barbarians would not know (how to do) at all. Another time (he sent against them) the barbarian soldiers of the detachment[194] garrisoned in the city, and sometimes, wherever he found it expedient, he ordered the total destruction of whoever resisted him.

(Also) he took a band of (the inmates), all who were there, from the hospice of the lepers, which was outside the city, and which was called "of Mar Romanos", sent and lodged them in the house of a believer who was thus forced to leave his house and flee from their hideous and horrible appearance, seeing their faces misformed and their bodies all festering and putrefying, discharging abominable purulence, while their hands were festering and dripping with blood and pus, fouler than those of corpses laid in graves. In addition also their souls were cruel and impious, and their intentions threatened the Christians with destruction [p. 38] since by their malice they dropped their rottenness and filthiness on (the owners') fine and clean household equipment and rolled in their beds filling them with filthy pus and making them repulsive. Also they put on fine clothes and seized everything which pleased them and carried it off. Nobody could restrain and stop them. When they had eaten up and made repulsive everything which was in the house to which they had been sent, and when they realized that they would soon be ordered to leave, they entered (the storeroom) and opened flasks of wine or jars of oil or honey and the rest (of the store). They gathered all and plunged their hands into these vessels leaving pus and making them (thereby) repulsive and filthy to such a degree that the people could not eat anything from them any more but they would afterwards have to throw them away and destroy them. The consequence was therefore the total destruction of the house to which the lepers had been sent. (The inhabitants) would have preferred that people who did not

---

[192] I.e. monks.

[193] Chabot's emendation: *tulqānē* (to be spelt *twlqn'*, ms.: *twlqy'*), but perhaps the word should be corrected to *tūliqē* (spelt *twlyq'*), 'eminent', distinguished'.

[194] The Syriac uses here the Greek term ἀριθμος = Lat. *numerus*, i.e. any detachment of the Roman army: *manipulus*, *cohors*, *legio*, or the like.

know God had been sent against them rather than the lepers. But Bar Kaili sent these (lepers) all the more against the people, threatening (them) with evil actions and destruction. Also (he did) other things impossible to tell and describe.

On Ephrem's arrival in the East, on the great persecution which he initiated and on the gathering of the Amidene monasteries.[195]
When this Ephrem Bar Aphiana,[196] an Amidene who was made patriarch of Antioch, arrived in the East, he (began to) persecute, trouble and disturb the whole of the East, God's Church and all Syria. He moved around and in every region or city he expelled (the monks from) big and little monasteries and caused (the stylites) to descend from (their) [**p. 39**] columns, which he also demolished, and (the recluses) to come forth from (their) hermitages. He administered communion by means of the sword, staves and barbarian troops.

(He launched persecution) also against the monasteries of Amid, not only against those in the vicinity of the city but in the whole region. He sent (to Amid) and expelled (the monks) by (the intermediary of) Abraham Bar Kaili, whom we have mentioned in the preceding narrative and (in) the book on this whole persecution which we wrote at that time.[197]

Having been driven out and (forced to) leave, numerous (monks) gathered, took their crosses[198] and departed. They arrived at an old monastery which had at one time been great and powerful: it was called Tella de-Tuthe.[199] When they had stayed there a few days and began to establish themselves in it, detachments of Roman soldiers, *chorepiscopi* and *periodeutae*[200] were sent to drive them out from there.

---

[195] Cp. John of Ephesus, *Lives, PO* 18:4, p. 607-623; see also Vööbus, *Asceticism*, III, p. 215-217; Harvey, *Asceticism*, p. 71f.

[196] PD *'pyn'* (Appianus?, Apion?; Land II, 294 *'phn'*). Before becoming patriarch of Antioch, Ehprem was *comes Orientis, PLRE II*, p. 394-396; to the literature given there add, G. Downey, 'Ephraemius, patriarch of Antioch', *Church History* 7 (1938), p. 364-370, and Gray, *Defense*, 141-154.

[197] An autobiographical note of John of Ephesus, who was among the persecuted monks; the book (*On the persecution,* or *On the whole persecution*) has not survived, see D'yakonov, *Ioann Yefesskiy*, p. 167f.

[198] See above n. 164.

[199] I.e. 'The Hill of the Sycamores'.

[200] According to Land's text; PD's provides singular forms (i.e. no *syāmē* for either term). For the titles, see above nn. 145-146.

When the Roman force arrived and saw long lines (of monks) standing one behind another at a service, God laid fear upon (the soldiers) and (the monks) appeared in their eyes as giants. They left and began to talk to each other:

"Let us avoid strife with these (giants) for if one of them raises a stick, he will defeat twenty of us."

Thus they withdrew and left the monks (alone). They went to stay in the villages nearby and started to oppress their (inhabitants) by plundering, killing their animals and eating (them). They said:

"We shall stay in your houses until you, men and women, go and by lamentation cause that congregation of monks to leave. (Until then) we shall stay in your houses and eat up and plunder everything you have."

Thus (the inhabitants of) all these villages gathered crying and lamenting, and implored (the monks) to have mercy [**p. 40**] upon them and to leave. So they complied and left. Indeed (the monks) were not prepared to fight with (the soldiers), yet they said:

"If, as you say, the emperor ordered you to evict us from our monasteries, in that case we have (already) left. But you have not been ordered to evict us from another place. And unless you produce the order (to that effect, even) if you are 5000 men, no matter whether we win or not,[201] you will not cast us out."

When however they saw the tribulation and (heard) the cries of the whole region they left of their own will, moved to the region called Madhbeha,[202] and stayed in the monastery called Hawranyatha.[203] In the wilderness a thousand men or more pitched tents in rows to the effect that now their camp, persecuted for the sake of Christ, seemed to be a city. So (the people of) all the surrounding villages rushed up (to them), not only to be blessed, but also to see something astonishing, especially (to watch them) standing in rows at a service or sitting by the table.

This monastery was (situated) right between three dioceses, those of Edessa, Amid and Samosata. Thus when Ephrem the patriarch arrived in Edessa he sent to (the monks) his brother John, who also was a

---

[201] Or "whether we are right or not".

[202] I.e. 'the altar' or 'the sanctuary'; this seems to be the correct reading; ms. *mdbdḥy'*, London ms. *mdbry'*; so Chabot after Michael the Syrian, p. 274. Likewise John of Ephesus, *Lives, PO* 18:4, p. 619, 21, which E. W. Brooks takes as a corruption from *madnḥā*, 'the East'.

[203] Syr. 'Poplars'; cp. John of Ephesus, *Lives, PO* 18:4, p. 619f & *PO* 19:2, p. 223f.

governor, together with *chorepiscopi* and many clerics, pretending persuasion (instead of violence). He sent them (this) message:

"Do you not [**p. 41**] realize that I am your son and your fellow citizen and grew up among you and in your monasteries? And I am anxious about your tranquillity and honour. In connection with that stumbling-block by which you have become indignant as regards the faith, let two or three men from every monastery come to me, and I shall give you explanation; or else I will come to you. But receive me in good will."

When thus these and many other things were told to our ears and to the whole congregation, the elders, the chiefs of the congregation, answered in these words:

"If, as he says, he is our son and our fellow citizen, let him cease the war against us, because, as it has pleased him and that person in Amid,[204] behold, they have had us evicted from our monasteries and now we sit in these rugged and harsh mountains. (So) what does he have in common with us? Let him know and (be) sure that none of us will come to him, neither shall we receive him if he comes hither, but as a persecutor and an enemy (shall we treat him). So whatever he may do to us we are prepared to endure (it)."[205]

And when these (words) were said briefly (but) firmly to John, his brother, he said:

"I am very sorry for you and for everything that you will suffer."

And so (the messengers) went off conveying (the answer). They informed (Ephrem) of everything which had been said. When "(their) son", as he put it, "and (their) fellow citizen" heard it, he kindled with anger like the furnace of the Babylonians,[206] and wrote to Amid that all the detachments which were garrisoned there should proceed against them, armed as if for battle, and that they should seize and bind [**p. 42**] them and so bring all of them to him.

Thus when Bar Kaili received this order he sent a strong armed force together with many clerics against that congregation. When these had gathered and set out in order to come (to the monks, the following) was written to the archimandrites:

---

[204] I.e. Bar Kaili.
[205] Read *nsybr* for *nsybd.*
[206] Dn. 3, 19-23.

"Now the force of armed horsemen is setting out against you. Be careful what you do!"

It was wintertime; all the archimandrites gathered and took counsel: "It is not laid down that we should fight". And it was agreed among them that every archimandrite should divide the brothers of his monastery among his clergy, and every cleric, be he priest or deacon, should take his band along and lead (it) to go to whichever place he might choose, (and) which was known to him, whereas all of the elders would assemble immediately, cross the Euphrates and wait until they saw the end of this affair.

So it was; every priest took his band and left. So also to our humble self (was committed a group of monks); although young of age, we had (already) received ordination to the priesthood.[207]

In this way the monastery was left supplied with everything—the contributions of the whole people—except for the vessels for the services and books, the brass and the vestments and other things of this sort, which each one, taking care of (the belongings of) his monastery, removed from before the (oppressors). Also a large building, a hospital, remained containing over 40 men brought down with various illnesses, some of them close to death. These committed their souls to God (since) because of the severity of the winter [p. 43] and the seriousness of (their) illnesses they could not escape before the oppressors.

The rest of (the monks), however, were forced to cross rough rivers, full (of water through which) they waded (immersed) up to their necks, while it snowed, (the wind) blew, and (there was) severe frost. It had been written in advance to all authorities that whoever in any village received one of them or invited him to his house, the house should be confiscated and he himself would risk being put to death. In this way many (monks), and among them our humble self, were forced to go in among steep rocks and into caves nearby the great river of Euphrates and to hide like beasts.

When these things became known in the neighbouring villages, all the people who kept God in their heart conferred secretly with each other, because of fear of the persecutors, and in the middle of the night they took bread, wine, dry pulses and other things necessary for sustenance, and secretly brought them to (the monks) having seen in what distress

---

[207] Michael the Syrian, who summarizes this story, preserves the information that John of Ephesus took care of 10 monks while still a deacon, 275b /II, 186b.

they were and in what miserable dwellings they lived, like the beasts among the crags.

(The monks) wept, lamented and cried woe upon themselves and upon Christianity (for) what happened to it. And they stretched their (hands) and lowered them in great lamentation. Others climbed to "bare places", that is, inaccessible mountains covered with snow, and out of necessity hid themselves in shelters intended for goats and sheep. And so did everybody everywhere. They were afflicted by the severity of frost and ice, the wretchedness of the place and other tribulations.

(But) God is good and rich in favours towards everyone who calls upon Him. When He saw them being persecuted because of His name, He did not leave them to be tormented.

(However), since previously, as we [**p. 44**] recounted above, we desisted from (writing) a full account of (these events) which would take many books, and we recorded them by some examples[208] at the same time as they took place one after another, (that is) in the time of our youth, (so now) we desist from relating again all that God's Church suffered in those times, (and) that we suffered for many years together with that spiritual congregation. And in order not to be distracted from the story which we have undertaken, we return to it.

The year 833 (A.D. 521/2): the holy doctor Mar Jacob, bishop of Batnae of Serugh, died. Moses came in his stead.

The year 836 (A.D. 524–5): waters entered Edessa.[209]

It seemed to us right not to conceal with silence (this) terrible thing and great disaster which came upon Edessa, the *metropolis* of Osrhoene, in our days, that is in the year 836. Then, as is written, "a decree of the Most High"[210] came upon many people, and there was a flood in (various) places. About the third hour of night, when many were asleep, many (others) were bathing in the public bath, and still others were sitting at supper, suddenly mighty amounts of water appeared in the

---

[208] See above n. 197.

[209] The flood of Daisan is also known from Malalas 418f/237, Procopius, *Buildings*, II, 7, 4-5 & *Secret History*, 18:38; (the Greek authors call the river Skirtos, 'Leaper', a Greek translation of Syriac *Daysān*). Among the Syriac sources the *Chr. Ed.* (10, 27-11, 2/37) has it under the same date, whereas Jacob of Edessa dates it to 832 Sel. (*s.a.* 196, *Chr. Min.*, 318, left col., 6f/240) and the *Chronicle to the year 724* (ibid., 150, 6/115) to 835 Sel.; see also Segal, *Edessa*, p. 187.

[210] Dan. 4, 24.

river Daisan, and they entered ...[211] that the river Daisan passed through the middle of the city. Suddenly in the darkness of the night the (city) wall was breached and (the debris) stopped up and held back [p. 45] the mass of water at its exit and (so) it completely inundated (the city). It rose (above) all the streets and courtyards of the city adjacent to the river. In one hour, or maybe two, the city was filled with water and became submerged.

Suddenly the water entered the public bath through all the doors and all the people who were there drowned while trying to (reach) the doors to get out and escape. (But) the flood just poured in through the gates and covered all who were in the lower storeys and all together they were drowned and perished. As for those on the upper storeys, when those who were there realized (the peril) and rushed to get down and escape, the flood overwhelmed them, they were submerged and drowned. Others were submerged while slumbering and, being asleep, felt nothing.

Houses which had not been firmly constructed were lifted up, (then) lowered and (so) they sank in (the waters of) the flood. Only those whom God the merciful wished (to keep) alive were saved, while their houses being firmly constructed did not fall, especially those which were built of stones and lime, in the whole district going down towards the river, whereas the places which were high and situated at the foot of the mountain remained intact as well.

On how the wall broke and water departed and the city was emptied, and on the damage (the flood) did over the whole plain of Edessa and Harran.

When thus most of the city was filled (with water) and inundated, apart from the places mentioned, the water was enclosed and the city became like a lake. Then the wall of the city broke, first (from) above and (then) below. Since it could not contain the power of the flood it broke suddenly, (producing) three breaches. Towers were overthrown, carried away [p. 46] and destroyed by the force of the flood of water, while it inundated and carried away the corpses of the drowned like flotsam. And not only this but it also inundated houses, courts, the palace, the public bath and other things of all kinds, that is people's belongings, and even stones and beams of numerous buildings.

---

[211] Two or three words missing.

(Also) the land outside the city became inundated and not much less damage and destruction was wrought there than inside (the city). As the river Daisan spread over into other rivers (reaching) as far as the Euphrates, the vehemence of its flood carried off corpses of human beings and cattle, objects and animals, causing them to float along.

When God showed His grace the flood ceased and the city was emptied (of water) as well as the land outside it; those who had survived spent many days digging in great sadness and bitter pain of the spirit uncovering and bringing out corpses and other things.[212]

On the blessed men whom the wicked Asclepius seized one day before the flood.

Thus the day before that disaster of the flood the wicked Asclepius, who was the bishop of the city, seized monks from all sides, about ten blessed and chaste anchorites,[213] and tortured them in order that they might accept communion with him. When they did not let themselves be persuaded he imprisoned them, threatening that the next day he would torture them and bring them to subjection. But that night the flood came, and so it seemed to everybody that it was because of the tribulation of these blessed men that God became angry with the bishop and the city. After the city had been emptied of the water, all who had survived took stones and rushed to the bishop's house to stone [**p. 47**] Asclepius. But he managed to hide himself, escape from them and flee to Antioch to Euphrasius,[214] whose opinions he shared. Euphrasius having received him had him come up together with himself to the *bema*,[215] where he preached about him to (the people of) the city in these words:

"Come and see the second Noah, who like (the first) in the ark has also been saved, from the second flood."

This Asclepius died there and never returned to Edessa. And there came peace for all the believers. Those who were imprisoned by him left after his escape and went each to his monastery.

---

[212] After the flood Justinian had the Daisan's course through Edessa regulated, and a wall built which, by diverting the excess of water around the city, would prevent further catastrophes, Procopius, *Buildings*, II, 7, 6-16; see the plan in Segal, *Edessa*, p. 264.

[213] Syr. *'abīlē*, lit. 'mourners'.

[214] Chalcedonian patriarch of Antioch 521–526; on his death see below p. 46, and n. 237.

[215] See above n. 87.

Famous at this time are: Abraham bishop of Anzitene, Mar Maron the stylite of the monastery of Hesikha,[216] Mar Simon the recluse, and Mar Sergius his disciple in Qolosh. Also famous are: Mar Mara, archimandrite of Surtha on the Tigris, Mar Addai, *sa'orā*[217] of the monastery of Pardaysa,[218] and Mar John of Zuqnin.

The persecuted patriarchs: Theodosius of Alexandria,[219] Severus of Antioch,[220] Anthimius of Constantinople;[221] the heretics: of Antioch, Euphrasius,[222] of Constantinople, Epiphanius,[223] of Rome, Hormisdas,[224] of Jerusalem, Peter,[225] of Alexandria, Timothy.[226]

The year 837 (A.D. 525/6): Antioch was overthrown.

In the seventh year of Justin,[227] that is the year 837, Antioch the Great was also overthrown, (this being) its fifth collapse, at the seventh hour of the day.[228] (It was) a terrible and distressing collapse, impossible for anyone to recount. Such was the violent and harsh disaster, which was (sent) from heaven, that **[p. 48]** fire set alight and consumed those who had escaped from the terrible vehemence of the cataclysm of the earthquake and the collapse: the sparks flew and set fire to everything

---

[216] I.e. 'Abstinent'.

[217] *Sā'orā*: 'visitor'; 'inspector'; 'administrator'; in a monastery a monk in charge of food supplies, economic affairs, and other dealings with the outer world; see the rules concerning *sā'orā* in the so-called *Canons of Marutha* (fifth century), *Syriac and Arabic Documents Regarding Legislation Relative to Syrian Asceticism*, ed., tr. ... by A. Vööbus, Stockholm 1960, p. 134-136; A. Palmer, *Monk and Mason on the Tigris Frontier: the early history of Tur 'Abdin*, (University of Cambridge Oriental Publications 39), Cambridge 1990, p. 82 & 92.

[218] I.e. 'Paradise'.

[219] 535–537, deposed; died 566.

[220] See above n. 83.

[221] 535–536, deposed.

[222] See above n. 214.

[223] 520–535.

[224] 514–523.

[225] 524-552.

[226] 517–535; a Monophysite.

[227] So exceptionally the ms. (*ywstyn'*, 'Justin' 47, 22), whereas Land's text (299, 10) has wrongly (against Chabot, PD 47, n. 6) *ywstnyn'*, 'Justinian'.

[228] The earthquake took place in May 526, according to Malalas (418f/238f), from whose original version this lemma, as well as the subsequent account of the fire of the Great Church, and that of the appearance of a cross, was taken over by John of Ephesus; for further witnesses, see Grumel, *Chronologie*, p. 478 (year 526); and the Great Chronographer, in *Chron. Pasch.*, transl., p. 195, n. 4; Stein, *Bas-Empire*, p. 242; Downey, *Antioch*, p. 521-525.

on which they settled.[229] The earth itself from below, from within the soil, surged, seethed and burned everything which was there. Thus the foundations as well, together with all the storeys above them, were lifted up, heaved up and down and burst apart, collapsed, fell and burned with fire. Those who had saved themselves (so far) and (now) tried to escape were met by fire, which set them alight, and burnt them up. They burned like wood and the tongues of flame blazed terribly[230] and grievously by (God's) mighty wrath. And now, like rain from the sky, flames rained down and so the whole city blazed like a burning furnace, while it collapsed completely, fell, was ruined and burnt with fire, except only for a few houses which remained at the foot of the mountain above (the city),[231] although even these were damaged and ready to fall. Every day these too collapsed (one by one), setting fire to those which (still) remained. (In the end) no house or church or building of any kind remained, not even the garden fences, which had not been torn asunder or damaged, or had not disintegrated and fallen. The rest burned, crumbled away and became like an extended putrefaction. And underground the earth seethed and humid dust rose up. The odour of a stinking sea and (something) like watery moisture appeared, so that also sea drops rose with the bubbling dust. [**p. 49**]

On the fire at the Great Church in Antioch seven days (after the collapse).

Still the Great Church, which had been built by Constantine the Victorious, (and) about which it was said that there was nothing comparable in the whole Roman empire,[232] remained, cracked, yet still standing. (But) suddenly on the seventh day it too caught fire from top to bottom, and it fell and crumbled away on the ground. So (it was with) other churches as well. Although they were saved from the collapse in the earthquake, in the end suddenly they burnt with fire by (God's) great wrath and were razed to the foundations. (Many) souls perished and were destroyed in this city of Antioch, which became like

---

[229] Cp. above, p. 22.

[230] Read *dhilā'īt*.

[231] Mount Silpius.

[232] Called also the Octogonal Church from its plan, or the Golden Church from its gilded roof; Downey, *Antioch*, p. 342-348.

"the wine-press of wrath"[233] to all its inhabitants, as John of Antioch[234] wrote. He (also) wrote this about (the city): how those who were (still) alive could count those who had died and were disinterred and (otherwise) found. They amounted to 250,000. It happened to be a feast[235] and therefore many people had gathered in (this) great city, magnificent in its buildings and objects. It was (famous for) its hospitality but suddenly became a tomb for the visitors as well as for its inhabitants. However, we are unable to state the number of those who perished as we have recorded only a few things out of many about this terrible disaster which suddenly came upon the great city of Antioch.

On the cross which appeared in the sky after this collapse of Antioch.
On the third day after the collapse, [**p. 50**] which was Sunday, a cross of light appeared in the sky in the western quarter. All who remained alive saw (it) and were moved and cried *Kyrie eleison.* They kept watching it for about one hour and then it was covered by clouds, while everybody was astounded. Thereafter God's mercy and grace were shown, in that 30 and 40 days after (the earthquake) people were found (still) alive—men, women, youths and children—amidst all that burning and flaming fire, so that all the people were astonished and praised the abundant mercy of God, who does not withhold His grace from His creation. (Yet), there were earthquakes all these days and nights for one year and a half, constantly, all the time.

On the hideous death of Euphrasius, patriarch of Antioch.
When people (of Antioch), who were (still) alive, having been rescued from the disaster, (those) from other places and (from) the neighbouring cities had gathered in the city of Antioch and were disinterring and bringing up the corpses of those buried in the catastrophe, the body of Euphrasius was found in a cauldron of pitch used by wineskin makers, who (worked) beneath his episcopal residence. When the residence collapsed and fell, he happened to fall into the cauldron. The whole of his body sank down in it, and he was cooked in the pitch. His head was found (hanging, as if he had) fainted, outside the rim of the cauldron. Thus he was recognized from his face, while

---

[233] Rev. 19, 15.
[234] I.e. John Malalas (419-421/238-241); Witakowski, 'Malalas', p. 299-310.
[235] The festival of the Ascension of Christ, as John Malalas (420/239) reports.

his bones were found [stripped of the flesh]^{236} in the pitch. Some [p. 51] heretics, his adherents, who were in Antioch, deceived the people by saying that he had been snatched away to heaven. God however, in order to expose their fraud, preserved his face unaltered as if he was alive. And fear and trembling seized all who saw (it).^{237}

For the believers, however, it was a wonderful thing, for they remembered the impudence of his evil deeds, his cruel plans, persecution, and pillage which he had done, and tribulations which he caused people to suffer. Not only did he do so himself, but also he urged all the bishops under his authority to do (the same), to persecute, plunder and torture the people. They took inspiration and power from him and all engaged in these evil deeds competing with each other and exerting themselves (as to) which of them would surpass his companions in persecution and evil deeds in every region and city. Many books would not suffice to tell about all these in full: tribulations, persecutions, as well as tortures, fetters and imprisonments which in all regions and cities were carried out by bishops, clerics, *periodeutae, chorepiscopi* and others by the orders and assiduity of Euphrasius and of his predecessor,^{238} all the days of their lives.

On the collapse of Seleucia and the neighbouring Daphne in a terrible (series of) earthquakes.^{239}

Seleucia in Syria and Daphne, which is above Antioch, were overthrown and destroyed for 20 miles^{240} in length and breadth, and were also (a cause of) terror to those who saw it, (although) not (because of) fire but only because of the earthquake. Thus when the emperor Justinian (the Elder)^{241} learned about such total destruction and the loss of Antioch, Seleucia and Daphne, he put off [p. 52] his crown in bitter pain and took off his purple robes and sat in sorrow wishing neither to hear nor to do anything at all, merely sitting, weeping and

---

^{236} After Michael the Syrian (273b, 10/II, 183); PD's manuscript has a lacuna and Martin's text printed by Chabot is corrupt.

^{237} According to Malalas, Euphrasius was burned during the earthquake (423/243); according to Evagrius, he died covered with debris (IV, 5); Ps.-Zachariah, VIII, 4 (II, 76, 16-19/205) agrees with PD but, since he is very laconic, cannot be John of Ephesus' source for this lemma.

^{238} I.e. Paul the Jew.

^{239} Cp. Malalas 421/241, an abbreviated version.

^{240} Roman mile: *ca.* 1.480 m.

^{241} The Elder, i.e. Justin, as is known from Malalas, 421/241.

groaning over Seleucia, Daphne and Antioch, for he knew them and loved them very much and admired them.

When the feast of the Pentecost came, the emperor went out to the church weeping in sorrow and without the imperial crown, while wearing garments of mourning and grief because of the destruction of (the cities). Likewise all his senators, on seeing the extent of his sorrow, themselves put on mourning garments like him. Then he sent five *centenaria*,[242] that is five hundred pounds[243] (of gold),[244] in order to dig out the city of Antioch and to rebuild it together with Seleucia and Daphne and that the corpses which had been buried in them might be extracted, (for) many thousand souls, which had not been counted, had perished in that terrible catastrophe. And so it was: Antioch, Seleucia and Daphne were rebuilt.

The year 840 (A.D. 528/9): there was a severe earthquake and Dyrrachium was overthrown by it. But who is able to report the terrible chastisements which the sins of the people bring about all the time, and the collapse of cities? Thus it also happened to that city of Dyrrachium, the *metropolis* of the new province called Epirus,[245] from which the emperor Anastasius had come, as it suddenly trembled and came to be ruined in the severe earthquake. Just at that time it collapsed and buried its inhabitants.

The year 841 (A.D. 529/30): there was a severe earthquake and the city of Corinth, the *metropolis* of Hellas, was also ruined in it. [p. 53]

The year 842 (A.D. 530/31): Anazarbos, the *metropolis* of Cilicia was also overthrown, its fourth collapse.[246]

After Euphrasius, Ephrem of Amid became patriarch of Antioch. He surpassed all his predecessors in his evil deeds and also ... so that people like Trajan and Diocletian might well have been (his) pupils.[247]

The year 842 (A.D. 530/31): Justinian the Elder made Justinian, his nephew, an emperor together with himself.[248]

---

[242] Centenarion: 100 pounds (*ca.* 32 kg; see next note).

[243] Roman pound (*libra /litra*): 327.45 g.

[244] Supplemented after Michael the Syrian, 273b, 18/183.

[245] I.e. the province of Epirus Nova, Malalas, p. 417/237.

[246] Earthquakes in Dyrrachium, Corinth and Anazarbos, Malalas 417f/236f; Grumel, *Chronologie*, p. 478 (years 522, 525); Stein, *Bas-Empire*, p. 241.

[247] The text after the lacuna (of two words) is not certain; a word also seems to have disappeared after the period.

[248] The correct date is 1 April 527.

The year 843 (A.D. 531/32): Rufinus[249] came and made peace between the Romans and the Persians.[250]

On the same day stars appeared leaping in the sky.

The year 844 (A.D. 532/33): Grepes,[251] the king of the Heruli, with all his army, all his nobles and twelve members of his family came to Justinian. He greeted (the emperor) and declared himself willing to become a Christian. The emperor Justinian rejoiced on hearing it, since he devoted much care and much zeal to converting erring peoples to the faith.[252] He gave instructions and (Grepes) was baptized on the holy feast of the Epiphany, along with his family, his nobles and his army; the victorious emperor was his godfather.[253] (Then) he gave (Grepes) many gifts and sent him back.

The year 845 (A.D. 533/34): Grod,[254] the king of the Huns, together with a numerous army, arrived in the capital and asked to become a Christian. He[255] was instructed (in the faith) and baptized, Justinian being his godfather. He honoured (Grod), gave him many gifts and dismissed him **[p. 54]** to his country. When he came to his country he found his brother, whom he had appointed chief over his troops, and he told him about his (conversion to) Christianity. Also, he showed him the riches and gifts from the Roman emperor, and (the brother) was astonished. Then (Grod) removed the idols of silver and gold which they used to worship, since he believed that only One was the true God, and those idols were deaf and were not gods. He broke them up and sent them to the city of Bosporos[256] to exchange them for *miliaresia*.[257] When his brother and all his troops saw it they became full of anger

---

[249] *Magister militum*, *PLRE II*, p. 954-957 (Rufinus 13).

[250] Cp. *Chr. Ed.*, 12, 29-13, 2/38; Ps.-Zachariah, IX, 7; Malalas 477/282.

[251] Following Malalas (427/247: Γρέπης); PD writes: '*gryps*, which suggests "Agrippas".

[252] On Justinian's missionary endeavours, see: I. Engelhardt, *Mission und Politik in Byzanz: ein Beitrag zur Strukturanalyse byzantinischer Mission zur Zeit Justins und Justinians*, Munich 1974.

[253] The institution of godfathership (on which see R. Macrides, 'The Byzantine Godfather', *BMGS* 11 (1987), p. 139-162) as practised by emperors over foreign rulers was a political means of creating alliances; ibid., p. 150f.

[254] After Malalas (431/250: Γρώδ); PD: *gwrdyws*.

[255] Ms.: 'they'.

[256] I.e. the Cimmerian Bosporos, at the eastern tip of Crimea.

[257] Syr. *zūzē*, which here translates *miliaresia* (Malalas 432/250), Byzantine silver coins = 1/60 or 1/72 of a silver pound, i.e. 5.45 or 4.55 g. in the fourth century; later reduced even more; K. Regling, s.v., *RECA* 15 (1932), col. 1661f; *ODB* II, p. 1373.

against him, and having devised a plot against him, together with the priests of the idols they killed him. Since they were afraid of the Roman emperor, they fled to another region.

The year 846 (A.D. 534/5): Justinian the Elder died and Justinian, his nephew, became emperor.[258]

On the kingdom of the Indians and how because of war they became Christians.

At the same time it happened that a war broke out between the kings of the Indians,[259] namely the king of the Indians whose name was Aksundon and another king of Inner India, whose name was Andug[260] (and) who was a heathen. When they stopped fighting each other Andug also became engaged in a war with the king of the Himyarites—these are Indians too—whose name was Dimnos.[261] The reason why they waged war between themselves was this:

The kingdom of the Ethiopians[262] is situated further to the interior than that of the Himyarites, (which is closer) to the lands of Egypt and Thebais[263]—these are outside India. Roman merchants used to pass through the countries of the Himyarites to come to the country of the Inner Indians, which is called [p. 55] the Auzalis in India,[264] and also to the countries (situated) further away than those of the Indians and of

---

[258] The correct date is 1 August 527.

[259] The term "Indians" according to a popular conception in the Greco-Roman antiquity included the inhabitants of India, South Arabia and Africa, being thus co-extensive with the term "Ethiopians", see A. Dihle, 'The Conception of India in Hellenistic and Roman literature', *Proceedings of the Cambridge Philological Society* 190 = n.s. 10 (1964), p. 15-23; J.Y. Nadeau, 'Ethiopians', *CQ* 64 = n.s. 20 (1970), p. 339-349.

[260] In Malalas (429/248 & 434/252) Andas; Theophanes (AM 6035): Adad.

[261] Ms. *dymnwn*. The name of the king varies in the sources. The form used here is that used by Malalas (433/251: Δίμνος), the source of the present lemma. On other names see Shahid, *Martyrs*, p. 260-268; also H. Z. Hirschberg, 'Yūsuf 'As'ar Yath'ar Dhu Nuwās (Masrūq)', *Encyclopaedia Judaica* 16 (1971), col. 897-900.

[262] Syr. *kūšāyē*, lit. *Cushites*, the usual Syriac term for the Abyssinians, based on Genesis 10, 6ff. Although here the Syriac renders Malalas' "Axumites" (433/251: Αὐξουμῖται) we keep the English "Ethiopians", since elsewhere *kūšāyē* is the usual Syriac counterpart of Αἰθίοπες.

[263] I.e. Lower and Upper Egypt, respectively.

[264] Probably Adulis ('Adōli, Azōli, 'Adawlā: F. Praetorius, 'Der Name Adulis', *ZDMG* 47 (1893), p. 396), south of Massawa on the Erythrean coast, which in the late Roman/early Byzantine epoch was a centre of Greek trade in the Red Sea.

the Ethiopians.[265] There are, namely, seven kingdoms of the Indians and of the Ethiopians: three of the Indians and four of the Ethiopians. These are (more) distant and are within the southern countries (situated) on the shore of the great sea which surrounds the whole world (and) which is called the Great Ocean.

When the above-mentioned Roman merchants passed through the countries of the Himyarites to enter the countries of the Indians to trade there as usual, the king of the Himyarites, Dimnos,[266] learned (about it), seized them, killed them and plundered all their merchandise, saying:

"(This is) because in the countries of the Romans the Christians wickedly harass the Jews who live in their countries and kill many of them. Therefore I am putting these men to death."

In this way he used to kill many (merchants) until many (others) were seized by terror and refused to come (to the country) and the trade in the inner kingdoms of the Indians and of the Ethiopians ceased.

On what message the king of the Ethiopians sent to the king of the Himyarites and on the war between them.

Then the king of the Ethiopians sent (this) message to the king of the Himyarites:

"You did wrong in that by killing the Christian Roman merchants you have stopped the trade and hindered supplies to my kingdom and other kingdoms. Especially my kingdom have you damaged."

Because of this they came to great enmity and declared war on each other. When they approached to fight a battle with each other, Andug, the king of the Ethiopians, said:

"If it be granted to me that I defeat this torturer, the king of the Himyarites, I will become a Christian. For it is the blood of Christians I intend to avenge on him."

---

[265] On Roman and Byzantine trade with the region of the Red Sea, see N. Pigulewskaja, *Byzanz auf den Wegen nach Indien: aus der Geschichte des byzantinischen Handels mit dem Orient vom 4. bis 6. Jahrhundert* (BBA 36), Berlin 1969; for an earlier period, see also S. E. Sidebotham, *Roman Economic Policy in the Erythra Thalassa 30 B.C.–A.D. 217*, (Mnemosyne Suppl. 91), Leiden 1986; on Byzantine economic and political interests in this region see also Stein, *Bas-Empire*, p. 265-267, 296-302; Vasiliev, *Justin*, p. 283-302; B. Rubin, *Das Zeitalter Justinians*, I, Berlin 1960, p. 297-319; Z. Rubin, 'Byzantium and Southern Arabia: the policy of Anastasius', *Eastern Frontier*, II, p. 383-420.

[266] Ms. here: *dymynws.*

Then they fought a battle with each other [**p. 56**] and the king of the Ethiopians was victorious over the king of the Himyarites. He took him captive, killed him, and plundered his kingdom. He conquered his countries and routed all his army.

Then, after his victory, he did not delay in fulfilling his vow, but sent two of his nobles to the emperor Justinian (asking) that he would send him a bishop and clergy. (The emperor) rejoiced greatly and gave orders that a bishop, whomsoever they chose, might be given to them. The envoys searched and found a man, a *paramonarios*[267] of the church of Saint John,[268] whose name was John (too), who was celibate, chaste and zealous (in faith). They asked for him and obtained him. They took him with them, together with numerous clerics, and departed. Rejoicing they returned to their country.

When they arrived before Andug their king, he received them, also with great joy, along with the bishop and the priests who had come with them. (The king) was instructed in the faith, was baptized and became a Christian together with all his nobles. They were eager that all the regions should become Christian and that churches be erected in them to the glory of the true God of the Christians. For such reasons God gave salvation to these erring peoples.

Again on the same kingdom of the Himyarites and on the evils and killings which the Jews wrought in it.

After some time the Himyarite Jews waxed stronger. When the Christian king whom the king of the Ethiopians had established there died, (the Jews) chose a king from among themselves over the people of the Himyarites and in bitter wrath slew and destroyed all the Christian people there, men, women, young people and little children, poor and rich. On account of that a testimony to the numerous martyrs there was written by the zeal of the blessed Simeon the Disputer. [**p. 57**] This fills all hearers with grief. We also put it (here) in order as follows.

---

[267] *Paramonarios*: church or monastery warden.
[268] In Alexandria, as we know from Malalas (434/252).

The letter which the holy Simeon, bishop of Beth Arsham, the leader of the believers of the land of the Persians, sent to Mar Simeon, the archimandrite of Gabbula,[269] being also an account of the martyrdom of the Himyarites.[270]
We inform you, O beloved, that on the 20th of January of the present year 835 (A.D. 524) we left Hirta de-Nu'man[271] together with the priest Abraham, son of Euphrasius, who had been sent by the emperor Justinian[272] to Mundhir, king of the Arabs, to make peace,[273] about which we already wrote in our previous letter.[274] We and all the believers here are indebted to his favour, for he assisted our faction.[275] He is acquainted with all those matters about which we wrote previously, as well as with these about which we write now.
We travelled through the desert towards the south-east—a ten days' journey—and we found Mundhir [**p. 58**] over against the mountains called Hala, and in Arabic, Ramla.[276] When we were entering Mundhir's encampment, heathen Arabs and Ma'addites[277] came to meet us and said:

---

[269] Gabbula: in Northern Syria, east of Aleppo.

[270] What follows is a "shorter" version of the so-called "first" *Letter* of Simeon of Beth Arsham (the "second" *Letter*, containing what seems to be an updated account of the martyrdom, was according to I. Shahîd, *Martyrs*, p. 31-37, written by the same author). The "longer" version of the "first" *Letter* has been preserved in a separate manuscript tradition (ed. by I. Guidi, 'La lettera di Simone vescovo di Bêth-Arsâm sopra i martiri omeriti', *ARALM* 3:7 (1881), p. 471-515; an English transl.: A. Jeffery, 'Christianity in South Arabia', *The Moslem World* 36 (1946), p. 204-216), whereas this "shorter" version is contained in historiographical works. PD copied it from John of Ephesus, who had probably taken it from Ps.-Zachariah of Mitylene. In a slightly abbreviated form it can also be found in Michael the Syrian.
Another text of the *Letter*, parallel to that of PD, is provided by the British Museum ms. Add. 14, 641 (= L). Its title reads: "The letter which bishop Simeon, that is the *apokrisiarios* of the believers, sent from Persia to Simeon the archimandrite of Gabbula, in which he reports on the martyrs killed in Najran, the capital of Himyar, in the year 835 of the Greeks, the year 6 of the reign of Justin, and it is also the story of the martyrs."

[271] Now Hîrâ in Southern Iraq, east of the Euphrates; it was the capital of the Arab Lakhmid kingdom, a vassal state of Sasanid Persia. Nu'man was the name of three Lakhmid kings.

[272] Scil. the Elder, i.e. Justin.

[273] On the diplomatic context of this visit, see I. Shahid, 'Byzantino-Arabica: the Conference of Ramla, A.D. 524', *JNES* 23 (1964), p. 115-131.

[274] This letter has not been preserved.

[275] I.e. the Monophysites in Persia, or among the Arab tribes under Persian allegiance.

[276] Both toponyms mean 'sand' in Syriac and Arabic respectively.

[277] Ma'addites: a collective name for the northern Arab tribes; W. N. Watt in *The Encyclopaedia of Islam* 5 (1979–80), p. 894f.

"What is there for you to do now, when your Messiah has been expelled by the Romans, the Persians and the Himyarites?"[278]

Being mocked by the Arabs, we became distressed. (Then even more) sorrow and distress came upon us because in our presence an envoy sent by the king of the Himyarites to the king Mundhir came and gave him a letter full of boasting in which it was written thus:

"Know, my brother, king Mundhir, that the king whom the Ethiopians established in our country has died. The winter season came and the Ethiopians could not set out to our country to set up a Christian king as they used to do, therefore I became king over the whole country of the Himyarites.

First I seized[279] all the Christians who confess Christ, if they would not become Jews like us. I killed two hundred and eighty priests who were there and together with them the Ethiopians who guarded the church. Of that church of theirs I made a synagogue for ourselves.

Then together with an army of 120,000 I went to Najran, their capital city.[280] When I had besieged it for a number of days but had not taken it, I gave them promises under oath.[281] (But) I decided not to keep my word to the Christians, my enemies. And I seized them and (required)[282] them to bring their gold, silver and (other) possessions. They brought them to me [**p. 59**] and I took (them).

I asked for Paul, their bishop, (but when) they told me that he had died I did not believe them till they showed me his grave. I dug up his bones and burnt them, as well as their church,[283] their priests and everybody whom I found inside taking refuge.

---

[278] In the case of the Romans the author has in mind the decision of the Council of Chalcedon, which, in the opinion of the Monophysites, denied Christ His divine nature. The presence of this apparently fictitious remark, put into the mouth of pagan Arabs, suggests the Monophysite propagandistic character of the *Letter*, L. Van Rompay, 'The Martyrs of Najran: some remarks on the nature of the sources', in *Studia Paulo Naster oblata, II* (Orientalia Lovaniensia Analecta 13), Leuven 1982, p. 307; W. Witakowski, 'Syrian Monophysite propaganda in the fifth to seventh centuries', in *Aspects of Late Antiquity and Early Byzantium: papers read at a colloquium held at the Swedish Research Institute in Istanbul... 1992*, ed. L. Rydén & J. O. Rosenqvist (Swedish Research Institute in Istanbul Transactions 4), Stockholm 1993, p. 57-66.

[279] 'First I seized: L (see above n. 270) has "I planned to make perish first all..."

[280] Zafār was the capital of Himyar, not Najran.

[281] L adds, "and their chiefs went out to [me]."

[282] Added from L.

[283] L "churches".

I put pressure on the rest (of them) to deny Christ and the Cross.[284] They would not (do so) but confessed that He was God and the Son of the Blessed, and chose to die for His sake. Their chief said many (words) against me and insulted me.[285] (Then) I ordered that all their nobles be put to death. We fetched their wives and while they watched the slaughter of their husbands for Christ's sake we told them to deny (Him) in order to have pity on their sons and daughters, but they would not. The daughters of the covenant[286] pressed forward to be killed first, and the wives of the nobles were indignant against them, and said, "It is our turn to die after our husbands"; and so they were put to death by our command, except for Ruhmi,[287] the wife (suitable) for a future king there.

We did not let her die, but required her to deny Christ and to stay alive taking pity on her daughters, and by becoming a Jewess to enjoy all that she possessed. We ordered her to go and consider (it), while guards of our army followed her. She went off to walk around on the streets and squares of the city, her head uncovered—a woman whose appearance nobody had ever seen on a street since she had grown up. She cried saying:

"O women of Najran, my companions, Christian, Jewish or heathen, listen! You know my family and tribe, and whose Christian daughter I am, [p. 60] and that I have gold and silver, servants and handmaids and numerous fields and (their) products. And now when my husband has been killed for Christ's sake, if I should want to marry a man, (I can do it for) I have 40, 000 *denarii*,[288] numerous golden and silver adornments, as well as pearls and beautiful and resplendent garments, in addition to my husband's fortune. There are among you some who know that I have not lied about these things. (Also, you know) that for a woman

---

[284] L adds, "and to become Jews".

[285] L "against us and insulted us".

[286] "Daughters of the covenant": lay virgins characterized by some sort of religious practices (e.g. ascetic), the nature of which is still debatable, see Vööbus, *Asceticism, I*, p. 184-208, and *III*, p. 24-27; G. Nedungatt, 'The Covenanters of the early Syriac-speaking Church', *OChP* 39 (1973), p. 191-215, 419-444; M. Breydy, 'Les laïcs et les bnay qyomo dans l'ancienne tradition de l'Église syrienne', *Kanon* 3 (1977), p. 51-75. By the seventh century the term designates simply nuns.

[287] Ms. *rwmy*; the name is spelled *rhwmy* below. In the *Book of the Himyarites* (p. xcvi) her name is given as Ruhm, and she is not the wife of any future king, but just a noble lady.

[288] Tiny Roman silver coins, in the 6th century worth 1/7000 - 1/8500 of a golden *solidus* (4.55 g.); *RECA* 5 (1905), col. 212.

there are no days of joy equal to those of the wedding feast, for
thereafter (come) griefs and groans at the birth of the children and again
when she is bereaved of them, and when she buries them. But from
today on I am free of all these things. (As) I rejoiced on the first day
of my[289] wedding feast, now, in the serenity of my mind, I have adorned
my five virgin daughters for Christ.

Look at me, my companions! You have seen me twice, at my first
wedding feast and at this, the second, for I went in to my first betrothed
with my face unveiled before all of you, and now with my face unveiled
I go to Christ, my and my daughters' Lord and God, (just) as he abased
himself in His love, and came to us and suffered for us.

Imitate me,[290] for I am not less beautiful than you, and am now going
to Christ resplendent in beauty, uncorrupted by the infidelity of the
Jews. Let my beauty testify before my Lord that (the king)[291] has not
been able to seduce me into the sin of denying (Him). [p. 61] I have not
loved my gold, my silver and everything I possess as I love my God.
This rebellious king has (tried to) persuade[292] me to deny (Christ) that
I might live. Far be it from me, my companions! Far be it from me to
deny Christ God in whom I and my daughters believe. I was baptized
in the name of the Trinity and I worship His Cross, and for His sake I
die with joy, I and my daughters, just as He suffered in the flesh for our
sake.

Now (I) leave upon earth all that is lovely to the eyes and the body
and is transient, and I go to receive from my Lord something which is
not transient. Blessed be you, my companions, if you hear me, listen to
the truth and love Christ God for whose sake I and my daughters die.
Let there be peace and well-being from now on for God's people. Let
the blood of these our brothers and sisters, who have been put to death
because of Christ, be a bulwark for this city if it perseveres in Christ,
my Lord. Behold, with unveiled face I leave this city, in which I have
lived as in a temporary dwelling place,[293] to go with my daughters to the
eternal city, (seeing that) I have betrothed them there. Pray for me, my

---

[289] L adds, "first".

[290] L adds, "and my daughters and understand".

[291] L "the Jewish king unbeliever".

[292] Read *'appis*, as in Michael the Syrian 275c21/II, 187, instead of PD 61, 2 & L *'appes li*, "permitted me, allowed me", which makes poor sense.

[293] Lit. 'tent of time', the term in the Syriac Bible for the Ark of the Covenant.

companions, that Christ my Lord may receive me and be gracious to me, for now I have tarried three days after my husband."

And then we heard the sound of wailing from the city. Those who had been sent (to follow her) returned, and on being asked told us what we have written above, how Ruhmi had been walking around the city talking to the women, her companions, comforting (them). There was wailing in the city and because the guards had let her do these things we became angry with them (enough) to kill them, had we not become persuaded (not to do so). In the end she came out from the city like an insane person with her head unveiled, together with her daughters. She stood in front of me without shame, [**p. 62**] holding her daughters, adorned as if for the wedding feast, with her hands. She loosed the braids of her hair, grasped it with her hand, stretched out her neck and bowed her head. She shouted:

"I and my daughters are Christians and we die for the sake of Christ. Cut off our heads that we may go and find our brothers and our sisters and the father of my daughters."

I, however, after all that madness, tried to persuade her to deny Christ and merely say that he was a man, but she would not. One of her daughters (even) insulted us for having spoken thus. And as I realized that there was no means to (make) her deny Christ, on my order—(intended) to frighten the other Christians—she was thrown down on the earth and her daughters were executed so that their blood flowed down into her mouth. Thereupon her head was cut off, and I swear by Adonai that I was very distressed because of her beauty and that of her daughters.

It seemed to my high priests and to me that it would not be right, according to law, that children should die because of parents. So I distributed the boys and girls among the soldiers that they might raise them. When they have come to maturity they will live if they become Jews, and die if they confess Christ.

I have written these things and informed Your Majesty, and I urge you not to allow any Christian (to live) among your people unless he deny (Christ) and become one of yours. As far as the Jews, my brothers, who are under your dominion are concerned, treat them kindly, my brother. Write and send me (your wish) in return for this, for I shall send you whatever you desire."

All these things were written to Mundhir by the unclean Jewish king.

When we arrived there, he assembled his army, the letter was read before him and the messenger told how the Christians had been put to death and expelled from the land of the Himyarites. Said Mundhir to the Christians of his army:

"Now, you have heard what has happened. Deny Christ now [**p. 63**] because I am not better than the kings who persecuted the Christians."

(Then) a certain Christian man of his army was moved with indignation and boldly said to the king:

"We did not become Christians in your time that we should (now) have to deny Christ."

Mundhir grew angry and said:

"Do you dare to speak (so) in front of me?"

And (the man) said:

"It is because of the fear of God that I speak (thus) fearlessly, and nobody will restrain me. For my sword is not shorter than the others', and I am not afraid to fight to the death."

But on account of his family and because he was a noble man, distinguished and courageous in battle, Mundhir remained silent.

When we returned to Hirta de-Nu'man in the first week of the fast, we found (there) an envoy who had been sent by the king of the Himyarites before he had died. When he heard about these who had been massacred by that Jewish tyrant, he quickly hired a man from Hirtha de-Nu'man and sent him to Najran to bring him a report. When he saw and found out what had happened there, he too, on his return, told the Christian envoy in our presence about the matters which we have described above, and that 340 nobles who had gone out from the city to (the Jewish king) had been killed, and about Harith son of Ka'b,[294] their chief, Ruhmi's husband,[295] whom the Jew insulted by saying to him:

"You have put your trust in Christ to revolt against me, but (now) spare your old age and deny him or else you will die with your companions."

He answered:

---

[294] Instead of Kalb (as in PD) or Kanb (as in Ps.-Zachariah II, 70, 11) read Ka'b (a known Arab name), according to I. Shahîd's emendation, *Martyrs*, p. 50. The forms with -l- or -n- must be misreadings of -'-, as these three characters are easy to confuse in Syriac script.

[295] According to the author of the *Book of the Himyarites* (36b, 24/cxxvii), who has more information to hand than Simeon had at the time he wrote his *Letter*, Harith was Ruhmi's relative, not her husband.

"Truly, I feel distressed for all my companions because they did not listen to me when I said to them that you were a liar and that we should not come out to you giving credence to your words, but (rather) fight against you. I have trusted in Christ that I might vanquish you and that the city might not be conquered because nothing was missing in it. And you are not a king but a liar. I have seen many kings who possess [p. 64] the truth and do not lie. I will not deceive Christ my God by becoming a Jew like you and an unbeliever. Now I know that He loves me.[296] I have lived long in the world and I have sons and grandsons and I have daughters and my family is numerous. I was victorious in wars by the power of Christ. It is clear to me that as the vine, once pruned, gives many fruits,[297] so our Christian people will increase in this city, and the church which has been burnt by you will grow up rebuilt and have dominion and give orders to kings. Christianity shall rule and Judaism shall be extinct. Your kingdom shall pass away and your power shall cease. Do not boast of what you have done. And when you swagger, you show yourself to be counterfeit."

So said noble Harith, the venerable old man. Immediately he turned round and said loudly to his companions, the believers, who (stood) around him:

"Did you hear, my brothers, what I have said to this Jew?"

They said: "We heard everything you said, our father."

Then he said: "Is it true or not?"

And they cried: "True."

He said: "If anyone is afraid of the sword and denies Christ let him separate himself from us."

They cried: "Far be it from us to be afraid, our father. We shall all die with you for the sake of Christ. None of us will remain after you."

Then he cried saying:

"You who are around me, Christians, Jews and heathens, listen! If anyone of my family, of my kinsmen or of my tribe denies Christ and adheres to this Jew, he will not have any bond with me and he will not inherit from that which is mine, but what I have will be (used) toward the cost of rebuilding the church. But if a man of my kin does not deny

---

[296] Read w-hāšā yed'et d-rāhem lī, as in the parallel text in Ps.-Zachariah II 70, 24; this is corroborated by Guidi's text (see above n. 270), 510, 4, which reads, "Now I know that Christ loves me".

[297] Cp. Jn. 15, 1f.

(Christ) and yet survives, he will inherit my possessions after me. Three villages, however, which the Church shall choose from among my properties, shall be for her expenses."

Having said this he turned to the king and said:

"I renounce [p. 65] you and whoever denies Christ. Behold, we are standing before you."

His companions took heart and said:

"Behold, Abraham the patriarch is looking upon you and upon us with you! (Let) everyone who denies Christ and remains (alive) after you be renounced."

(The king) gave orders to take them to a dry river-bed, called *Wadiya*,[298] to cut off their heads and to throw their bodies into it. (Harith) stretched out his hands towards heaven and said:

"Christ God, come to our help, give us strength and receive our souls. Let the blood of Thy servants, which has been shed for Thy sake, be pleasing to Thee. Make us worthy to see Thee, and acknowledge us before Thy Father, as Thou didst promise.[299] Let the church be rebuilt and let there be a bishop in this city in place of Paul, Thy servant, whose bones were burnt."

They bade each other farewell and the old man Harith made the sign of the Cross over them. He bowed his head and received (the blow of) the sword. His companions rushed up and in a throng smeared themselves with his blood. And they all died the death of martyrs.

A three-year-old child, whose mother, holding him by her hand, went out to receive death, saw the king as he was sitting dressed in royal garments. He left his mother and rushed to kiss the king upon the knees. The king took him up and began to fondle him. And he said to him:

"What do you prefer: to go and die with your mother or to stay with me?"

The boy said to him:

"My lord, I prefer to die with my mother. And this is why I have gone (out) with my mother. She told me, 'Come, my son, we shall go to die for the sake of Christ.' So leave me alone that I may go to my mother lest she die without my seeing her, for she told me that the king

---

[298] Ms. *wdy'*; it was thought to be simply Ar. *wādi*, but the newly discovered Simeon's "second" letter has *lwdy'* (Lawdiya?); Shahid, *Martyrs*, p. XIX, 6, transl. p. 54.

[299] Cp. Mt. 10,32.

of the Jews gave orders that everybody who would not deny Christ should die. And I do not deny Him."

(The king) asked him:

"Whence do you know Christ?"

The boy said to him:

"I see Him every day when together with my mother I come to [p. 66] the church."

He said to him:

"Do you love me or your mother?"

And he said:

"By our Lord—my mother!"

And again (the king) said to him:

"Do you love me or Christ?"

He said:

"I love Christ more than you."

Said (the king) to him:

"Why (then) have you come and kissed my knees?"

He answered:

"It seemed to me that you were a Christian king, one whom I had seen in the church. I did not know that you were a Jew."

Said (the king) to him:

"I will give you nuts, almonds and figs."

The boy said:

"No, by Christ, I shall not eat Jewish nuts; just let me go to my mother."

And he said to him:

"Stay with me and you will be a son to me."

Said the boy:

"No, by Christ, I shall not stay with you, for stinking and rotten is your smell, and not sweet like my mother's."

(Then) the king said to those who stood nearby:

"Look at this bad root, whom from his childhood Christ has led astray that he might love him."

One of the nobles said to the boy:

"Come with me. I shall bring you to the queen that you may be a son to her."

Said the boy to him:

"May your face be slapped! My mother is better to me than the queen, for she takes me to the church."

And when he realized that they were seizing him, he bit the king upon the thigh and said:

"Leave me, evil Jew, that I may go to my mother and die with her." (But the king) gave him to one of his nobles and said to him:

"Guard him till he has grown up. (Then) if he denies Christ, he shall live, and if not, he shall die."

When a servant of that man carried him out, he kicked (the servant's) legs and cried to his mother:

"My mother! Come and take me that I may go with you to the church!" She called to him saying:

"Go, my son, you are entrusted to Christ. Do not cry. Wait for me in the church with Christ until I come!"

And when she had said this, they cut off her head.

Through these writings and tidings which were heard, grief came upon all the Christians here. [**p. 67**] And we have written to the reverend bishops, the (true) believers, about what happened in the land of the Himyarites that they might know and commemorate these holy martyrs. We suggest to you, O beloved, that it should quickly be made known to the archimandrites and bishops and especially to the chief priest of Alexandria that he may write to the king of the Ethiopians (inviting him) to get ready at once to help the Himyarites. But let also the chief priests of the Jews in Tiberias be seized and forced to send a message to this Jewish king who has appeared that he may put an end to the strife and persecution in the land of the Himyarites.

The rest of the letter contained greetings to hierarchs of that time and to believing archimandrites.

Again on that little boy concerning whom it was written above in the story of the martyrs.

It seemed to us proper also not to pass in silence over that little boy concerning whom it was written above in this narrative that he bit the king upon the thigh, saying, "Leave me that I may go and die with my mother." But (the king) kept him, and although he coaxed him, (the boy) did not hearken to him. (The king) handed him over to one of his nobles to raise him. If he would not deny Christ when he reached adulthood he was to die.

Since however that Jew was killed by the Ethiopians and all the Jews among the Himyarites were eradicated, this boy survived and grew up. When it became known to the Christian king who ruled there, he took the boy (to live) with him. When thereafter (the boy) made progress in his education and reached adulthood, (the king) treated him with great honour as a witness to Christ and made him the chief of his patricians. He became (king's) confidant and advisor. His name was Baysar. Thus [**p. 68**] finally he sent him on an embassy to the emperor Justinian. For a long time we[300] were in his company. We admired the man's good intentions, his gentleness, his humility and nobility depicted upon his face, and his constant sadness. His mind was occupied in constant prayer, when he walked around from dawn till dusk from one church to another in the capital, praying and giving alms from what he had been given by the king. He fasted constantly for entire days until the evening. Finally, when all who saw him marvelled at these things and spoke about him with admiration, it became known that he had been that little boy who had renounced that Jew and had insulted him publicly and in the end had bitten him upon the thigh, although he did not wish these things to be known about him. (But) we have recorded them (as) concerning a witness to God.

On the king of the Ethiopians, on his expedition and his killing of the tyrant and the Jews with him.

Thereafter, when the king of the Ethiopians—the one who had killed the former king of the Himyarites and because of this had become a Christian—learned this, and about the slaughter of the Christians and the tyranny of the Jews, he flamed up with zeal and led off his army. He set out against the tyrant, seized and killed him and routed his troops and all the Jews in the country of the Himyarites altogether. Also he established there a king, a zealous Christian whose name was Abraham.[301] Thus all the Christians who had been dispersed by the persecution and the fear of the Jews gathered there (again) and the country was restored to Christianity.

He sent a message to Alexandria and before the Council of Chalcedon was imposed (there) he received (from there) a bishop. The latter after a short [**p. 69**] time in that country died. But when the king of the

---

[300] It is John of Ephesus, the main source of Ps.-Dionysius, who speaks here of his own experience; that these are his words is confirmed by the testimony of Michael the Syrian (276c, last two lines/189).

[301] Most probably identical with the Abram of Procopius, *Wars*, I, 20. In Ethiopian tradition he is known as (Ella) Abreha: Yu.M. Kobishchanov, *Axum*, University Park, PA, 1979, p. 105-108. On Abraha(m) in Arabic tradition, see M. J. Kister, 'The Campaign of Ḥulubān: a new light on the expedition of Abraha', *Mus* 78 (1965), p. 425-436.

Himyarites learned that the Council of Chalcedon had been imposed in Alexandria and the patriarch Theodosius had been deposed[302] because of (his) belief and had departed as he had refused to accept the Council, (the king) also took offence and did not want to accept a bishop from Alexandria.

The year 850 (A.D. 538/9): the Persians attacked Antioch and it was conquered, ravaged and burnt.[303]

At the same time, in the fourteenth year of Ephrem('s episcopacy) powerful Persian troops, coming together with their king Khosraw,[304] approached and conquered the city of Antioch. They burned it with fire and destroyed it. They stripped it and removed even the marble slabs, with which the walls (of the buildings) were overlaid, and took them away to their country, since they also were building in their country a city like this one and named it Antioch (too).

Ephrem fled before them to hide himself in shame after (the capture) of his city and its devastation which took place in his days. And so it befell him, and thus four years later in shame he passed away from life here. But there—God knows what was in wait for him.

The year 857 (A.D. 545/6): the holy Timothy, patriarch of Alexandria, died and entrusted his see to a man by the name Theodosius from among the people of the church there.[305]

The year 841 (A.D. 529/30): the great river Euphrates was obstructed above the region of Claudia[306] facing Cappadocia, beside the village [Pro]sedion.[307] A great mountain(side) [p. 70] slipped down and as the mountains there are very high, though set close together, having come

---

[302] The chronicler here anticipates the course of events; see below, the lemma for the year 857 Sel.

[303] The correct date of Khosraw's invasion and of the capture of Antioch is 540; on this Persian-Roman war, see Procopius, *Wars*, II; see also, Bury, *Later Empire*, II, p. 93-100; Stein, *Bas-Empire*, p. 485-502; Barker, *Justinian*, p. 119-121; G. Downey, 'The Persian Campaign in Syria in A.D. 540', *Speculum* 28 (1953), p. 340-348; Frye, *Ancient Iran*, p. 326f.

[304] Or 'Chosroes' (Χοσρόης); Khosraw Anūshirwān ("of the immortal soul"), king of Persia 531–578/9.

[305] The correct date is 535, see above n. 226; Timothy is there called "heretic"; Theodosius was elected patriarch in 535 and deposed in 537, d. 566.

[306] South-east of Melitene.

[307] *[Prw]sydyn*, the first three letters supplemented by Chabot according to the parallel account in the *Chr. 1234*, I, 199/156; in the (Latin) translation Chabot writes "Praesidium".

down it obstructed (the flow of the river) between two (other) mountains. (Things) remained (thus) for three days and three nights, and (then) the river turned its flow backward towards Armenia and the earth became inundated and villages were submerged. It caused much damage (there), but downstream (the river) ran dry in some places, dwindled and turned into dry land.

Then people from many villages gathered in prayers and services and with many crosses. They came in sorrow, with tears streaming down and with great trembling carrying their censers and burning (incense). They offered (the eucharist) further up on that mountain which had obstructed (the flow) of the river in its midst. Thereafter it gradually receded to produce an opening and in the end it suddenly burst and the mass of water gushed out and came down. There was great terror in the whole of the East as far as the marches of Persia, since many villages, people and cattle were flooded as well as everything which was standing in the way of the sudden mass of water. It destroyed many communities. But some of the houses of the village which lay upstream from the mountain with its vineyards remained as they were firmly embedded on the other shore. (Although) weakened by (the flood),[308] they have lasted until today. So (was it) too with the whole land above the blockage; while flowing down (the tide) overwhelmed it and caused damage.

The year 842 (A.D. 530/1): the sun darkened and stayed covered with darkness a year and a half,[309] that is eighteen months. Although rays were visible around it for two or three hours (a day) they were as if diseased, with the result that fruits did not reach full ripeness. All the wine had the taste of reject grapes. Then the Lord let his mercy appear to [p. 71] his creation and shine upon it. And again the people reverted to hardness of heart without fear, just as before.

The year 849 (A.D. 537/8): the holy Mar Severus, patriarch of Antioch, departed this world on the 8th of February,[310] and on the 6th

---

[308] The text seems to be corrupt.

[309] Syr. ša(n)ttā (spelt šnt'), which seems to be an early scribal mistake for ša 'tā, 'hour' (spelled š't'), the letters: ' and n are extremely easily confused. The explanation "18 months" seems to be a later rationalisation of the confusion. Michael the Syrian (296a, 10-end/II, 220f) accepted the reading "year", though with some surprise, whereas the author of the Chr. 1234 (I, 199, 11-13/157) corrected it to "hour". The lemma may have originated from the Original Chronicle of Edessa (Witakowski, 'Chr. of Edessa'), from which, via John of Ephesus, it reached PD, Michael the Syrian and the Chr. 1234.

[310] I.e. 8 February 538.

of the same month died the holy Mar John Bar Qursos,[311] and on the 4th of November died Mar John Bar Aphtonia.[312]

The year 850 (A.D. 538/9): Pompeiopolis was struck.[313]

This (city), Pompeiopolis, was not (only) overthrown like other cities by a heavy earthquake which befell it, but (also) a terrible sign took place in it, when the earth suddenly opened and also was torn apart from one side of the city to the other: half of (the city) together with (its) inhabitants[314] fell in and was swallowed up in (this) very frightful and terrifying chasm. In this way it "went down to Sheol alive", as is written.[315] When the people had fallen down into this fearful and terrible chasm and were swallowed up into the depth of the earth, the sound of clamour of all of them together rose bitterly and terribly from the earth to the survivors for many days. Their souls were tormented by the sound of clamour of (the people who had been swallowed up), which rose from the depth of Sheol, but they were unable to do anything to help them.

Later the emperor, having learned (about it), sent much gold in order that they might, if possible, help those who had been swallowed up in the earth. But there was no way to help them—not a single soul of them could be rescued. The gold was given to the living for the restoration[316] of the rest of the city which had escaped and had been saved from that cataclysm of (this) terrible horror caused by our sins. **[p. 72]**

---

[311] John Bar Qursos, bishop of Tella, removed in 521 because of his Monophysitism. After his expulsion he became a wandering bishop ordaining in the Monophysite spirit a great number of priests, thus laying foundations for the separate Monophysite Church organization. He is known from two biographies, one by his disciple Elias (*Vitae virorum apud Monophysitas celeberrimorum*, ed. E. W. Brooks, (CSCO SS 3:25, textus & versio), Paris 1907, p. 19-94/21-60), and one by John of Asia (*Lives, PO* 18:4 (1924), p. 513-526).

[312] John Bar Aphtonia (not to be confused with John the archimandrite of the Monastery of Beth Aphtonia) is known to have founded the monastery of Qenneshre on the Euphrates, a centre of Greek studies; Wright, *Literature*, p. 83-85.

[313] Pompeiopolis in Mysia (Malalas 436/253) in Western Asia Minor (i.e. apparently distinct from Pompeiopolis in Paphlagonia); on the earthquake: Grumel, *Chronologie*, p. 478; the Great Chronographer, 6, *Chr. Pasch.*, tr. p. 195, n. 6.

[314] Read '*mwr*' rather than '*wmr*': "dwellings", or "monasteries".

[315] Cp. Num. 16; 30.33.

[316] Read *l-quyyāmā*, closer to Malalas 437/253: εἰς ἀνανέωσιν, 'for the reconstruction (of the city)', than ms. *l-qāyūmā*, "to the prefect".

The year 851 (A.D. 539/40): Antioch was overthrown—(its) sixth collapse—in the time of Justinian.[317]

Two years after the fifth collapse of Antioch[318] it was overthrown again, for the sixth (time), on the 29th of November on Wednesday, at the tenth hour in the seventh (year of) indiction, that is, according to the computation of the Antiochenes, in the year 576.[319] On that day there was a heavy earthquake for one hour. At the end of the quake there was heard (a sound) like a great, powerful and protracted thunder coming from the sky, while from the earth rose a sound of great terror, powerful and frightful, as from a bellowing bull. The earth trembled and shook because of the terror of this horrible sound. And all the buildings which had been built in (Antioch) since its (previous) collapse were overthrown and razed to the ground as well as the walls and the gates of the city, especially the Great Church,[320] not to mention other churches and martyria and the rest of the buildings, even the small ones, which had escaped (being destroyed) in the previous earthquake.

So (the inhabitants of) all the surrounding cities, on hearing of the disaster and the collapse of the city of Antioch, sat in sorrow, pain and grief. All the villages around (Antioch) were overthrown too, those which had been rebuilt previously, as far as 10 miles (from Antioch). Seleucia and Daphne[321] fell in the fifth collapse but in this, the sixth, did not fall nor were they damaged.

(Most of)[322] the citizens who had been dug out died, apart from those who were (just) wounded, of whom some got (their limbs) broken [**p. 73**] and others were struck with various injuries. (But) God's mercy and grace appeared and did not allow fire to kindle and burn (the city) as in

---

[317] The correct date of the sixth earthquake is 29 November 528, corroborated by Theophanes, AM 6021; Grumel, *Chronologie*, p. 478; Malalas 442f/256f, and n. 27 for parallel sources; the Great Chronographer 5, *Chr. Pasch.*, tr. p. 195, n. 5.

[318] For Antioch's fifth collapse, see above lemma 837 Sel., p. 44-48 and n. 228.

[319] The era of Antioch began on 1 October 49 B.C. (Julius Caesar's granting of freedom to the city), and the year 576 (November) of the era gives A.D. 527 (Grumel, *Chronologie*, p. 215), i.e. one year earlier; the 7th indiction, November, = A.D. 528 (ibid. p. 244).

[320] The Great Church must have been rebuilt after the fire which followed the fifth earthquake, see above p. 45, the lemma for year 837 Sel.

[321] Land's text adds (302, 8-10): "which are upstream from Antioch were overthrown and destroyed for 20 miles' length and breadth, and also they became (a cause of) trembling to the people who saw it, although not because of fire but only because of the earthquake".

[322] So after Land's text (302, 11).

the previous collapse. Most of those, however, who were alive, fled to other cities and left Antioch deserted and desolate. On the mountain above the city others made for themselves shelters of rugs, straw and nets and thus lived in them in the tribulations of winter.

On the harsh winter which came and on prayers made by those who remained in the city.
Immediately after the earthquake in which Antioch was shaken and collapsed a harsh winter came. It had snowed three cubits deep and those who stayed in the city made lamenting supplications in great pain, walking barefoot in the snow and holding olive twigs in their hands. They went out of the city on to the plain at a distance of one mile, while it snowed upon them; (there) they threw themselves down on the snow and so stayed gasping out in painful suffering and in bitter weeping, crying *Kyrie eleison.* To watch them as they were making their way[323] through the snow, their colour altered, made a painful and terrible sight. They threw themselves on their faces shouting in great pain of body and of soul, their faces being miserable and distorted with tears, pain and the harshness of the winter frost.

On the vision which appeared to a believer in that time and on the rebuilding of the city.
Thus in that time, when they were sending up prayers, a vision appeared to a Christian, [**p. 74**] a (true) believer, that he should bid all who had remained in Antioch to write on the gates of the courtyards, houses and shops[324]—those which had lasted and had not fallen—"Christ is with you, stand upright!" Thus all who had survived wrote (this) on the houses which had not fallen, and thus heartened they entered (them). And (the houses) which had remained standing, stood (firm).[325]

Ephrem the patriarch was with them, he who together with the nobles (of the city) who had escaped (death), informed the emperor about all this.

---

[323] Ms. *srwdyn*; read *srw dyn*.

[324] Lit. 'rooms'.

[325] A similar episode can be found in Leontius of Neapolis' *Life of Simeon the Fool* (Léontios de Néapolis, *Vie de Syméon le Fou et Vie de Jean de Chypre*, éd. par A. J. Festugière & L. Rydén (BAH 95), Paris 1974, p. 84, 20-28, tr. 139), where in the time of Maurice (582-602) before an imminent earthquake Simeon whipped columns in Antioch saying to them, "Your master has said, 'Stand upright'". After the earthquake it turned out that the whipped columns did not fall.

On hearing about it (the emperor), together with all the senate sat in sorrow for many days because of Antioch. And again he sent much gold giving orders that the city be made smaller and limited, that the outer wall be destroyed and a wall in the midst of the city be built, and as for the rest most of it should remain (as) an open space outside. And so it was. When the (newly) wall was built, it (appeared to) be at a distance from the river Orontes, whereas most of the city remained outside in ruin. The emperor gave orders that (a channel) should be dug outside the (newly)-built wall in order that there might be a (new) passage for the river (leading) it to pass close to (the city) from one side to another. So the river was blocked in (in its old bed) and (directed to) pass through the channel along the (newly)-built wall. This was done with much toil and at great expense through the emperor Justinian's care and zealousness.[326]

The year 852 (A.D. 540/41): on the second of the month of January, at the eighth hour, in the seventh year (of indiction),[327] **[p. 75]** that is the year 76 of the reckoning according to the era of Laodicea,[328] an earthquake took place and Laodicea was razed to its foundations from the Antioch Gate as far as the Jewish quarter and the sea. The left side, however, where the Church of the Blessed Mother of God stood, did not fall. According to reckoning, seven and a half thousand souls had perished in (the quake). Many Jews but only a few Christians were found alive, although wounded with heavy blows: 274 Jews and 4 Christians. All the churches however by God's help did not fall and were not (even) shaken, neither did fire overwhelm the ruins. The emperor sent also much gold for the rebuilding of Laodicea. And thus it was rebuilt and its walls erected (again).

---

[326] On the reconstruction of Antioch: Procopius, *Buildings*, II, 10:2-25; see also, Michael Whitby, 'Procopius on Antioch', in *Eastern Frontier*, p. 537-553.

[327] 'In the seventh year': Land (303, 9) prints *š't* (i.e. "hour", instead of *šnt*', "year") *d-tš*', "the ninth": this is also wrong, see next note.

[328] So Land's text (303, 10), whereas the Vatican ms. here has a lacuna. Originally it must have read, '576th year' of the Laodicean era (of Julius Caesar). The Laodicean era began from 48 B.C. (Grumel, *Chronologie*, p. 215), giving a date of (January) A.D 529; the seventh indiction, January, is also A.D 529. Grumel, ibid., p. 478, has taken John of Ephesus' date (A.D 541) at face value. Malalas (443/258) places this earthquake in the same year as Antioch's sixth collapse, cp. above n. 317.

At the same time Manichaeans were found in Const(antinople)[329] *and they were burnt with fire.*

At that time many people were found seized by the pernicious error of the Manichaeans.[330] They gathered in houses to perform the mysteries of their abominable and erroneous doctrine. When they were arrested the emperor gave orders to bring them before him, [**p. 76**] since he hoped to be able to admonish them and to convert them from their pernicious error. Thus when they had been brought he debated with them on many (issues), admonished and showed them from the Scriptures that they were caught up in the error of paganism. They would not let him convince them, but in haughtiness (instigated) by Satan they cried out before him without fear, saying:

"We are ready to be burnt for the sake of the doctrine of Mani, and to endure all sorts of tortures and tribulations. But we shall not change (our mind concerning) it."

Then (the emperor) gave orders that their desire be fulfilled and that they be thrown upon a boat and burnt with fire on the sea, and thereby be drowned in the sea, and that their possessions enter the imperial treasury,[331] since well-known women and nobles and patricians[332] could also be found among them. Thus numerous Manichaeans perished by this sentence of burning with fire, yet they would not be persuaded to turn from their error.

---

[329] Abbreviated in the ms.

[330] Manichaeans, adherents of the religion of dualistic character with elements of Zoroastrianism, Gnosticism and Christianity, which was founded by the Persian Mani (216–276), were probably the most persecuted religious minority in the late Roman/early Byzantine empire. Anastasius was the first emperor to impose the death penalty on Manichaeans (S. N. C. Lieu, *Manichaeism in the Later Roman empire and Medieval China: a historical survey*, Manchester 1985, p. 168), as did Justin I and Justinian (as Justin's co-regent) in 527 (Lieu, p. 170), and later Justinian alone (ibid. 174). By these measures Manichaeism became extinguished in Byzantium during this emperor's reign (p. 175).

[331] The Syriac uses here the Greek loanword ταμιεῖον, 'treasury'.

[332] An honorary title granted to the highest dignitaries of the Byzantine empire and other distinguished persons; it was reintroduced by Constantine the Great in imitation of the ancient Roman *patricii*; Guilland, *Institutions*, II, p. 132.

Again on pagans which were found in the capital in the days of the emperor Justinian.[333]

In the 19th year of the emperor Justinian (A.D. 545/6) by encouragement of our humble self the affair of the pagans was investigated. There were found in the capital famous persons, nobles and others—*grammatici*,[334] sophists,[335] *scholastici*[336] and physicians, and when they were exposed, on being tortured they denounced each other. They were arrested, scourged and imprisoned. (Then) these patricians and nobles were sent into churches to learn the faith of the Christians, as befitted pagans.

One noble and rich pagan among them, whose name was Phocas,[337] and who was a patrician, seeing the intensity of the investigation and also (knowing) that those (pagans) who had been arrested informed (the authorities) that he was a pagan (as well), and that a heavy sentence was prepared against him because of the emperor's severe zealousness, took poison in the night [p. 77] and ended (his) life here. When the emperor was informed of it he made a very just decision giving instructions that (Phocas) should be buried (with) the burial of an ass,[338] that is without people attending or any prayer for him. So members of his household carried him on a bier at night, went out (of the city), opened a tomb and threw him in like a dead beast. Thus for some time fear seized all the pagans.

---

[333] Notwithstanding the legislative efforts of Theodosius I (379–395), who prohibited sacrifices and other cult practices, paganism survived up to the sixth century (and beyond) both in villages and among the upper classes of traditional background and education. The *Code of Justinian* reduced the number of laws against the pagans (they were not allowed to possess property, hold public office, or teach; once baptized they would be punished with death for backsliding), but their enforcement was hence the more vigorous: three major persecutions of pagans were launched during Justinian's reign, in 528–29, 545–46, and 562; cp. Maas, *Lydus*, p. 67-78; on paganism before the Justinianic epoch, see F. R. Trombley, *Hellenic Religion and Christianization c. 370–539*, I-II (Religions in the Graeco-Roman World 115), Leiden 1993–94.

[334] At this period, professors of literature.

[335] Teachers and practitioners of rhetoric.

[336] Lawyers, or officials with a legal education.

[337] *PLRE II*, p. 881f, Phocas (5); Maas, *Lydus*, p. 78-82; Phocas who had been a *silentiarius* (court attendant in charge of order and silence—hence the name—in the imperial palace; see R. Guilland, 'Silentiaire', in idem, *Titres et fonctions de l'Empire byzantin*, London 1976, art. XVII) and a patrician, survived Justinian's first purge of the pagans in 529 without any harm to his further career; he became *praefectus praetorio* (see n. 63), and a judge; he took his life in the second persecution campaign (545–46), as he may have expected to be accused of backsliding.

[338] Jer. 22, 19.

The year 853 (A.D. 541/2): God's grace visited the countries of Asia, Caria, Lydia and Phrygia by the zealousness of the victorious Justinian. It proceeded from him abundantly by the mediation of our humble self, that is John of Asia, to the effect that by the power of the Holy Spirit 70, 000 souls were instructed in the faith and turned away from the error of paganism, idolatry and the celebration of the demons to the knowledge of the truth. They were converted, signed with the Cross and baptized in the name of our Lord Jesus Christ. Having renounced the error of their fathers they joined the ranks of the Christians. (For) the expenses and the baptismal robes the victorious (emperor) gave abundantly and he also took care to bestow upon every one of them a *trimision*.[339] So when God opened the minds of all of them and enlightened their understanding with the truth, together with us, they destroyed their temples with their own hands and hewed down rows of their idols, cast down the sacrifices set in order everywhere, and overthrew their altars which were stinking and impure with the evil smell of blood from the sacrifices to demons, and hewed down the innumerable trees of their cult, while deriding the entire error of their fathers.

Thus [p. 78] the sign of the Cross of salvation was set up everywhere among them, and God's churches were consecrated with much zealousness and care in every place, on high and habitable mountains, in valleys, and in other places, where paganism had disappeared. As many as 96 of them were built and erected, and 12 monasteries, in the places where paganism had disappeared. Where the word "Christianity" had never been pronounced since the foundation of the world until (this) time, (there) 55 churches were built (with money) from the public treasury,[340] but the new Christians built 41 at their own (expense), whereas the victorious emperor through our humble self abundantly gave silver and linen garments, books and brass (vessels) gladly and willingly from the public treasury.[341]

---

[339] Τριμίσιον, or in Latin *tremissis* = 1/3 of a golden *solidus*; H. Chantraine, *RECA* 24, col. 890f.

[340] The Syriac uses here the Greek loanword δημόσιον.

[341] Another account in John of Ephesus, *Lives, PO* 18 (1924), p. 681; and idem, *Third Part*, II, 44-45, III, 36-37, p. 111f; 169-172/159f; 229-232; see also, Bury, *Later Empire*, II, p. 371; Stein, *Bas-Empire*, p. 371f; F. R. Trombley, 'Paganism in the Greek world at the end of antiquity: the case of rural Anatolia and Greece', *HTR* 78 (1985), p. 329-336; M. Whitby, 'John of Ephesus and the pagans: pagan survivals in the sixth century', in *Paganism in the Later Roman Empire and in Byzantium*, ed. M. Salamon, Cracow 1991,

The year 854 (A.D. 542/3): there was an earthquake and the city of Cyzicus[342] was overthrown and most of it collapsed. Most of the wall disintegrated, fell and broke open. The rest which had not fallen in (the quake) remained, although heavily damaged, tottering and as if on the verge of falling.

Since at that time we were passing through it we saw the columns of the public building[343] tilted, and lying on (their) sides ... outer ... their side ... them, the people were removing.[344] And thus most of the city rested on the cedar beams [p. 79] and was propped up (by these). Also many (other) cities were in that shape.

In the same year a great and terrible star, similar to a spear of fire, appeared at evening in the western quarter (of the sky). A great flash of fire rose up from it and it shone brightly too, and from it went out little rays of fire. Thus terror seized all who saw it. The Greeks called it a "comet". It rose and was visible for about twenty days.[345]

Thereafter when many (people) were awaiting what was about to happen in the wake of this sign, they saw many wars and drought of the air and thirstiness and shortage of rain. The (sign) brought about the desolation of the cities. We are unable to record in full the memory of these misfortunes (about which we have heard) from all sides.

---

p. 111-131; S. Mitchell, *Anatolia: Land, Men and Gods in Asia Minor*, II, Oxford 1993, p. 117-119.

[342] Cyzicus: on the Asiatic shore of the Sea of Marmara; the exact date is 6 September 543, Grumel, *Chronologie*, p. 478; Downey, 'Earthquakes', p. 598; & the Great Chronographer, 9, *Chr. Pasch.*, tr. p. 196 & n. 9.

[343] Δημόσιον: any building for public use may be meant here, treasury, archive, prison, bath, etc.

[344] The text is partly lost.

[345] Malalas 454/266; Grumel, *Chronologie*, p. 470 (year 542/3); Schove, *Eclipses*, p. 292.

The year 855 (A.D. 543/4) of Alexander:[346] there was a great and mighty plague in the whole world in the days of the emperor Justinian.[347]

Now, for the beginning of this narrative the blessed prophet Jeremiah has proved most helpful to us, being versed in raising songs of lamentation amid groans over the afflictions and the ruin of his people. Thus he would be a model for the present writer—or lamenter—in (putting down) the story of this terrible and mighty scourge with which the whole world was lashed in our days; though this time not over the afflictions of one city, Jerusalem, or of one people only, the Jews, would he have to weep and lament, but over (those of) many cities [p. 80] which (God's) wrath turned into, as it were, a wine-press and pitilessly trampled and squeezed all their inhabitants within them like fine grapes.

(He would have to weep and lament) over the whole earth (upon) which the command went out like a reaper upon standing corn and mowed and laid down innumerable people of all ages,[348] all sizes and all ranks, all together;

—over corpses which split open and rotted on the streets with nobody to bury (them);

—over houses large and small, beautiful and desirable which suddenly became tombs for their inhabitants and in which servants and masters at the same time suddenly fell (dead), mingling their rottenness together in their bedrooms, and not one of them escaped who might remove their corpses out from within the house;

—over others who perished falling in the streets to become a terrible and shocking spectacle for those who saw them, as their bellies were swollen and their mouths wide open, throwing up pus like torrents, their eyes inflamed and their hands stretched out upward, and (over) the

---

[346] Another term for the Seleucid era.

[347] The Great Plague under Justinian, 541–544; see P. Allen, 'The "Justinianic" Plague', *Byzantion* 49 (1979), p. 5-20; and J.-N. Biraben & J. Le Goff, 'La peste dans le Haut Moyen Age', *Annales: Économies, Sociétés, Civilisations* 24 (1969), p. 1484-1510. This, the longest known account of the Great Plague, although less informative (but much more replete with Biblical quotations) than the accounts of Procopius (*Wars*, II, 22), Evagrius (IV, 29) and Agathias (V, 10), comes from John of Ephesus, who devoted to it a separate work, subsequently incorporated into his *Church History*; D'yakonov, *Ioann Yefesskiy*, p. 168f; from this source it was also copied by Michael the Syrian (305b&c, 1-308 end/II, 235–240).

[348] A pun on the words *qāymātā*, "standing corn" and *qawmān*, "man's ages".

corpses rotting and lying on corners and streets and in the porches of
courtyards and in churches and martyria and everywhere, with nobody
to bury (them);
—over ships in the midst of the sea whose sailors were suddenly
attacked by (God's) wrath and (the ships) became tombs for their
captains and they continued adrift on the waves carrying the corpses of
their owners;
—over other (ships) which arrived in harbours, were moored by their
owners, and remained (so), never to be untied by them again;
—over palaces which groaned one to the other;
—over bridal chambers where the brides were adorned (in finery), but
all of a sudden there were just lifeless and fearsome corpses;
—over virgins which (had been) guarded in bedchambers and (now)
there was nobody to carry them from (these) bedchambers [p. 81] to the
tombs;
—over highways which became deserted;
—over roads (on) which (the traffic) was interrupted;
—over villages whose inhabitants perished all together;
—over many things of this kind, which defeat all who have the power
of speech in (their skill with) words and stories.

Thus over these things the prophet might weep and say, "Woe upon
me not 'because of the destruction of the daughter of my people,'[349] but
because of the desolation of the entire habitable earth of humanity,
which has been corrupted by its sins; and because the world in its
entirety has already been made desolate for some time and has become
empty of its inhabitants". He might, I imagine, use the words of the
prophecies of his fellow prophets to bring forward and say to the
remnant among humanity who had survived, "'Lament, wail, O
ministers of the altar. Go in, pass the night in sackcloth, O ministers of
my God, not only 'because the cereal offering and the drink offering are
cut off from the house of your God',[350] but because (God's) wrath, due
to sins, has suddenly turned the holy house of God into a tomb for dead
corpses and it reeked of dead bodies instead of living worshippers".
Again he might also repeat these words, "The earth shall sit in sorrow
and all its inhabitants mourn".[351] Also not very remote (from the case)

[349] Lam. 2, 11.
[350] Cp. Joel 1, 13 and 1, 9.
[351] Is. 24, 6 (Peshitta).

is this, "Call for the mourning and lamenting women, "[352] that together they may make lamentation, not over one corpse, or over one people, or over an only-begotten son, or over a young man who was snatched away by death, but over (whole) peoples and kingdoms, over territories and regions and over powerful cities which were seized (by the plague) and their dwellings groaned over the rotten corpses (lying) in them.

Thus when I, a wretch, wanted to include these matters in a record of history, my thoughts were seized many times by stupor, and for many reasons I planned to omit [p. 82] it, firstly because all mouths and tongues are insufficient to relate it, and moreover because even if there could be found such that would record (at least) a little from among the multitude (of matters), what use would it be, when the entire world was tottering and reaching its dissolution and the length of generations was cut short? And for whom would he who wrote be writing?

(But) then I thought that it was right that through our writings we should inform our successors and transmit to them (at least) a little from among the multitude (of matters) concerning our chastisement. Even if together with us they are knocking on the gate of the consummation, perhaps (during) this remainder of the world which will come after us they will fear and shake because of the terrible scourge with which we were lashed through our transgressions and become wiser through the chastisement of us wretches and be saved from (God's) wrath here (in this world) and from future torment.

It was upon us that (the chastisement) came at that time (and so now) it is time that we should weep together with the prophet saying, "Death has come up into our windows, it has entered our gates, and made our palaces desolate".[353] Perhaps the eye of the prophecy watched these present events and prophesied concerning us, especially since in very deed it has appeared that, "My sword will be drawn forth out of its sheath and will destroy both righteous and sinners",[354] so that it also happened that at a single sign they became a single wine-press, and corpses which were split open, were eaten by dogs and exposed, having been cast about in great terror.

---

[352] Cp. Jer. 9, 17; PD has added, "and lamenting".

[353] Cp. Jer. 9, 21.

[354] Cp. Ezek. 21, 3.

Now when the chastisement had been fulfilled[355] it began to cross the sea to Palestine and the region of Jerusalem; furthermore some terrible shapes also appeared to people at sea.

When this plague was passing from one land to another, many people saw shapes of bronze boats and (figures) sitting in them resembling people [p. 83] with their heads cut off. Holding staves, also of bronze, they moved along on the sea and could be seen going whithersoever they headed. These figures were seen everywhere in a frightening fashion, especially at night. Like flashing bronze and like fire did they appear, black people without heads sitting in a glistening boat and travelling swiftly on the sea, so that this sight almost caused the souls of the people who saw it to expire.

In this way they were seen proceeding to Gaza, Ashkelon and Palestine and simultaneously with their appearance the beginning (of the plague) took place there. Also (horrors) exceeding by far those previously narrated about the city of Alexandria[356] took place from now on in the whole of Palestine, with the effect that villages and cities were left totally without inhabitants.

Now (we shall speak about) another sign of menace and of God's just sentence. Since in this way the riches of many people were left unguarded, gold, silver and other things,—the pearls of the world—gates standing open and treasures abandoned, houses full of all (kinds of) objects and everything one could desire in the world, so if it happened that somebody wished to take and gather something in order to take possession (of it), thinking that he would escape, on the very same day the sentence would come upon him.

Thus it was told about one city on the Egyptian border (that) it perished totally and completely with (only) seven men and one little boy ten years old remaining in it. The (men) having made common cause with each other went around the whole city and saw [p. 84] that there was nobody alive in it but themselves, the corpses of the rest (of the people) being mixed together in a decaying state. And when after one, two, and as much as five days, these (seven) were (still) alive, they took counsel among them(selves) and said:

---

[355] In Alexandria; we know this from Michael the Syrian (305b-306/II, 235–238), who retains the beginning of John of Ephesus' account of the plague, omitted by PD.

[356] PD has forgotten that he omitted the beginning of John of Ephesus' account of the plague, cp. previous note.

"Perhaps we shall escape (from death), but since now it is easy for
us—come, let us enter the large houses and gather for ourselves gold,
silver and whatever (of other riches) is in them (so that) we shall (be
able to) fill one house. Perhaps we will survive and so it will be ours."
    In fact as they had said so it was. They dared to enter the houses
which were rich and empty of inhabitants. For three days they gathered
only gold and silver and with it filled one large house. On the third day
(when) they were carrying (the booty) and entering the house, there,
inside the house, (God's) wrath came upon them. Immediately they fell
and all of them except that little boy within one hour perished on top
of (the booty) they had gathered.
    And so that boy alone survived. Seeing that all of them had died and
from that time on there were no living persons in the whole city he
intended to go and leave the city. He went, but when he reached the
gate of the city something in the shape of a man seized him, brought
him back and set him in the doorway of the house filled with what the
(seven men) had gathered. Many times it treated him in this way.
    A certain rich man who had previously left his property (in that) city
on hearing that it had become desolate, took fright and stayed away
from (the city) saying:
    "Perhaps God will have mercy upon me and let me live."
    When he was persevering in prayer, repentance and supplications he
heard news that the entire city had perished totally. A few days later he
(could) not restrain himself (any longer) from sending to find out about
his household and about the whole city. He sent an agent[357] together
with other servants saying:
    "Come, go [p. 85] and find out the truth about what has happened to
my household and to the whole city."
    So these people went to the city, entered it and went around in it,
but they found nobody alive at all except that boy sitting and weeping,
his soul (being) close to expiring from weeping. On finding him they
asked him:
    "Why are you sitting here and have not fled?"
    He told them of all that had happened and of those seven men and of
everything they had gathered and of what had happened to them. He
also showed them their corpses and what they had collected. When the

---

[357] The Syriac uses here the Greek loanword ἐπίτροπος, 'guardian', 'overseer'.

agent saw that great amount of gold, its sight excited him too, and he
said to the assistants accompanying him:
"Let us take some of this gold."
They, however, being frightened said:
"We shall not approach it. But you do as you wish."
Thus he entered and carried out as much of that gold as he was able
(to load) on his pack animals. Then he also took along that boy and
tried to leave, but when he reached the gate of the city (something)
resembling a man rushed after him, caught him, bound both him and the
boy and brought them back. Being seized, he took thought that (all) this
was happening because of that gold, while the others called out to him:
"Come back and put it in its place and perhaps you will be released."
Then he and that boy came back to the house and when they entered
(it) both of them perished. The rest of them fled and thus they were
saved.

Again it was told that at the same time in another city on the border
of Palestine, demons appeared to (its inhabitants) in the shape of angels.
They deceived them saying that they should make haste to worship an
idol of bronze which had been left like other bronze statues which now
stand in cities. Previously it had been (one of) the idols of the pagans
and also [p. 86] it had a name and it was even now secretly worshipped
by those few who were caught up in paganism. Thus the demons made
the entire city worship (the idol) saying:
"If you first worship such and such an idol, death will not enter this
city."
So what is said in the psalm would also apply to these wretches:
"they reeled and staggered like drunken men and were at their wits'
end".[358] Thus since they "were drunk", their devices "were at an end"
and were of no effect through the vehemence of (God's) wrath. To this
they were led by their error, for (they thought) they would escape death.
Knowing not the second death[359] after this one, all of them fell down
and worshipped that idol. But because (of that) the divine power
revealed itself on account of their error: when they (were standing)
gathered before the statue, suddenly, in order that others might not yield

[358] Ps. 107, 27.
[359] For the Jewish origin of this term for 'Judgement Day', see S. P. Brock, 'Jewish
traditions in Syriac sources', *Journal of Jewish Studies* 30 (1979), p. 220f (repr. in idem,
Studies in Syriac Christianity, London 1992, ch. 4).

to such error, a whirlwind as it were entered into this idol and lifted it about 1000 fathoms, as far up as the eye could see, and threw it down with force from all that height upon the surface of the earth. It was broken into pieces and scattered like water on the surface of the earth and was no more.

And the sword of death fell upon (these people) and towards evening no living soul could be found in the city, but it was as is written in the prophet, "Now all of them have perished since they did not remember the name of the Lord".[360] So it befell them too.

Chapter two[361]
On that bitter suffering and on the rest of the cities in all the regions.

We are incapable of telling not only (about) those (events) which took place in Egypt and Alexandria but (also) about those many times as numerous (which) took place (in) the rest of the cities and regions of Palestine, of the whole North and the South and the East as far as the Red Sea [**p. 87**].

At the same time that in the region of the capital these things were as yet known (only) by rumour, since they were still remote, and also before the plague (reached) Palestine, we were there. (Then) when it was at its peak we went from Palestine to Mesopotamia and then came back again when the chastisement reached there also, as well as (going) to other regions—Cilicia, Mysia, Syria, Iconium, Bithynia, Asia, Galatia and Cappadocia, through which we travelled in terror (on our way) from Syria to the capital (during) the height of the plague. Day by day we too—like everybody—knocked at the gate of the tomb. If it was evening we thought that death would come upon us in the night, and again if morning had broken, our face was turned the whole day toward the tomb.

In these countries we saw desolate and groaning villages and corpses spread out on the earth, with no one to take up (and bury) them;
—other (villages) where some few (people) remained and went to and fro carrying and throwing (the corpses) like a man who rolls stones (off his field), going off to cast (it away) and coming back to take (another

---

[360] Is. 1, 28.
[361] The account of the plague is copied (or excerpted) by John of Ephesus from his own previous work devoted solely to it. This otherwise unknown book was apparently divided into chapters. Although out of place in PD's *Chronicle*, John's chapter numeration was left unaltered; see above n. 347.

stone) and again having thrown (it) upon a heap, returns to pull forth (the next one) and thus rolls (them) the whole day;

—others, heaping them up, dug tombs for them;

—(still) others who had totally disappeared, having left their homes void of (their) inhabitants;

—staging-posts on the roads full of darkness and solitude filling with fright everyone who happened to enter and leave them;

—cattle abandoned and roaming scattered over the mountains with nobody to gather them;

—flocks of sheep, goats, oxen and pigs which had become like [p. 88] wild animals, having forgotten (life in) a cultivated land and the human voice which used to lead them;

—areas that were tilled and full of all kinds of fruits (which) had become overripe and fallen for lack of anyone to gather (them);

—fields in all the countries through which we passed from Syria to Thrace, abundant in grain which was becoming white and stood erect, but there was none to reap or gather in;

—vines for which the time to be stripped of their fruits had come and passed: the (following) winter being severe, they shed their leaves while the fruit still remained hanging on the vines, there being no one to pick or press them.

How is one to recount or to write anything about this sight full of terror, the appearance of which was bitter, and the lament over it painful, which we met day after day on our journey, unless he who saw (it) should say together with the prophet, "the earth will sit in sorrow and all its inhabitants will mourn".[362] And not only this but also another passage, which reads, "The earth mourned and sat in sorrow, the world mourned and sat and made lamentation, the height of the earth mourned ...", and so on.[363]

At the sight of these things we had occasion also to recall what had previously been said by the blessed prophet when he prophesied saying, "The earth shall be laid utterly waste and be utterly despoiled",[364] and "the earth shall be utterly stirred up and shall utterly totter and shall be utterly shaken and shall quiver like a hut, and its iniquity shall prevail

---

[362] Based on Is. 24, 6.
[363] Is. 24, 4 Peshitta.
[364] Is. 24, 3.

over it",[365] and, "it shall be burned again like a terebinth or an oak, which fell out from its acorn cup;"[366] all these things were completely fulfilled in our days, not over a long period but in a short time.

However, in the year preceding the plague, earthquakes [**p. 89**] and heavy tremblings beyond description took place five times during our stay in this city.[367] These which occurred were not rapid as the twinkling of the eye and transient, but took a long time until the hope of life expired from all human beings and was cut off, as there was no delay after the passing of each of these earthquakes. And thereafter they ceased, (or), as is written in the prophecy, after "the earth had been violently shaken".[368]

But three years before the plague, and even in the fourth, until this year, the whole Western land was stirred up and the wars multiplied and grew violent in the city of Rome and in Ravenna which is beyond it,[369] as well as in Carthage which is in the land of Africa.[370] Again powerful, innumerable peoples to which this empire is opposed—some of them indeed with God's help—were subdued by this empire, that is Rome and Africa and their countries and their kingdoms. Also their kings were led (in triumphal procession) and brought in to this city.[371] Until their end we had watched how they, as well as the rest—everyone of their chieftains together with the captives of their countries—were enslaved.

These are barbarian peoples, which, as is written, "were stirring from the farthest parts of the earth",[372] waxed strong and conquered, laid waste, set fire and plundered. Also they came up to the wall of the city when we were there. They carried off booty from suburban farms and

---

[365] Cp. Is. 24, 19f.

[366] Is. 6, 13.

[367] I.e. in Constantinople.

[368] Is. 24, 19.

[369] Syr. *lgaw*, to be understood as 'beyond' [S. P. Brock].

[370] PD or rather John of Ephesus, means here Byzantine campaigns which resulted in recovery of parts of the Western Roman provinces (Africa, Italy) for the empire, putting an end to the Germanic states there. In 533–534 the Vandal state (in Roman Africa) was brought under Byzantine authority by Belisarius. The kingdom of Ostrogoths in Italy was overpowered in two protracted campaigns, by Belisarius 535–540, during which both Rome (536) and Ravenna, the capital of Ostrogothic Italy (540), were seized, and by Narses 544–554 (after Ostrogothic recovery under the leadership of king Totila; the second capture of Rome 552); Stein, *Bas-Empire*, p. 311-319 (Africa), 339–368 & 564–611 (Italy); Barker, *Justinian*, p. 139-145, 145-166; H. Wolfram, *History of the Goths*, Berkeley 1988, p. 353-361.

[371] Gelimer, the Vandal king 530–534, in Belisarius' triumph in Constantinople.

[372] Jer. 50, 41.

abducted some of its inhabitants, not for one year only but for three, one after another. Because of their power nobody could withstand them.[373]

They held this empire in such light esteem that they sent by their envoys the (following) message:

"Prepare your palace for us, for [p. 90] behold we are coming thither."

Terror fell even upon the emperor and the nobles, and from now on the gates of the palace were covered with iron and made secure; (it was) as if the whole (of the rest) of the city had (already) been taken by them, and (the authorities') only concern was to make secure the palace. Thus something unheard of happened (now), which had not happened ever since this city was built.

Being frightened they ordered that all the trees up to 100 cubits around the city should be cut down and, since it was the capital, all its contents were faithfully and securely guarded between one wall and the other on the western side, because only there was the wall of stone and elsewhere (there was) the sea.

Tall and strong trees, cedars, cypresses, nut and fig trees, as well as vineyards and gardens, had grown there for one hundred years previously. Now all of them were cut and felled, and people were not able to remove them from their places because of their (great) mass. This destruction of the trees struck everyone with terror, and all were astonished and said:

"Had they not been unaware that (something) evil was decided, things would not have come to this point." But (the authorities) replied and pressed on in confidence, as well as (their) opponents.

Thereafter also the wind of the East, that is the kingdom of Persia, awoke, gathered its strength and made itself ready (for war) together with all the mighty peoples of the whole East.[374] It stirred up all the kings of the land of the East and they went straight to this land of the Romans. They conquered, marched across (it) [p. 91] and subjugated (all the territory) as far as the great city of Antioch which they besieged.

---

[373] John of Ephesus describes here the Bulgarian onslaught on Byzantium in 540, during which they menaced Constantinople itself; Stein, *Bas-Empire*, p. 309f.

[374] The Persian attack of 540; cp. above, p. 64 & n. 303.

And because it was gathering its strength to resist (the Persian king),[375] he overcame it, ravaged, captured, burnt, plundered and destroyed it to its foundations. He even carried off marble slabs with which the (outer) walls and the houses had been overlaid. He drove all (the inhabitants) into captivity. He also (did) other things, whereupon he turned back to his country in order to ...[376]

Now, what am I to tell about things which exceed (the power) of narrative ...[377] is the challenge[378] of the story, but in order that we may know the words of the prophecy, which every day sound like trumpets in our ears, yet we do not want to listen, so that one after another all of them now show us in practice the power of their explanations, (and) not at a distance. And this one (chastisement) exceeds all others and is also the most terrible of them all. It arrived and devoured and surpassed all others.

Nothing else was known about it but only this. Like that species of wretched cows which appeared to Pharaoh, and having devoured the good ones were recognized only for being bad,[379] so this chastisement surpassed and devoured not (only) the previous good (events) but also the bad ones. Like the previous scourges also[380] (this) by its power caused suffering to those who were scourged.

Chapter three
(On) when this plague of pestilence arrived at the capital, Constantinople.[381]

Thus returning to the story and to the series [**p. 92**] of afflictions, which because of our sins came upon us, we shall now, omitting other matters, tell with sighs and in bitter lamentations about what happened to the city of the emperors, because these (events) are more than anything worthy of lament. Not only we, the miserable, should make lamentation for them, but if it be possible (also) the heavens and the earth.

---

[375] The ms. here use singular when referring to the Persians; on the Persian king who led the expedition, see n. 304.

[376] Lacuna of two words.

[377] Lacuna of two words.

[378] If *darrāh* is read; or perhaps 'cycle' (of the story), if *dārāh* is read.

[379] Based on Gen. 41, 18-21.

[380] The ms. adds here "not" which does not seem to make sense.

[381] From Land's text, p. 312, 11f; this caption is omitted in the Vatican ms.

(The signs of plague) were still too few for the measure of sorrow (meted) against (the people) to be judged to be fulfilled.

Who then, O brothers, would describe this hideous and cruel sight! From whose heart, on hearing of these things which happened there, would not sighs break out, and (whose) limbs would not melt as wax melts in front of fire? Leave then those who with their (own) eyes watched that spectacle of misery, destruction and groans, those about whom there is nothing else to say except the word of the prophet whose question should be asked by everyone who saw these things, "Who gave water to my head, and to my eyes—fountains of tears? I wept day and night[382] and did not cease, over the destruction and ruin of Babel the great, which up to now has been roaring in the kingdom, but now, behold, her kingdom is humbled and defeated and it is only an angel of wrath who has been made king and destroyer over all her inhabitants."

Now when the chastisement came upon that city, in truth the abundance of the benignity and grace of God appeared in it. Although this (chastisement) was very frightening, grievous and severe, it would be right for us to call it not only a sign of threat and of wrath but also a sign of grace and a call to repentance. For the scourge used patience and moderation until it should arrive at the place. [p. 93]

Just as when a king prepares to go to battle and gives orders to the commanders of his army saying, "Prepare yourself, make your arms ready and take care of your provisions, for, behold, you will proceed with me to war on such and such a day", and likewise he sends a message in writing to the neighbouring cities, "Now I am coming; be prepared, for when I have come there will be no lingering", so this scourge of the benign grace of God by its silence sent as it were numerous messengers from one country to another,[383] and from city to city and to every place, just as if somebody were to say, "Turn back and repent and beg for (forgiveness of) your wrongdoings, and make ready for yourself provisions of alms from your possessions, for behold I am coming, and I am going to make your possessions superfluous."

God's providence informed (us) about it in such a way that (news) was sent to every place in advance, and then the scourge arrived there, coming to a city or a village and falling upon it as a reaper, eagerly and swiftly, as well as upon other (settlements) in its vicinity, up to one, two

---

[382] Jer. 9, 1, Peshitta. The source of the rest of the quotation is unclear.

[383] Read *lhbrh* for *lhrbh*.

or three miles (from it). And until what has been ordered against (one city) had been accomplished, (the scourge) did not pass on to enter the next. In this way it laid hold on (cities and villages) moving slowly.

This is what (also) happened to this city: the visitation came upon it after (the city) had been perceiving the movement[384] of the visitation by hearsay from all over the place for one or two years; (only) then did it reach (the city). But (God's) grace towards it was both eager and encouraging and in some people here it was truly active.

As in the days of Noah, when that blessed man together with his family heard the message of the threat and of perdition, he grew afraid and did not disregard (it) but took care to build [**p. 94**] the ark which became (a salvation) for him, for his own life and for all he had, so also in this time in like manner as did that blessed man, many people managed in a few days to build ships for themselves consisting of almsgiving, that these might transport them across that flood of flame; others in pain of tears (achieved it) by almsgiving and also by distributing their possessions to the needy; (still) others by lament and humility, vigils, abstinence and woeful calling upon God. In this way many people who feared and trembled were able to buy for themselves the kingdom.

Then the onslaught came upon them. Those, however, who neglected and refused to send their riches in advance, left them to others and themselves were snatched away from their possessions, whereas the possessions remained. Both (misfortunes) happened to many people in this city very often.

Chapter four
Again on the same matter, how, once the plague had arrived at the capital, Grace descended[385] first upon the poor to gather together and to encompass them in honour not mixed with wrath.

When thus the scourge weighed heavy upon this city, first it eagerly began (to assault) the class of the poor, who lay in the streets. It happened that 5000 and 7000, or even 12,000 and as many as 16,000 of them departed (this world) in a single day. Since thus far it was (only) the beginning, men were standing by the harbours, at the crossroads and

---

[384] Read *mardūteh*, instead of *mardūteh*, 'his punishment', or 'his revolt', Chabot, p. 93, n. 6.
[385] Read *'aggnat* instead of *'agg'at*.

at the gates counting (the dead). Thus having perished they were shrouded with great diligence and buried; they departed (this life) being clothed and followed (to the grave) by everybody.

Thus [**p. 95**] the (people of Constantinople) reached the point of disappearing, only few remaining, whereas (of) those only who had died on the streets—if anybody wants us to name their number, for in fact they were counted—over 300,000 were taken off the streets. Those who counted, having reached (the number of) 230,000 and seeing that (the dead) were innumerable, gave up (reckoning) and from then on (the corpses) were brought out without being counted.

When those for whom the enshrouders and grave-diggers were (too) few had been removed and (put) in a large common grave, He stretched His destructive hand over the rulers of the world and the renowned in the realm of earthly men, the mighty in riches and those resplendent in their power. From now on the common people, together with the nobles could be seen to be smitten by a single great and harsh blow, and suddenly to fall, apart from a few. Not only those who died, but also those who escaped sudden death (were struck) with this plague of swellings in their groins, with this disease which they call *boubones*,[386] and which in our Syriac language is translated as 'tumours'. Both servants and masters were smitten together, nobles and common people impartially. They were struck down one opposite another, groaning.

As to God's sentence, it was explained (as being decreed) so that the people should be astonished and remain in amazement about His righteous judgements which cannot be understood, nor comprehended, by human beings, as it is written, "Thy judgements are like the great deep".[387]

Also we saw that this great plague showed its effect on animals as well, not only on the domesticated but also on the wild, and even on the reptiles of the earth. One could see cattle, [**p. 96**] dogs and other animals, even rats, with swollen tumours, struck down and dying. Likewise wild animals could be found smitten by the same sentence, struck down and dying.

This terrible sign came upon the people of this city suddenly after removal of the poor.

---

[386] PD transcribes here Greek βουβῶνες.

[387] Ps. 36, 6.

Another sign would separate those to be snatched away from those who would survive and remain (waiting) for either death or life. It appeared in this way: three signs became visible in the middle of the palm of a man's hand in the form of black pocks which did not depart (from the skin) but (remained) deep (in it). They were like three drops of blood deep within. On whomsoever these appeared, the moment they did so the end would come within just one or two hours, or it might happen that (the person) had one day's delay. These (signs) were (to be found) on many (people).

To others however, neither this (happened) nor that, but as they were looking at each other and talking, they (began to) totter and fell either in the streets or at home, in harbours, on ships, in churches and everywhere. It might happen that (a person) was sitting at work on his craft, holding his tools in his hands and working, and he would totter to the side and his soul would escape. It might happen that (people) came to the bath to bathe as usual and they would not be able to take off their clothes, but would fall and expire. It might happen that (a person) went out to market to buy necessities and while he was standing and talking or counting his change suddenly the end would overcome the buyer here and the seller there, the merchandise remaining in the middle together with the payment for it, without there being either [**p. 97**] buyer or seller to pick it up.

And in all ways everything was brought to nought, was destroyed and turned into sorrow alone and funeral lamentations: everyone's hands were weakened, buying and selling ceased and the shops with all their worldly riches beyond description and moneylenders' large shops[388] (closed). The entire city then came to a standstill as if it had perished, so that its food supply stopped. There was nobody to stand and do his job, with the result that food vanished from the markets and great tribulation ensued, especially for the people prostrate with exhaustion from illnesses. Only a few were strong (enough) to bring to any bazaar anything worth one obol, but if they wished they took a dinar for it. Thus everything ceased and stopped.

What was most pressing of all was simply that everybody who was still alive should remove corpses from his house, and that also other (corpses) should disappear from the streets by being removed to the

---

[388] Or 'silversmiths', ἀργυροπρατεία, the ms. reading is *'rgwrpsys*.

seashore. There boats were filled with them and during each sailing they were thrown overboard and the ships returned to take other (corpses).

It would be seemly for the hearer of these things to shed tears for us rather than for the dead and to lament with sighs for what our eyes saw. Alas, my brothers, for this cruel sight! Alas for those corpses (worthy of) lamentations at that time!

Standing on the seashore one could see litters colliding with each other and coming back to carry and to throw upon the earth two or three (corpses), to go back again and to bring (further corpses). Others carried (the corpses) on boards and carrying poles, bringing and piling (them) up [p. 98] one upon another. For other (corpses), since they had rotted and putrefied, matting was sewn together. People bore them on carrying poles and coming (to the shore) threw them (down), with pus running out of them. And they would return bringing (corpses) again. Others who were standing on the seashore dragged them and threw them down upon boats, piling them up in heaps of two or three and (even) of five thousand (each). Innumerable (corpses) piled up on the entire seashore, like flotsam on great rivers, and the pus flowed, discharging itself down into the sea.

With what tears should I have wept at that time, O my beloved, when I stood observing those heaps, full of unspeakable horror and terror? What sighs would have sufficed me, what funeral laments? What heart-break, what lamentations, what hymns and dirges would suffice for the suffering of that time over the people thrown in great heaps torn open one upon another with their bellies putrefying and their intestines flowing like brooks down into the sea? How too could the heart of a person who saw these things, with which nothing could be compared, fail to rot within him, and the rest of his limbs fail to dissolve together with him (though still) alive, from pain, bitter wailing and sad funeral laments, having seen white hair of the old people who had rushed all their days after the vanity of the world and had been anxious for gathering (means) and waiting for a magnificent and honourable funeral (to be prepared) by their heirs, who (now were) struck down upon the earth, (this) white hair (now) being grievously defiled with the pus of their heirs.

(With what tears should I have wept)[389] for beautiful young girls and virgins who awaited a joyful bridal feast and preciously adorned (wedding) garments, (but were now) lying stripped naked, and defiled with the filth of other dead, making a miserable and bitter sight, not even inside a grave, but in the streets and harbours [p. 99], their corpses having been dragged (there) like those of dogs;

—(for) lovable babies being thrown in disorder, while those who were casting them onto boats seized and hurled them from a distance with great horror;

—(for) handsome and merry young men (now) turned gloomy, (who were) cast upside down one under another (in a) terrifying (manner);

—(for) noble and chaste women, dignified with honour, who sat in bedchambers, (now with) their mouths swollen, wide open and gaping, (who) were piled up in horrible heaps, all ages lying prostrate, all statures bowed down and overthrown, all ranks pressed one upon another, in a single wine-press of (God's) wrath, like beasts, not like human beings.

And what shall we say about (all) them (if not) to call out upon (God's) mercy with the words, "Right are Thy judgements, O Lord![390] Thou didst not wish that these things should befall Thy creation but through the abundance of iniquity and through our erring from Thy commandments and Thy wish, Thou hast delivered[391] us (to the cataclysm)".

And again in our same clamour we shall speak about and say together with the prophet, "O Lord, in Thy wrath remember Thy mercies".[392] "Have pity for Thy name's sake, O Lord, over Thy people and renounce not Thy inheritance."[393]

Thus when the bearers became few, the whole city, (once) rich in inhabitants, splendid with power, and opulent, suddenly became a gloomy and putrid tomb for its inhabitants, so that now also the graves were insufficient. And this was more painful than anything, for the (corpses) from the city collected together in tribulation were cast down on boats (and having been transported) from this side across (the bay),

---

[389] The author seems to resume here the harangue which he began in the previous paragraph.

[390] Ps. 119, 137.

[391] Read 'ašlemt, instead of 'ašlem.

[392] Hab. 3, 2; for the opening words cp. Jer. 14, 7.

[393] The quotation is unidentified.

were thrown there like dung on the earth and nobody would gather (them).

Also "the empire was sitting [**p. 100**] in sorrow", as it is written,[394] for (the authorities) learned that the hands of the people who were bringing out the corpses grew weak because they also became fewer and (began to) disappear. The city stank with corpses as there were neither litters nor diggers and the corpses were heaped up in the streets.

Thus when the merciful emperor, in whose days these things took place, learned of it, he stirred himself up with zeal and showed diligence, giving orders for 600 litters to be produced. He appointed a man, his *referendarius*,[395] whose name was Theodore,[396] who was also zealous in good deeds, and gave him instructions to take and spend as much gold as should be necessary for supervising these matters and for encouraging people with great gifts not to be negligent but to dig large ditches and to fill them by piling up the corpses. This man proceeded with application. He crossed (the bay) northward to the other shore called Sykai[397] and climbed the mountain which was above the city. He took along many people, gave them much gold and had very large pits dug, in every one of which 70, 000 (corpses) were put. He placed there (some) men who brought down and turned over (corpses), piled them up and pressed the layers one upon another as a man might heap up hay in a stack.[398] Also he placed by the pits men holding gold and encouraging the workmen and the common people with gifts to carry and to bring up (corpses), giving five, six and even seven and ten dinars for each load. So also he walked around in the city urging (people) to bring out (the corpses). He himself was ordered to fill every grave he could find, to whomsoever it might belong. Thus by his application the city [**p. 101**] was gradually rid of the corpses. Everyone who had many

---

[394] The quotation is unidentified.

[395] *Referendarius*: the emperor's secretary for transmitting orders to the *magistri* and receiving petitions from the people; Guilland, *Institutions* II, p. 91-98.

[396] *PLRE III*, p. 1248 (Theodorus 10).

[397] Sykai: the modern Galata on the other side of the Golden Horn.

[398] According to Procopius, *Wars* II, 23, 9-11, Theodore used the towers of the fortifications in Sykai as graves.

corpses (to be buried) went to inform him and he would have them removed.[399]

When this man was walking around in the city, a deacon from our (people) appeared who also was very zealous in these matters. (The *referendarius*) became aware of him and took him up and now appointed him in charge of the matter of the gifts and (general) custody together with himself.

When they went about they came and found a house all closed up and stinking, while people trembled at its smell. They entered and found in it about twenty people dead and rotten, with worms creeping all over them. Although terror seized them, they brought people, who having received large payments, picked them up in cloaks and removed them bearing them on carrying poles.

Others were found all dead but with babies alive and crying; other women were dead in their beds[400] but the babies, their children, were alive sleeping beside them, holding and sucking their breasts although (the mothers) were dead.

In (some) palaces life expired totally, in others, one remained out of a hundred (nobles), each of whom had been attended by many servants, but (now) had remained alone, or perhaps with few (servants only). But sometimes neither he nor any of his people (remained). Also those who (once) had been served by a multitude of servants, (now) stood and served themselves and the diseased in their homes.[401]

The (imperial) palace was overwhelmed and overcome by sorrow. The emperor and the empress to whom myriads and thousands [**p. 102**] of commanders and the whole great senate had bowed and paid honour every day, (now) were miserable, and like everybody sank into grief, being served only by few.[402]

(We omit) the rest of these matters which cannot be reported by people at all, (which took place) when devastation and destruction befell this (city), coming upon innumerable people of all kinds, upon many times as many as anywhere else, including the great city of Alexandria. Only now the hearts of people were numb and therefore there was no

---

[399] Burials *intra muros* were forbidden; C. Mango, *Le développement urbain de Constantinople (IVe-VIIe siècles)*, (Travaux et memoires du Centre de recherche d'histoire et civilisation de Byzance: Monographies 2), Paris 1985, p. 48, 58.

[400] Read '*arsāthēn*.

[401] Cp. Procopius, *Wars* II, 23, 4f.

[402] According to Procopius, *Wars* II, 23, 20, Justinian was also ill.

more weeping or funeral laments, but people were stunned as if giddy with wine. They were smitten in their hearts and had become numb.

What however was painful was that corpses should be dragged out and thrown down, people dealing with other people—with (their) dead—as with dead beasts: they dragged and threw, dazed and upset, (fulfilling) thus what was called in the Scripture "the burial of an ass".[403] It befell everybody here. From now on, as in Alexandria,[404] nobody would go out of doors without a tag (upon which his name was) written and which hung on his neck or his arm.[405]

Chapter five
Again on a lamentable matter—on wills and inheritances.

There was nobody to tell about wills and inheritances, and if it happened that somebody required it according to the secular (law), or appointed heirs, these might quickly precede (their) benefactors (in death). Whoever they may have been, no matter whether poor or rich, or (whatever) open treasure (was involved), or large shop, or whatever [p. 103] one might desire, (the moment that), in hope that perhaps he would escape (death) and come into possession, he put his hands upon it to take (it), immediately the angel of death would appear, as if standing behind the man, and he would faint and be struck down. Therefore the needy did not give heed to[406] any gifts which someone might wish to grant them, and they would not accept (them) from him. Those who did accept, perished.

There were, however, (some) needy people (who) having survived until then thought:

"Perhaps we shall escape (death), so if a man (is willing to) give, let us ask and accept the gift. Without having to enter someone's house and take something from those who have died, let us just ask for a favour."

And they came to one big shop belonging to a moneylender. They found an old man sitting on his door(step) in whose family everybody had perished. They approached him and said:

---

[403] Jer. 22, 19.

[404] The author (John of Ephesus) refers here to an earlier fragment of his account of the plague, which was omitted by Ps.-Dionysius, but is preserved by Michael the Syrian in his *Chronicle*, tr. II, 237; see above n. 355.

[405] Presumably for identification of the person in case of sudden death.

[406] Read *ḥāyrīn*.

"Grant us a gift. Perhaps we shall live and (so) we will be able to commemorate you."

And he said to them:

"My sons, behold, the whole shop (is) before you. Enter and carry off whatever your soul desires and go, and do not fear. Take as much as your hands are able to carry, and go in peace."

If somebody said that in that shop there were only 1000 pounds of gold and silver, it would still be (as if) nothing. So these people entered and took freely. They looked and were astonished. They cast their eyes on many things, especially on gold, and took (it) and wished to leave. When (one of them) crossed the threshold and the other came along to go out, (it was) as if a sword came between them and cut both of them, one here and the other there. They fainted and fell and their souls fled and their load was scattered. Thus [**p. 104**] great terror fell upon the rest of them; from now on gold, silver and also all material goods were despised in everybody's eyes. A frightful and zealous power laid hold of everything and therefore from now on nobody relied on either gold or other riches, but the faces of all were turned toward and prepared for the grave.

Those who remained healthy lifted and carried the corpses, some for more pay than others, some for little (remuneration) as they scorned it; some, on the other hand, did not accept any payment at all. Whoever was strong and desired gold was able to collect up to a pound of gold a day and up to 100 dinars, because having no fear for God they took as it pleased them.

There were two strong young men who carried stoutly and demanded greedily, without fear. In the end they requested from the emperor's *referendarius* (payment for) one, two and three days (more). When he realized how much they took from him alone he said to them:

"Go, my sons, it is enough for you. For how much are you arguing? Go, keep what you have earned. Do not be a bad example for others."

But they said to him:

"We shall not be idle."

He did not press them to, but said to them:

"You know."

Then those wretches rushed off to carry (corpses) and reached those ditches into which the corpses were cast. When they arrived there both of them suddenly fainted, fell [**p. 105**] and died. Then the man seeing (it) wept over them and said:

"Woe to thee, covetousness of Adam, whose mouth is stopped this hour!"

Then he ordered one of his servants:

"Come near, and see if there is upon them anything which they have collected. Take it and give to others (who) come bringing (corpses). And as for those (two), throw them in, to go down together with the rest."

Again three others gathered 450 dinars and finally said to each other: "It is enough for us. Let us take this and leave this city."

They went off taking (the money) along to divide (it) between themselves. Sitting on a marble slab they counted 150 dinars for each of them, but when they had divided their shares and each was about to stretch out his hand to take his portion, each twisted round to his side, fell and died. Thus their shares were found before them, divided up and placed there with their owners prostrate in front of them.

Such was the message of that angel who was ordered to fight people with this scourge until they should spurn all matters of this world—if not of their own will, then against it—so that everybody who might incite his mind to revolt, and still covet things of this world, was by him quickly deprived of life.

Thus now in this city, once mighty in (the number) of its inhabitants, desolation and emptiness increased from one day to another.

What more is there to say?—also on those pits into which people were thrown and trodden upon, while men stood below, deep as in an abyss, and others above: the latter dragged and threw down (the corpses), like stones being thrown from a sling,[407] and the former grabbed and threw them [p. 106] one on top of another, arranging the rows in alternative directions. Because of scarcity (of room) both men and women were trodden upon, young people and children were pressed together, trodden upon by feet and trampled like spoiled grapes. Then again from above (other corpses) were thrown head downwards and went down and split asunder beneath, noble men and women, old men and women, youths and virgins, young girls and babies.

How can anyone speak of or recount (such) a hideous sight, and who can watch this burial, even though his soul should remain in his body and not waste away from bitter lamentations over so much iniquity

---

[407] Read *qāla 'tā* as in Land's text, p. 323, 25; the Vatican ms. has *bāla 'tā*, 'throat'; 'one who devours'.

which would suffice to destroy the children of Adam? How and with what utterances, with what hymns, with what funeral laments and groanings should somebody mourn who has survived and witnessed this "wine-press of the fury of the wrath (of God)"?[408]

Those who trampled stood (below) and when a man or a woman or a young man or a child was put (down) they would tread (them) with their feet to press them down and to make place for others. The (corpse) which was trampled sank and was immersed in the pus of those below it, since it was after five or as much as ten days that (the corpses) reached (this place of) pernicious prostration.

What mind could bear and endure this suffering of white hairs of old age which were not even, as is written, buried "by the burial of an ass"?[409] Whom would compunction of heart, terror and sadness not seize as he stood (there) and in great terror and bitter sadness disconsolately watched lovely young men like flowers being seized by their hair, dragged and cast from above into the depths of lowest Sheol: as they fell their bellies were split asunder, and the sight of their youthfulness was laid bare down there: (it was a matter) of great horror, shattering and bitter, with no (hope of) comfort. [p. 107] How can any eye endure seeing these heaps of little children and babies piled up in mounds like dung on the earth? Who would not weep more over us, who behold the sight to which our sins have brought us, rather than over the dead? Even if we shall later be blamed for deficiency of mind by the wise, it becomes us, confronting this sight, O brothers, to raise wailing and lamentations for ourselves and not for those (dead) and say:

"Woe to you, our eyes, for what you see! Woe to you, our bitter life, for the destruction you have encountered, which has come upon the kindred of your body, while your eyes look on."

It would be much better for us who saw (it) to be mingled with those who drank the cup of wrath,[410] who ended their journey and did not experience that destruction; or with those whose heart is darkened together with their eyes, mind and thought.

What words or what mouth, tongue, voice and word would suffice a man to tell about (all this)? How can I, miserable, who have wanted to recount (it), not resemble someone who has fallen into the depths of the

---

[408] Based on Rev. 19, 15.
[409] See n. 403.
[410] Cp. Is. 51, 17 & 22.

sea and, being buffeted hither and thither by[411] waves, can neither touch the bottom, nor is close to reaching the shore, but (instead) is battered and dashed by the heavy and powerful waves and therefore is close to perishing by drowning?

And what more is there to say or tell about the unspeakable things which befell this city more than any other, to the extent that even the wise lost their mind and "the stratagems of the crafty",[412] as it is written, were dissolved and brought to nought? Therefore it was not easy to find anyone who was firm in mind, but, as it is [p. 108] written, "they reeled and staggered like drunken men, and were at their wits' end".[413] It happened in this way: being stupefied and confused each talked to his friend like men drunk as a result of liquor, thus through drunkenness resulting from the chastisement people were easily led to madness of mind.

(The latter) happened indeed in this city: the demons wanted to lead people astray and to laugh at their madness. A rumour from somebody spread among those who had survived, that if they threw pitchers from the windows of their upper storeys on to the streets and they burst below, death would flee from the city. When foolish women, [out of their][414] minds, succumbed to this folly in one neighbourhood and threw pitchers out ...[415] The rumour spread from this quarter to another, and over the whole city, and everybody succumbed to this foolishness, so that for three days people could not show themselves on the streets since those who had escaped death (in the plague) were assiduously (occupied), alone or in groups, in their houses with chasing away death by breaking pitchers.

Again it was effected by demons who deceive people that when those who had acted so foolishly by breaking pitchers (started) to lament that they had failed in what they imagined their deception (would achieve, but instead) were drawing closer each day to utter perdition, (the demons then) appeared to them, wishing to mock the garb of piety, that is the (monastic) habit of the "shorn"—of the monks and of the clerics. Therefore [p. 109] when either a monk or a cleric appeared the (people)

---

[411] Land's text adds "heavy and powerful" here, instead of at the end of the sentence.
[412] Suggested perhaps by Job 5, 13; cp. also Is. 29, 14; 1 Cor. 1, 19.
[413] Ps. 107, 27.
[414] Chabot's suggestion, p. 108, n. 3.
[415] Two words missing.

gave a yell and fled before him, supposing that he was death (in person) who would destroy them. Thus this foolishness was manifested in (the idea) that death would come in the likeness of the "shorn" ones. It befell simple people especially and the populace of the city, so that hardly anybody wearing the monastic habit would appear on the streets, for on seeing him they fell upon each other, fled and huddled together crying:

"Where are you going? We belong to God's Mother! We belong to such and such a martyr (patron)! We belong to such and such an apostle!"

This foolishness persisted with some even longer, for as long as two years: on seeing a monk or a cleric they cried, "We belong to God's Mother!"

(All in all) not many (people) but (only) few in number could now be seen in this great city, the queen of the world, out of (once) innumerable (inhabitants), thousands and tens of thousands.

Although at the beginning we desisted from recording the memory of these events, three years later, arranging in a story the lamentations one after another, we recorded those matters for the remembrance of the sorrow and afflictions which happened before our eyes.

Also the eastern regions were overwhelmed by the same (horrors) which have not yet come to an end.

We have left these matters for the remembrance of other (people) who will come after (us), in order that when they hear about the chastising of us, fools and provokers, and about the sentence for our sins, they may "become wise", as it is written,[416] and that they may cease to anger that One for whom everything is easy to do, and that they may repent and ask mercy continually, lest this chastisement also be thrown upon them.

The story of the violent plague as was written by the holy John, bishop of Asia, is finished. [**p. 110**]

Patriarchs who were famous at this time:

in Antioch, Ephrem Bar Aphiana of Amid is famous; in Alexandria, patriarch Zoilos; in Rome, Agapetus; in Constantinople, Menas; in Jerusalem, Macarios.[417]

---

[416] Pr. 8, 33.
[417] Ephrem: 527–545; Zoilus: 540–551; Agapetus: 535–536; Menas: 536–552; Macarios II: October-December 552.

The orthodox and persecuted are these: Theodosius, patriarch of Alexandria; Sergius, patriarch of Antioch; of Constantinople, patriarch Anthimius; Theosebeios of Ephesus; Thomas of Damascus;[418] Jacob of Edessa from the Monastery of Pesilta;[419] Theodore of Hirta de-Nu'man.[420]

Kings who are famous: Khosraw, king of the Persians; Justinian, the emperor of the Romans; Arethas son of Jabala, king of the Arabs, a Christian;[421] Abraham, king of the Himyarites, a believer; Andug, king of the Ethiopians, a Christian.[422]

Famous are: Ahudemmeh, *catholicos* in Persia, a martyr;[423] Joannes, *catholicos* of Armenia;[424] Eunomius, bishop of Amid; John of Pergamon; Photius of Smyrna; Sergius, bishop of Harran; John,

---

[418] Theodosius, see above n. 219; Sergius: 557–561 (Honigmann, *Évêques*, p. 192-195); Anthimius, see n. 221; Theosebeios of Ephesus, 502/3–518 (see above p. 20, and discussion in Honigmann, ibid., p. 119-123); Thomas of Damascus, see above, p. 19, and John of Ephesus, *Lives*, *PO* 18:4 (1924), p. 540f, (only the beginning preserved); Honigmann, ibid., p. 97f.

[419] Jacob of Pesilta, better known as Jacob Baradaeus (*ca.* 500–578), was responsible for numerous priestly and episcopal consecrations, thus creating the 'second generation' (after the bishops deposed in 518 together with Severus of Antioch) of the Monophysite hierarchy, separate from the Chalcedonian. In memory of this the Syrian Monophysite ("Syrian Orthodox") Church is often called 'Jacobite'. For his life, see John of Ephesus, *Lives*, *PO* 18:4 (1924), p. 690-697 (= 488–495), and another life attributed to the same author (*PO* 19:2 (1925), p. 228-268 (= 574–614); D. D. Bundy, 'Jacob Baradaeus: the state of research, a review of sources and a new approach', *Mus* 91 (1978), p. 45-86.

[420] Theodore of Hirtha: most probably the Theodore who was ordained bishop together with Jacob Baradaeus. His normal residence was Hirta of the Arabs (Hīrtā d-Ṭayyāyē; John of Ephesus, *Lives*, *PO* 19, p. 154, 3), the main encampment of the Ghassanids, and thus Hirta de-Nu'man, in the Lakhmid territory (today in Iraq), must be a mistake.

[421] Arethas (Hārith ibn Jabala), the ruler (*phylarch*) of Ghassanids (Banū Ghassān), the Arab vassal tribe of Byzantium in the Syrian desert, christianized to a degree. It was on his request that Jacob Baradaeus and Theodore were ordained bishops (John of Ephesus, ibid., p. 153); see I. Kawar (I. Shahid), 'Arethas, Son of Jabala', *Journal of the American Oriental Society* 75 (1955), p. 205-221; Trimingham, *Christianity among Arabs*, p. 178-185; Guilland, *Institutions*, II, p. 137.

[422] See above, p. 63, 50 and n. 301, 260 respectively.

[423] Ahudemmeh (spelt here 'Ahūhd'emmeh, Syrian missionary among the Arab tribes of Mesopotamia (under Persian rule). He had been Nestorian bishop of Beth Arabaye, but later converted to Monophysitism and was appointed in 559 metropolitan of the East (i.e. for the Monophysites in Persia, the dignity which in a later epoch was called *maphrian*) by Jacob Baradaeus. His life: *Histoires d'Ahoudemmeh et de Marouta, métropolitains jacobites de Tagrit et de l'Orient*, ed. by F. Nau, *PO* 3:1 (=11), Turnhout 1982 (= 1905), p. 7-51; see also Trimingham, *Christianity among Arabs*, p. 171-174.

[424] I.e. Hovhannes II Gabeghian, 557–574; F. Tournebize, 'Arménie' *DHGE* 4 (1930), col. 372.

bi(shop)[425] of Qenneshrin, John, bi(shop) of Callinicus; John bi(shop) of Asia, who has written this; Qashshish of the island Chios.[426]

Famous are: John and Bar Sahde, bi(shop) in Persia.

Also the holy Constantine, bishop of Laodicea is famous.[427] He fought bravely against patriarchs, emperors, bishops and the wicked Council of Chalcedon. The emperor and all his senate (tried to) persuade him with many (arguments) to unite with (the imperial Church), but he would not agree; on a Saturday the emperor gave sentence [p. 111] saying with many oaths:

"Until Monday you will not go from here unless you do this."

But that holy man and God's noble armed himself with the power of the Holy Spirit; having heard the emperor's sentence, he took courage in his Lord and said:

"If Christ knows me, He will not let Monday come upon me, lest I see your face."

And thus he finished his (life's) course on Sunday in accordance with this blessed man's (own) word. The Lord glorifies those who glorify Him. When the emperor learned about the death of the holy man and because he saw how the sentence of his word had been fulfilled, he trembled, became frightened and (so) somewhat alleviated the persecution.

In the same time there was great trouble for the kingdoms of the Ethiopians, Himyarites and Indians, because of a lack of priests. Every year they sent envoys with great honours to the emperor Justinian asking him to give them a bishop who would not accept the Council of Chalcedon. They (tried to) persuade him with many (arguments); he however, since he fought on the side of the Council, advised and admonished them to accept a bishop from (the patriarch) who stood by the Council and lived in Alexandria. They, however, were obstinate, (saying) they would not accept any Chalcedonian but only somebody

---

[425] Abbreviated in the ms.

[426] Eunomius: Monophysite (titular) bishop of Amid, *fl.* 563-568, Honigmann, *Évêques,* p. 206f; John of Pergamon: bishop 558, Honigmann, ibid., p. 216; Photius of Smyrna: unidentified; Sergius of Harran: d. 578, Honigmann, p. 190; John of Qenneshrin (Chalcis): ordained *ca.* 557, Honigmann, p. 235; John of Callinicus: perhaps John of Shura is meant here, as Honigmann (ibid. p. 191, n. 6) thinks; Qashshish, who took the name John, was ordained bishop in 558; his life: John of Ephesus, *Lives, PO* 19:2, p. 159-164.

[427] Constantine had been *magister militum per Orientem* before he was ordained bishop of Laodicea in 510; Honigmann, *Évêques,* p. 36-38; *PLRE* II, p. 314 (Constantinus 15).

who should not have accepted the Coun(cil).[428] But he gave orders that their wish should not be met. Thus they returned empty-handed, but every year the envoys from these three kingdoms came and went for approximately 25 years, until priests disappeared and were no longer found among those peoples. [**p. 112**]

When they became wearied by many (efforts) and failed to receive a bishop who did not adhere to the Council, they went so far as to transgress canonical rules, deciding that priests should gather and put the Gospel book upon the head of one of them and behold! so he was made bishop. In this way, they thought, they followed the rules of (appointing) a bishop. Since they did not wait for (the acceptance) of the lay attendants either, most of (the latter) became indignant, did not consider this imposition of hands[429] (as valid) and did not accept it; on the contrary, a great schism arose among them.

Thus because of the lack of bishop(s) yet another heresy appeared there. The error of the Melchizedekians—these presumptuously (used to) say, "Melchizedek is the Messiah"[430]—seized (those regions), so that among a single people not only was the church torn asunder, but also as a result of this the kingdom split into two, and wars, dissensions and disagreements were to occupy those countries for a long time. In the

---

[428] Abbreviated in the ms.

[429] The Syriac uses here the Greek word χειροτονία.

[430] It is not known whether these Melchizedekians of Ethiopia and South Arabia have anything to do with those of the fourth century described by Epiphanius of Salamis (†403) in his *Refutation of all Heresies*, or those of the sixth century (in Phrygia), known to observe the Sabbath; G. Bardy, 'Melchisédéciens', *DTC* 10:1 (1928), col. 513-516. The Syriac heresiological tradition follows Epiphanius (e.g. Theodore Bar Koni, *Liber Scholiorum, II*, ed. A. Scher, Paris 1912 (CSCO SS II:66), p. 307, 8-11; trad. par R. Hespel & R. Draguet, Louvain 1982 (CSCO 432, SS 188), p. 129. There exists also a Syriac translation of the *Memra against the Melchizedekians* by Mark the Hermit (*fl. c.* 431), cp. O. Hesse, 'Markus Eremita und seine Schrift "De Melchisedech"', *OCh* 51 (1967), p. 72-77, & idem, 'Markus Eremita in der syrischen Literatur', *ZDMG Supplement* 1 (1969), p. 450-457.

end, however, Phantasiasts of Julian's and Gaianus' (brand)[431] came to all those countries and corrupted them.

The year 858 (A.D. 546/7): the famine, the plague, the madness and fury began in the regions of Mesopotamia. This great and grievous plague, which was all over the earth, extended from the year 855 to the year 858, that is for three years.

Now let us relate something about the calamity [p. 113] which was sent upon the regions of Mesopotamia. Again it is right and proper that we include in the record of our story also those (events), which took place at that time in the city of Amid in Mesopotamia and in other cities (there).

For the beginning of this story of ours, full of bitter sufferings (and) of terrible and awful things, like that frightening plague, it would be suitable for us now (to learn from) the blessed (and) sorrowful prophet Jeremiah who was well trained in the raising of lamentations sorrowfully over the cities of his people, since from this prophet we have also learned to say, "Who will give water to my head and to my eyes fountains of tears? For I wept day and night and did not cease, for the slain of the daughter of my people".[432]

Now it is time for us to relate the affliction of the city in which we grew up, that is the city of Amid, and (that) of the other cities in its vicinity, and the chastisements by earthquakes and (other) terrible things which were sent especially against this harassed city, after all the grievous troubles, bitter vexation and tribulations during her protracted

---

[431] Phantasiasts: a name given by their opponents to the Aphthartodocetae, a sect within Monophysitism which taught the impassibility of Christ and incorruptibility of his body from the time of the incarnation; this doctrine was elaborated by Julian, bishop of Halicarnassus (till 518), but was strongly opposed by Severus of Antioch; see R. Draguet, *Julien d'Halicarnasse et sa controverse avec Sévère d'Antioche sur l'incorruptibilité du corps du Christ*, Louvain 1924; and English reviews by R. P. Casey in *HTR* 19 (1926), p. 206-213, and W. Telfer in *JTS* 27 (1925/26), p. 81-86; see also Severus's anti-Julianistic writings: Sévère d'Antioche, *La polémique antijulianiste, I-III*, éd & tr. R. Hespel, Louvain 1964–69 (CSCO 244-5, 295-6, 301-2, 318-9, SS 104-5, 124-7, 136-7).

Gaianus was elected the Monophysite patriarch of Alexandria by his followers in 535 but after three months he was deposed as a result of the empress Theodora's intervention. Julianists must have become numerous in South Arabia, since 150 years later Anastasius Sinaita (†700) calls them Ναγρανῖται, 'Najranites' (M. Jugie, 'Gaianites', *DTC* 6 (1920), col. 999); see too F. Altheim & R. Stiehl, *Christentum am Roten Meer*, 2, Berlin 1973, p. 347-349; Frend, *Rise*, p. 270.

[432] Cp. Jer. 9, 1.

persecution, of no shorter duration than forty years.[433] With all those afflictions of persecution from which she suffered and scandals which she endured before her accusers, she treated the plunder of her property lightly, without murmuring. For the entire city, the small and the great, endured a heroic struggle for the sake of the truth of her faith, although some few of her sons turned (against her) and became her persecutors. She fought bravely, valiantly and heroically, though by (her) struggle not only was she subjected to judgement, but also to the crucifixion of her children [p. 114] and the burning of her priests. She suffered cruel tortures of all kinds without mercy, enduring (them) with thanksgiving. All that time she was also delivered to cruel beasts instead of true shepherds—to two (such) in succession: to a deceitful man, and to the one (originating) from the foolish-minded Galatians.[434] They were violent and irascible, cruel, thirsty for blood, addicted to plunder and threatening with persecution more than all those who held office in any other place and city.

After all those hard struggles and heroic battles for the sake of the orthodox faith which (the city) had suffered and endured either because of sins, or as a test of chastisement, there was first sent against her and against the whole of her region the painful and bitter trial of famine for about eight years.[435] It came in small steps until it should seize that place where ...,[436] so that three or four *modii* of wheat ...[437] were very difficult to find for purchase.

The fields were now unsown because no seed was left, so that even people who were industrious and wealthy would find (only) a little to sow. The earth covered (the seed) but it did not germinate, or when it did sprout and come up, suddenly it faded and withered, to the effect that people were in difficulty and many would flee from one region to another and from one city to another, as a result of the tribulation of that bitter and harsh famine.

---

[433] Starting perhaps with the capture of Amid by Kavad in 503.

[434] John of Ephesus has here in mind Abraham Bar Kaili (bishop 529–559?) and his successor, also a Chalcedonian, whose name is unknown, and who apparently was a Galatian by birth, which is why John alludes to Gal. 3, 1.

[435] 546/7–554/5 (?) as would appear from lemma 858 Sel., see above p. 102, and below p. 107.

[436] Three or four words missing.

[437] One word missing.

Then, after eight years, when God's mercy stirred again for his creation and He looked particularly upon the tribulations and torments of the poor, widows and orphans who had reached the point of death, the grass of the field began [p. 115] to sprout[438] strongly. While other regions were (still) dead, the people began to sow[439] and to work many times harder on what was sown. By God's grace the grass began to appear and everybody rejoiced and praised the good Giver, being satisfied that He did not withhold His mercy from His creation and from all who relied upon Him and awaited (the fulfilment of their) hope in Him.

Then again in the year (called) in Greek *enate* [440] (of the indiction), that is the year 871 of Alexander the Macedonian (A.D. 559/560) together with the terrible chastisements and baleful signs which at that time again and again kept suddenly appearing everywhere in the sky and on the earth, as has been recorded above, the trial of another terrible, abominable and hideous affliction was sent upon that city of Amid, that is, fury, madness and demoniacal possession and, together with them, also an evil error.[441]

First, as if by the operation of the insolent demons, consternation and terror would suddenly fall upon many people when vain rumour spread among them (saying):

"Look, the Persian king with all his army is about to enter the city and to massacre the whole city."

So with great turbulence people would flee, leaving the city in all directions and on all sides, spreading rumours, inspiring agitation, fleeing and causing all whom they met to flee, whether on the roads or in villages or in all the neighbouring cities, all those through which they passed. Fear and commotion would rise in all the regions and cities through which they passed as they were spreading rumours and confirming that Amid [p. 116] had been captured by the Persians, laid waste and (its inhabitants) taken captive, "So flee!" And now (whole) regions all of a sudden went into exile and for many days great

---

[438] Read: *lm(')ī'ā*.

[439] The ms. repeats here "sprout strongly".

[440] Ms. *hnt'*, i.e. the Syriac transcribes the Greek word ἐνάτη, 'the ninth'.

[441] On the attack of madness, cp. Michael the Syrian, 323b, 4-29/II, 267f; *Chr. 1234*, I, 199, 18-200, 14/157; see also S. Ashbrook [Harvey], 'Asceticism in adversity: an early Byzantine experience', *BMGS* 6 (1980), p. 1-11, esp. 3f; and Harvey, *Asceticism*, p. 64f & 171f.

confusion and destruction ensued everywhere, until the trial which came upon the miserable people became known and exposed.

After that, people began to bark like dogs, to bleat like goats, (to howl)[442] like cats, to crow like cocks and to imitate all the voices of every dumb animal. Men and women began to throw themselves upon each other, especially the young, boys and girls; most people were (thus) led astray so that (only) few escaped from that chastisement.

Finally they gathered in groups, confused, disturbed, troubled and disordered, rushing here and there, in the night to the cemetery, going on madly ...[443] singing and behaving furiously, biting each other and imitating bugles and trumpets, speaking meaningless and gross words as if (uttered) by a demoniac, bursting out in laughter, using licentious speech and evil curses. Also they jumped, clung to the walls, hanged themselves head downwards, fell, wallowed naked (on the earth) and (did) other things of the kind, so that none of them could even recognize his home or his house.

But those who were spared from this madness managed by allurement or coercion and angry menaces to gather (the mad) in churches so that now all the churches and martyria of the city were filled with them entirely. (Brought) together in the churches they were seen (to act) in various ways, some of them behaving like mad dogs and foaming (at the mouth), others brawling and speaking gross words as if [p. 117] demoniacs, saying:

"There are so and so many myriads of us. And if Thomas the holy apostle does not come out against us, we shall capture the whole city, lay waste, kill and strangle (the people in it). Apostles and martyrs who are buried in this city, encounter us and restrain us from laying waste (the city), or we shall not leave a (single) human soul alive (there)!"

Some of them bowed and knelt as if to pray; others jumped and mounted them to ride—sometimes three or four were riding one upon another by the instigation of the demons. If it happened that some of those who had not gone mad entered the churches to pray, the (mad ones) would stand up to deride and insult them. They spoke to them with impure and filthy words, so that many (of the sane) would leave the churches, fleeing out of modesty.

---

[442] Chabot, p. 116, n. 2 supplements *m 'wsyn* from *Narrationes variae*, (*Chr. Min.*, p. 331, 15), which contains a similar account.

[443] Two words misssing.

At another time many of them became alarmed together and cried saying:

"Behold, rulers[444] are coming! Behold, kings are entering! Let us run out to meet them!"—and so they became confused and many of them together went out in great commotion starting to run rapidly hither and thither all over the city, misbehaving, roaming and rushing, boisterous and confused. Some of them laughed lecherously and spoke filthy, gross and crazy words. Some wept painfully and (then) again spoke in a crazed way. Others blasphemed and cried with hideous and strange sounds of folly. Then those who were not struck with this harsh affliction of frenzy went out and gathered them together again and brought them (back) into the churches. They prepared various and numerous meals (for them), having pity [p. 118] and being sorry for them. These or their wives brought (the meals) into (the churches) and so they were fed.

This illness of madness and frenzy lasted one year, especially in the city of Amid. Whereas in other cities, Tella, Edessa and other ones, few [people][445] were chastened by this scourge, this harassed (city) was particularly chastened, and only God knows for what cause and because of what sin this abandonment took place, whereby Christian people would be affected by such chastisement, (and) vicious spirits would possess (them), especially the young people, to the point that abominable lasciviousness would take place, that they would throw themselves upon each other inside the churches. When this became known, people stopped giving them oily food and wine to drink, giving them (only) bread and salt or dry pulses without any oil to eat, and *posca*[446] to drink. Also guards were posted (to prevent the mad) from defiling the churches and fulfilling the wish of the demons.

Some time after these people had been struck with this strange scourge, each (of them) began little by little to come to his wits. They wept in contrition, groaning and all the time humbling themselves in prayer and supplicatory [invocations].[447] At the same time some of those

---

[444] Or 'magistrates'; the Syriac uses here the Greek loanword ἄρχοντες.

[445] One word missing.

[446] The Syriac employs here the Greek loan-word πόσκα, from Lat. *posca*, a beverage made of water and vinegar or a sour wine drunk by Roman soldiers.

[447] One word missing.

who had returned to their wits now went in groups on pilgrimage[448] to Jerusalem and the other holy places, in contrition, wearing black clothes, uttering entreaties, praying and weeping. Thus thanks to the assistance of our Lord's grace and mercy upon His creation, He redeemed His people and expelled from them [**p. 119**] the evil powers.

That great plague came in the year 855 (A.D. 543/4) and it remained for three years.

In the year 858 (A.D. 546/7) famine began to appear and continued for eight years until the year 866 (A.D. 554/5),[449] but only three (of them) were severe, when there was nothing to reap or to thresh.

In the year 867 (A.D. 555/6) that madness which was described above took place, and it lasted for one year.

In the year 869 (A.D. 557/8) there was once more a plague in the same city of Amid in Mesopotamia, the third affliction after those two severe chastisements. At first the great plague came upon (Amid) in such a way that nearly all of those who had been struck with madness were to perish, (but also) others, so that within three months 35,000 were reckoned to have departed (this life) by the plague in this vexed and miserable city, until it was grievously reduced to a terrible[450] desolation.

In order not to weary the reader we have recorded briefly these matters concerning the chastisements by these three bitter scourges which took place at that time because of people's angering (God) with their sins. We have put them down for the memory of posterity, in order to stir the minds[451] of all future generations to repentence and prayer, just as our Lord also taught us in His Gospel, "Pray that you may not enter into temptation";[452] but, as it is written, "He who has ears to hear, let him hear";[453] and again, "Let him who is wise observe these (things)".[454]

These things were written by the holy John, bishop of Asia, who was an eye-witness to them.

---

[448] Literally 'for prayer'.
[449] See above n. 435.
[450] Read *dhīlā*.
[451] Lit. 'memories'.
[452] Mt. 26, 41.
[453] Mt. 11, 15; 13, 9.
[454] Cp. Jer. 9, 12; Hos. 14, 10.

The year 857 (A.D. 545/6): there was confusion [p. 120] in the capital, in Alexandria and in all the regions of the East about the beginning of Fast,[455] and great disorder spread in the whole Church, that is when (the decisions of) the Council of Chalcedon were in force. There were (people) who began the fast two weeks in advance and others (who began) one (week) later. In the capital, however, when we were there, after the Fast had been observed for a week, in accordance with (church) law, the emperor and his nobles turned round and decided that Fast would only begin after a further week. So, once the (original) Fast had been in force, meat was withheld from the city. Then, subsequently, butchers were required to slaughter and produce meat for sale, following the emperor's strict order, on the grounds that "the Fast has not yet begun". Forced against their will they slaughtered sheep, oxen and pigs and hung (the meat) out for sale. While the whole city looked at it as if it were brought for sacrifice, nobody approached it, except for a few who were given to greediness and gluttony. Many people took up dust, ash and lime and scattered it over every (piece of) meat which was hung out. When it had become tainted and nobody bought it, the tavern keepers were again required to slaughter animals. When they went to appeal to the prefect of the city, who had required them to slaughter, the prefect informed the emperor. He gave orders to slaughter (the animals) and if they should suffer loss (as the meat) would not sell, they would be reimbursed from the public treasury. Thus, being able to receive the price of sheep and oxen from the public treasury, they would not perish. In such great confusion passed not only the beginning of Fast but (also) the holy Feast of Unleavened Bread.[456]

Now concerning the non-canonical priestly consecration by the hand [p. 121] *of a dead man, (which) was carried out in the city of Ephesus by the Julianists in the year 860 of Alexander (A.D. 548/9).*
    Now Paul, the wise architect and builder of the Church, admonishes (us) saying, "I appeal to you, brethren, to be wary of those who create

---

[455] Cp. Malalas 482f/287f & n. 96, whose account is very much abbreviated, as compared with that of John of Ephesus as preserved in PD and Michael the Syrian (325b,3-15/II,271); see also A. Mentz, 'Zur byzantinischen Chronologie, I: Eine Osterreform zur Zeit Justinians', *BZ* 17 (1908), p. 471-474; R. Scott, 'Justinian's Coinage and Easter Reforms and the date of the *Secret History*', *BMGS* 11 (1987), p. 215-221, and for parallel sources, ibid., p. 220, n. 24.
[456] I.e. Easter.

dissensions and difficulties, in opposition to the doctrine which you have been taught; avoid them. For such persons do not serve our Lord Jesus Christ, but their own appetites, and by fair and flattering words they deceive the hearts of the simple-minded".[457] And again he instructs all saying, "Test everything, hold fast to what is good, abstain from every form of evil".[458] And again, "Look out for the evil-workers, look out for the dogs".[459]

Therefore we are vigilant now of the ungodly error of the "evil-workers" of *phantasia*, and it has appeared to us, O friends of truth, that we should not be oppressors of your zeal and should not cover with silence this evil crime, the ruin of people's souls, the transgression of all the norms of Christianity, and the reversal of all the ecclesiastical canons, (perpetuated) by the followers of the error and fanciful ideas of Julian of Halicarnassus.[460] It was wrought wickedly and deceitfully in God's church, namely by those who were seized by that heresy in the city of Ephesus. Particularly there it gained (followers), and spread because of four *scholastici*[461] from that region, who had become acquainted with Julian in the city of Alexandria and adopted his opinion.

Together with others they fancifully attacked the honourable rule of priesthood and dared to do a hideous thing which was far from every rule of decency, and is alien and hideous, as it is written,[462] even to [p. 122] speak about.

So by the efforts of the *scholastici* (a follower) of this fanciful error, a bishop whose name was Procopius, came to the said city and settled there. He was deceitfully led to the fanciful opinion of the Phantasiasts, but after some time he learned from many (people) that, by errors like that of Julian and all his followers, all the hope of the Christians then turned out to be baseless and false, and (thus) vanished (leaving only) *phantasia* and dreamlike illusions. As that man was opposed for this by many people, he later repented, turned from Julian's opinion and anathematized him. He wrote a *libellum* of recantation which is still

---

[457] Rm. 16, 17f.
[458] 1 Thess. 5, 21f.
[459] Phil. 3, 2.
[460] See n. 431.
[461] See n. 336.
[462] Quotation unidentified.

kept in the main monastery of the region of Asia. Then he erred again and turned back to the same heresy, like a dog to its vomit.[463] He came and lived in Ephesus for several years, until the end of his life, seized by the idea of *phantasia*. When [he reached] the peak of old age, he was requested by people of his party to ordain a bishop in his place, (but) at least in this he kept the rules and declined saying:

"The canons do not prescribe (so), and I will not ordain a bishop to be anathematized myself together with him."

Thus he did not accept that he might do it alone.[464] When he became ill to the point of death, they pressed him again, but as long as he lived he did not agree to ordain a bishop. After he had died, however, seven presbyters, as is reported, gathered there, about whom it might almost be said that they [**p. 123**] drank gall, became intoxicated and went out of their minds, with their intellects blinded. In a contentious spirit of error and paying no attention to the whole order of ecclesiastical canons they took counsel and brought another man, a monk whose name was Eutropius, made him bow over the corpse (of Procopius), lifted up the hand of that dead man and laid it upon (Eutropius's) head. And, instead of the dead (bishop), they themselves recited the prayers of episcopal ordination over (the monk). And behold! so he became a pseudo-bishop by transgression of the law and against all the ecclesiastical rules.[465]

For that wretch Eutropius, who had become an empty vessel, perdition from vain error and the gain of a purse full of holes—for he thought that he would profit from the hand of a dead man—was not enough, but in his intellect too he again became blind and dull to the observation of all the canons and ecclesiastical customs. As he himself, (being ordained) by a dead man, had become a vessel of corruption, he added (another) transgression to his previous misdeed and immediately ordained ten pseudo-bishops. (Thus) they too were ordained spuriously. This fool forgot that the late (Procopius) when alive and well declined to ordain a bishop on his own, and so disregard the canons. (Eutropius) too should have shrunk with fear and trembling from daring to ordain

---

[463] Cp. 2 Pet. 2, 22.

[464] According to canon 4 of the Council of Nicaea the presence of at least three bishops was required for episcopal ordination; see also next note.

[465] This story, most probably fictitious, was used in Monophysite (Severan) propaganda against the Julianists. In an anti-Julianistic dossier of the seventh century, published by R. Draguet ('Pièces de polémique julianiste, 3: l'ordination frauduleuse des julianistes', *Mus* 54 (1914), p. 59-89) it was supplemented by excerpts of relevant canons of the ecclesiastical law.

bishops alone, quite apart from the fact that (his own ordination) was from the hand of a dead man. So he too was shown to be someone dead[466] (to the ecclesiastical rules), and a useless cold corpse, with no spiritual awareness, together with all those who were (ordained) by him and those who were (subsequently ordained) by them.

About the truth of these matters testify not only we but also all the regions of Asia.

Then this man sent [p. 124] those whom he had (ordained) in all directions to be advocates of their error, that is of the heresy of illusion and of *phantasia*. They did it eagerly, and they went east and west, to the capital, to Alexandria, to the whole of Syria, and even crossed over to Hirta de-Beth Nu'man and to Persia. One of them, whose name was Sergius, even rushed off to the lands of the Himyarites. Previously he had been a 'mourner' (monk), and had taken the tonsure; he too became an empty vessel, and went to disturb, corrupt, lead astray and destroy all those countries, ordaining priests by name (only). Also he, as rumour has it, consecrated a man by the name of Moses, an instrument of destruction and perdition, (to be) a bishop in his stead, to the effect that both he and the one whom he had appointed were (bishops at the same time). He died in the land of the Himyarites before four years elapsed.

But others from among them directed their course to the countries of Sophanene and Arzanene[467] and entered also Armenia, whereby many of them, erring themselves and leading (others) astray, have persisted in those countries until now. They corrupted and totally lured into their heresy the countries of Arzanene and Sophanene especially ...[468] and that corrupter of souls [did] damage there (by) transgression of the law ...[469]

When [the people] (of Ephesus) realized (their fault), they became indignant at this ordination, having perceived that it was a false and not a true (one). They blamed and attacked each other and split into two[470] factions. Having realized [p. 125] that it was wrong of them (to accept) the ordination by a dead man, they rejected it totally and founded a separate church in the same city of Ephesus, and so they received communion from the old priests, as (these priests) specifically assured

---

[466] Read *mītā*.
[467] North of Upper Tigris, east of Amid.
[468] Two words misssing.
[469] One word missing.
[470] Read *tartēn* (instead of a doubtful *tlātīn*, 'thirty', printed by Chabot on the basis of Martin's copy; the ms. is here illegible).

us that they did. If it were not (for them) we would not allow ourselves to transmit the record of the story of these matters by distant hearsay, because we were not close at hand for those (events). Now, however, let all this be accepted by you and by everybody without dispute, with no one doubting the exactness of its truth, that it all took place in this way. Be steadfast in our Lord.

On the flood which was in the river that flows through Tarsus in Cilicia.
The year 861 (A.D. 549/50): most of Tarsus, the great city of Cilicia, was overwhelmed, submerged and destroyed by the water of the flood of the river which flows through it.[471] Also other villages of the region at a great distance were flooded and the fields, vineyards and other establishments were devastated and destroyed. Once they had dried up they were covered with earth.

At this time the destructive heresy of Montanus[472] was put to shame and uprooted. We have written the story of how it sprang up in (the section about) the apostolic times.[473] Now, however, at the incitement of John bishop of Asia the bones of Montanus were found, who used to say of himself that he was the Spirit Paraclete, and (the bones) of Kratis, Maximilla and Priscilla, his prophetesses. (John) burned them with fire and pulled their temples down to the foundations.[474] **[p. 126]**

The year 862 (A.D. 551): there was a great earthquake in the capital on Sunday the 7th of the month of August.[475]

There was a terrible, violent and mighty earthquake in the capital in the night, as Sunday was dawning. Numerous houses were overthrown by it and became dreadful tombs for their inhabitants. (Also) numerous churches and baths and the walls of cities collapsed, particularly the

---

[471] The Cydnus; cp. Procopius, *Buildings*, V, 5, 14-20.

[472] This ecstatic apocalyptic sect sprang up in the second half of the second century in Phrygia. The Montanists expected the imminent arrival of the Holy Spirit (Paraclete) and the duration of New Jerusalem for a thousand years.

[473] In PD I, 130, 7–18/97.

[474] A more comprehensive account (i.e. using other sources in addition to John of Ephesus) survives in Michael the Syrian (323c, new ch.-325, 15/II, 269-271); see also S. Gerö, 'Montanus and Montanism according to a Medieval Syriac source', *JTS* 28 (1977), p. 520-524.

[475] The correct date is 554, cp. Malalas 486f/293f; for parallel sources, see Grumel, *Chronologie*, p. 478 and Downey, 'Earthquakes', p. 598, to which add the Great Chronographer 8 (in *Chr. Pasch.* transl., p. 196).

wall of the capital which was called "of the Golden Gate".[476] And again many souls perished everywhere in this earthquake and many cities were overthrown and devastated. Nicomedia, the metropolis of Bithynia, was overthrown and totally destroyed. Most of it was swallowed up by the sea and the rest was buried in the collapse. (Later) many people were found alive in the ruins. Some of them were retrieved unhurt, some with injuries.

These terrible earthquakes had taken place for forty days, coming one after another. The mercy of God the compassionate being mingled with (the earthquakes) summoned the people to life in repentance and thus everywhere all the people were constant in supplication in the churches, (even) spending nights in them in sorrow and tears of repentance.

(Later) commemorations of these earthquakes took place on the vast and broad (plain called) the Kampos,[477] seven miles from the capital; every year on those days on which (the earthquakes) occurred there were many communal supplications with virtually the whole city [p. 127] going out. (Also) some of the nobles went out eagerly (to take part) in these supplications on the Kampos.[478]

At this time these bishops are famous among the believers: Theodosius, patriarch of Alexandria: persecuted; Anthimius patriarch of Constantinople: persecuted; Paul, patriarch of Antioch: persecuted;[479] Jacob, bishop of Edessa from the monastery of Pesilta; John, bishop of Amid from the monastery of Qartmin; Theodore, bishop of Hirta de-Nu'man.[480]

---

[476] Ms. 'Gates'; the Golden Gate, used for triumphal entries to the capital, was situated in the southern end of the city wall.

[477] An open space at the Hebdomon (on which, see below, n. 529), a suburb of Constantinople, south-west of the city; Janin, *Constantinople*, p. 408-410 and map 3 at the end of this volume.

[478] For the liturgical commemoration of the disasters caused by earthquakes, see B. Croke, 'Two early Byzantine earthquakes and their liturgical commemoration', *Byzantion* 51 (1981), p. 122-147.

[479] For Theodosius and Anthimius, see above n. 418; Paul the Black, Monophysite patriarch of Antioch: 564–577; Honigmann, *Évêques*, p. 195-205.

[480] For Jacob and Theodore, see above nn. 419 & 420; John of Qartmin had been the bishop of Dara (until its capture by the Persians in 573), and then seems to have been transferred to Amid; Honigmann, *Évêques*, p. 239-241.

Among the Chalcedonians these patriarchs are famous: Vigilius of Rome, Eutychius of the capital, Apollinarius of Alexandria, Domninus of Antioch.[481]

The year 863 (A.D. 551/2): the Jews and Samaritans revolted in the country of Palestine.[482]

At this time the Jews and Samaritans conspired together against the Christians in Caesarea of Palestine. United they revolted under the name of the Greens and the Blues.[483] They attacked Christians, routed (them) and caused many to perish, all whom they met. They rushed into the churches of the Christians, plundered them and desecrated and scoffed at the holy vessels. When the *proconsul*[484] of the city set out to push them back and drive them away, they gathered and surrounded him. When he saw the multitude of the people who had gathered against him he fled to his *praetorium*. They rushed after him, caught up with him and killed him.[485] (Also) they cut to pieces many commanders and all his guard, and killed [**p. 128**] many of the newly baptized, clothed in white garments. They took much booty.

When the emperor Justinian learned about these matters he became very angry[486] and gave orders to Amantius, a *stratelates* in the East,[487] who was a Christian and zealous in the Christian faith, and he went to Caesarea and throughout the whole country of Palestine. (There) he seized and crucified some of the Jewish and Samaritan rebels, (others) he burnt or beheaded, cut off their hands and legs, tortured (them) with

---

[481] Vigilius: 537–555; Eutychius: 552–565 and again 577–582; Apollinarius: 551–570; Domninus: 545–559.

[482] The correct date of the revolt in Caesarea is 555, Stein, *Bas-Empire*, p. 374, n. 2. The revolt may have been caused (as was that of 529, not reported by John of Ephesus/PD) by the anti-Samaritan legislation *De haereticis et Manichaeis et Samaritis*, promulgated by Justin in 527 and repeated by Justinian (as the sole emperor) in 529 *(Cod Just. I. 5. 12-19).* See *The Samaritans*, ed. A. D. Crown, Tübingen 1989, p. 75f; also Avi-Yonah, *Jews*, p. 251; Sharf, *Byzantine Jewry*, p. 29f.

[483] The Syriac employs the Greek names, Πράσινοι and Βένετοι. For the circus factions, see above n. 19.

[484] The Syriac uses here the Greek loanword ἀνθύπατος; for the office, see Guilland, *Institutions*, II, p. 68-79.

[485] The name of this *proconsul Palaestinae Primae* was Stephanus, *PLRE III*, p. 1186 (Stephanus 14).

[486] Read *rgez*.

[487] Amantius was apparently *magister militum per Orientem* from 555; he was renowned for his persecution of pagans, Manichaeans and heretics in Antioch; *PLRE III*, p. 52-54 (Amantius 2).

various tortures and thus remunerated them. Terror and the (feeling) of defeat fell upon all of them who escaped (from death).

The year 864 (A.D. 552/3): there were great and violent earthquakes. Many cities and villages were destroyed by them in the country of Syria.

In the month of June of this year there was a heavy and severe earthquake together with other ones (subsequently). Many cities were overthrown by it: cities of Phoenicia, Arabia and Palestine; that is[488] Berytus, Tripolis, Tyre, Sidon, Sarepta, Byblos, Antarados and other cities and villages with their vicinities collapsed and were ruined. By (this) wrath (of God) resulting from sins many souls were buried in their houses as well as the cattle and other things.[489]

The year 865 (A.D. 553/4): numerous groups of patriarchs, bishops, monks, hermits and laymen from all quarters gathered in the capital concerning the faith. However, we are not able to give an accurate and exact account of these gatherings, which flamed up with ardour [p. 129] and (of how) they rushed to the emperor (to discuss) the matter of the unity of the Church one after another at different times.

Thus, first of all, (the group) of persecuted bishops, especially the Eastern ones, appeared. They gathered, urged and led (to the capital) hermits, anchorites, "perfect ones",[490] wonder-workers and others versed in knowledge, words and the divine Scriptures, experts in the dogmas of the true faith. They arrived, entered, explained, stood up and showed prowess for the sake of truth. When, however, it was revealed spiritually to the holy men who accompanied them that nothing could be (achieved) at that time, they secretly went on board a ship and sailed away from the capital. This very much worried the believing empress Theodora also and she sent (inquiries) in all directions, but not one of (the holy men) was found and it was not known whither they went. Some of those who reached their homes did not obey either by answering or by leaving their abodes (again), and thus they ended their

---

[488] In the ms. the expression 'that is' is placed before 'Arabia'.

[489] Grumel, *Chronologie*, p. 478: July 551 (on the basis of Theophanes, AM 6043; cp. also Malalas 485/291 and Agathias II, 15, 2-4. One of the results of the fall of Berytus was that the famous law school of that city moved temporarily to Sidon.

[490] Syr. *gmīrē*; although the context suggests that some special category of monks is meant the term seems rather to denote ascetics generally; it is probably derived from Mt. 19, 21, "If you want to be perfect, go, sell your possessions and give to the poor... then come, follow me."

lives. The gathering itself was disbanded, no result whatsoever having been achieved.[491]

The year 866 (A.D. 554/5): there was (sent) fire from heaven upon the great and mighty idol temple in Baalbek, The City of the Sun[492] which is in Phoenicia between the Mountains of Lebanon and Senir.[493]

Again during the reign of the emperor Justinian, a great miracle took place through the fire [**p. 130**] (sent) from heaven[494] upon the great and mighty structure of the idol temple in Baalbek, the city of paganism which in the Greek language is called "The City of the Sun". In it there was a large and massive temple of idols, which, as people used to say, was one of those mighty constructions which Solomon had built. Its length measured 150 cubits and its breadth 75 cubits. It was built of squared stones which were carved. The length of some of them was twenty cubits and of some others fifteen cubits. The height of each of them was ten cubits and the thickness (as measured) within the structure four cubits. The construction of its building (was supplemented) with high and massive columns, wonderful moreover to see. Its roof was of huge cedars of Lebanon, and on the top it was overlaid with lead, whereas its doors were of bronze, with the rams' heads above (them also) of bronze. Inside the nave under the entablature of the roof three cubits (of free space) could be seen. The rest of the details of that temple were wonderful (too). The erring pagans were deceived by the hugeness of that temple and boasted (of it) very much. Innumerable sacrifices, votive offerings and oblations for the demons took place continuously in that temple.[495]

---

[491] This lemma on religious discussions is erroneously dated since Theodora, who died in 548, features here. We may have to do here with an account of the discussions of 532, on which see E. Stein, *Bas-Empire*, p. 376-381; S. Brock, 'The Conversations with the Syrian Orthodox under Justinian (532)', *OChP* 47 (1981), p. 87-121.

[492] The author translates the Greek name of the city, Heliopolis.

[493] Mount Hermon.

[494] Ps.-Zachariah (II, 76, 6/204), from whom the lemma comes, specifies lightning as the cause of the fire.

[495] It was the temple of Jupiter Heliopolitanus, or of the Triad, Jupiter (Baal-Hadad), Venus (Atargatis), Mercury (Adonis/Eshmun). On the temple and its gods, see Y. Hajjar, 'Baalbek, grand centre religieux sous l'empire', in *Aufstieg und Niedergang der römischen Welt, II: Principat*, Bd. 18:4, ed. W. Haase, Berlin 1990, p. 2459-2508, esp. 2490-96. According to Malalas 344/187, already in the fourth century Theodosius the Great (379–395) "destroyed the large and famous temple of Helioupolis, known as Trilithon, and made it a church for the Christians".

Nobody indeed was able to destroy it or put an end to the error of the worshippers of the idols within it. God however, who saw the aberration and error of the people resulting from the immensity of that temple, suddenly sent upon it fire from heaven, (which) flamed up in (the temple) and consumed it. It destroyed its beams, its bronze, its lead and the idols inside it. (The fire) also cracked its stones and the statues which had been arrayed in it for the worship of the pagan error; it even licked up the dust of the ground. Only few stones remained in it—as if [p. 131] a sign—being cracked by the fire. Thus a great terror suddenly came upon all the idol worshippers, especially those of that temple. Weeping, mourning and bitter groans (overwhelmed) all the adherents of paganism when they assembled, having come from all quarters on hearing about that terrible thing which had befallen them and their gods—dumb, indeed, dead and with no sensibility—and also the temple in which they had been arrayed. Having gathered, (the pagans) stood around it and wept bitterly for many days. And the temple burned to the point that there was fire within fire.

But all the Christians who saw and heard what had happened to that temple rejoiced and exulted, being astonished at the miraculous sign performed by God. Then in God's entire Church their mouths were filled with glory and their tongues with thanksgiving, and they rejoiced and glorified (God) because of this great marvel which had been done by God in the sudden destruction of that temple by the power of the burning flames (sent) from heaven.[496]

The year 867 (A.D. 555/6): the Great Church[497] *of the capital collapsed.*

On the third of the month of May half of the eastern side of the Great Church in the capital, to be exact the dome, was suddenly shaken and collapsed. By the care of God's mercy who does not wish the destruction of His creation, (the church) was closed and nobody was in it: otherwise it would have buried thousands and tens of thousands

---

[496] Notwithstanding the fire, Baalbek remained a pagan centre until the second year of Tiberius II (579) when, as it seems, the final blow of persecution put an end to the heathen population there, as John of Ephesus himself writes in the third part of his *Church History* 3:27 (*Third Part*, 154, 9-155, 17/209f).

[497] I.e. the church of Hagia Sophia erected in 537; the correct date of the collapse is 7 May 558, a result of the weakening of the structure during the earthquake on 14 December 557 (Grumel, *Chronologie*, p. 478, Downey, *Earthquakes*, p. 598). Malalas, 489–490/297 provides a somewhat different report.

(people). By this terrible and violent earthquake it burst apart and cracked. The emperor and the whole city were greatly shocked by the collapse (of the church).

The part which did not fall was more resistant [p. 132] to collapse than that which did fall, because there was a great and strong arch (which) supported it. The workers could not pull down the semidome[498] (of the apse) being afraid that it would fall and strike the columns and the 'pinnacles'[499] below and that the whole church would collapse. The eastern side which fell, also struck and broke to pieces the whole magnificent *ciborium*[500] with all its marvellous columns and the whole balustrade[501] surrounding the altar, the altar itself, the whole platform (on which) the columns (stood), and the rest.

The emperor then gave orders, and in fear and with much labour the other side was dismantled. He had (the church) rebuilt firmly and stoutly, raising it by twenty feet above its former (height), and some people said by as much as thirty. He expended much gold on it and thus its construction was imposing; (in fact), no other church in the world was believed to be more imposing than this.[502]

The year 868 (A.D. 556/7): there was a violent earthquake and the city of Botrys collapsed in this earthquake. A great cliff called "The Face of Stone"[503] broke asunder and fell into the sea.[504]

---

[498] The ms. *q̇wnk'* (from Gr. κόγχη) has the plural mark (*syāmē*), but this is sometimes used to denote a Greek word [S. Brock], and the singular object suffix appended to the verb 'pull down' suggests that this is the case here.

[499] Syr. *'ā'yātā*. Possibly the author has in mind the columns of the gallery, smaller than those on the ground level.

[500] *Ciborium* (Syr. *qīburyōn*): a canopy-like construction over the altar in a church.

[501] Syr. *qenqellē*, from Latin *cancelli*, via Greek κάγκελλα (pl.).

[502] The reconstruction of Hagia Sophia was completed in December 562; on the collapse and reconstruction of the church, see W. Emerson & R.L. Van Nice, 'Hagia Sophia: the collapse of the first dome', *Archaeology* 4 (1951), p. 94-103, and iidem, 'Hagia Sophia: the construction of the second dome and its later repairs', ibid., p. 163-171; cp. also the account of the reconstruction in Agathias V, 9, 3-5; Malalas 495/303; for the celebration of the reinauguration of the church Paul the Silentiary wrote a special poem, which is an important source of our knowledge of Hagia Sophia's architectural structure; see Mary Whitby, 'The occasion of Paul the Silentiary's *Ekphrasis* of S. Sophia', *Classical Quarterly* 35 (1985), p. 215-228; R. Macrides & P. Magdalino, 'The architecture of ekphrasis: construction and context of Paul the Silentiary's poem on Hagia Sophia', *BMGS* (1988), p. 47-82.

[503] Known as Λιθοπρόσωπον; cp. Malalas 485/291, who dates the event to the 14th indiction (= A.D. 550/551.).

[504] The collapse of Botrys was caused by the same earthquake which hit Berytus in 551, see above p. 115 & n. 489; Plassard, 'Crise', p. 14.

Thus when Botrys of Phoenicia, which is on the sea-coast, collapsed in this violent earthquake, a great cliff which was close to it, called "The Face of Stone", was suddenly shaken and cleft asunder by the force of the earthquake. A large part broke off from it and fell into the sea. The earthquake shook (the sea-bottom) at a great distance in the sea, and (the part of the rock) fell and blocked off the city for a great distance, while the sea-water entered between it (and the city. The rocks which fell into the sea) left an opening on one side (creating), as it were, a spacious and astonishing harbour. [p. 133] *Centenaria*[505] of gold and the effort of emperors would not be able to make anything similar. And thus a large and spacious harbour which (was able to) receive large ships came into being. Everybody was astonished and amazed at God's providence with whose wrath also grace is mingled.

The emperor Justinian sent much gold to all the cities which were overthrown by the earthquake, and step by step they were rebuilt and their walls repaired, but the evil will of those who survived neither changed much nor was diminished.

The year 869 (A.D. 557/8): there was gathering of the Egyptian monks on the matter of the faith in the capital. Burning with zeal, they gathered, arrived (in the capital), and talked, discussed, reproved, and persuaded. When they realized that there was no softening (on the part of their opponents) they turned back, went on board ships and departed to their country, having achieved nothing.[506]

The year 870 (A.D. 558/9): there was a great earthquake and Berytus and many (other) cities on the coast were again overthrown, as well as villages in Galilee, Arabia, and also in Palestine and in the land of the Samaritans. Also the sea turned and drew back for about two miles along the whole (coast of) Phoenicia.[507]

(Now) about the terrible horror and the tremendous sign and portent which took place in Berytus, the city of Phoenicia. For the knowledge of those who will come after (us) we wished to present in (this) commemorative record (what happened) when the earthquake took place and the cities collapsed. [p. 134]

---

[505] See above n. 242.

[506] E. Stein (*Bas-Empire*, p. 828) suggested that this account of Chalcedonian-Monophysite discussions is dated 21 years too late, i.e. it refers to the discussions of the year 532 (cp. above n. 491).

[507] Cp. above lemma 864 Sel. (p. 115, and n. 489; Malalas 485/291). It seems that PD repeats here the account of the earthquake of 551 under a different date.

Thus when the terrible earthquake suddenly took place, by God's order the sea was restrained, turned back and held; it drew back to a distance of two miles from the city of Berytus and the other cities on the coast of Phoenicia. The awesome depths of the sea were revealed and in it also many large and astonishing objects, ships which had sunk full of various merchandise, and other things became suddenly visible by the withdrawal of the sea away from the land. Those (ships) which were moored in the harbours sank and settled on the bottom, having been pounded and broken in pieces, when the sea left them and withdrew by the order of its Lord, in order that this terrible thing might move people and bring them to contrition and to repentance. At the sight of this terrible cataclysm they should have despised not only these worldly things but also their lives; but they (were) like Pharaoh, (though it was) not God long ago, as was written,[508] but Satan now (who) hardened the hearts of all of them, like Pharaoh's.

People from the cities and villages who happened to be on the shore, (moved) by the power of audacity and hardness of heart, rushed and stepped onto (the bottom of) the great sea in order to plunder the awesome treasures that had been hidden in the depths of the sea. Through the sin of covetousness disastrous to their lives, thousands of people in destructive commotion rushed into the depths of the sea and began carrying objects from among the (sunken) goods and hurried to bring them up (on land). Others seeing them carry the riches of their perdition (also) hurried with great commotion in order not to be deprived of the hidden treasures which, due to the earthquake, suddenly became uncovered. While they were rushing down into the depth, [p. 135] others were striving (to come) up and (still) others were caught in the midst, all moving to and fro confusedly in their daring.

Then by a hidden sign the terrible mass of the sea suddenly surged forth to come (back) to its former (place in) the deep and it covered and buried at the bottom of the deep all those miserable people who had rushed after the riches of the bottom of the depths. Like Pharaoh "they went down into the depths and sank like stones", as is written.[509] God brought back upon them the water of the sea, and the mass of water gushed forth and inundated all of its former (place). Whereas those who were still on the outer shore were swiftly rushing (further) down, those

[508] An allusion to Ex. 10, 20 & 27.
[509] Ex. 15, 5.

who were close to dry land, seeing that the mighty height (of the wave) of the sea was returning to its former place, fled off.

When they were fleeing, close to them, as it were, a mighty earthquake took place which shook buildings of the cities, especially in Berytus. Falling, they buried those who had escaped from the sea. None of them survived, for when the sea rose up against them from behind, in front of them the earthquake shook the city. Because of the evil of their covetousness they found themselves between two horrors. Also the priestly word was fulfilled concerning them, "Although they were rescued from the sea justice did not let them live".[510] Thus they attained utter perdition: those who had gone down after riches caused the breath of their lives to perish, and their corpses were found floating like dung on the surface of water.

Later, after the city had been overthrown, by God's order fire was lit in the ruins and burned [p. 136] and glowed amidst the ruins for two months, until even the stones caught fire and turned into lime.

After that the Lord sent down rain from the sky for three days and three nights and so the fire which had burnt in the city of Berytus was quenched. The people in it who escaped from being drowned by the sea and from the collapse of the city were exposed to (the fire) and were severely hurt and injured. They were tormented by lack of water because the aqueduct[511] of the city was destroyed.

When the merciful emperor Justinian learned (of this) he sent gold and selected men from among his (servants) and they dug out and extracted the corpses of innumerable people. Also they rebuilt the city a little.

The year 871 (A.D. 559/60): the emperor gave orders that *scholastici, grammatici*,[512] monks (and) shipowners of Alexandria, Lower and Upper Egypt should gather in the capital for a discussion concerning the faith. Now, as all the shipowners who transported wheat for the state (distribution)[513] were (true) believers, they appeared together before the emperor Justinian, who, knowing that they opposed the Council, discussed the faith with them. After a long talk they said to him:

---

[510] Acts 28, 4.

[511] The Syriac employs here the Greek loanword ἀγωγός.

[512] See nn. 336 & 334.

[513] Δημόσιον: lit. 'public treasury'; the shipowners transported *annona*, food to be distributed free among the inhabitants of the capital.

"Because we are people who struggle with the sea but are not experienced in discussions, if you command, give the orders, (and) monastic fathers, *scholastici, grammatici* [**p. 137**], who are learned in the Scriptures, as well as the nobles of the city (of Alexandria), (and monks[514] will come with us when we return next time; in this way all the matters concerning the faith may be examined and talked over."

These words pleased the emperor and he did not delay to put them in effect but immediately pronounced the firm order which allowed and commanded that they should come. (The shipowners) raised (the anchors) and sailed off. When they arrived in Alexandria, they gathered, the (emperor's) order was read and they (began to) consider among themselves (what to do). As the matter was for the sake of the true faith, they should neither neglect it, nor hesitate, nor be afraid. And thus a large group of monks and laymen gathered, boarded ships and arrived together in the capital.

In our presence they entered (the hall), bowed to the emperor and the discussion started. They were found to be prepared, so that the emperor was astonished—he who himself was experienced in discussions—and he supposed that there was neither a bishop nor any other man who could withstand him in a discussion. When he realized that they did, he dismissed them and appointed a meeting for the next day. So they gathered again and talked at length and (so it continued) for many days. And again he let the matter drop, began to dismiss them and adjourned (the discussion) for as long as one year. Thus when they realized that it seemed unlikely that he would be ready to do anything (assenting to their view), they too returned to their country having achieved nothing.

In this way all the time similar groups used to gather. [**p. 138**] Some of them stayed in the city, but through the care of the empress, resting in peace, many of the believers also lived in the palace (itself).[515] In this way they many times gathered, discussed and persuaded and obtained unreliable promises, but nothing at all would become of it.

---

[514] Added after Land's text.

[515] Another palace where many Monophysite ecclesiastics lived was the Palace of Hormisdas; John of Ephesus, *Lives, PO* 18, p. 677 [= 475]; the palace was within the precincts of the imperial Great Palace, Janin, *Constantinople*, p. 334. On the allusion to Theodora, see n. 491.

The year 872 (A.D. 560/1): a synod gathered in the capital by the order of the emperor Justinian.[516]

Among these (meetings), in the 26th year of Justinian's reign a synod of patriarchs and bishops, gathered in the capital. Having gathered, it examined and anathematized Origen, this being (prompted) by the emperor Justinian himself.[517] It also anathematized the *Three Chapters,* that is Theodore of Mopsuestia, the *Letter* of Ibas (to Maris) and the writings of Theodoret (of Cyrrhus).[518] For this reason the whole country of Italy, that is of Rome and of all its surroundings, was (set) in commotion, so that as a result Vigilius, patriarch of Rome, came to the capital. At first he showed himself to be opposed and strongly resisted the anathemas against those *Three Chapters,* but finally he did agree and accepted what this synod decided. Thereafter serious dissensions, disagreements, [p. 139] persecutions, many (other) evils and also schisms arose in all the regions of the West.

At the synod itself three patriarchs were present, which had never happened before: Eutychius of the capital, Apollinarius of Alexandria and Domninus of Antioch.[519] While Vigilius of Rome too was in the capital, he did not participate in the synod.[520] Thus all four of the

---

[516] The correct date of the synod, in fact the Fifth Ecumenical Council, is 553.

[517] The condemnation of Origen, who had lived 300 years earlier († 254), was the result of the Origenist controversy, which flared up in Palestinian monasteries, but had repercussions in the capital. One of the adherents of Origenism was Theodore Askidas, who had been favoured by Justinian until the latter condemned the doctrine in an edict of 543. Allegedly it was Theodore who, in order to take revenge against anti-Origenist adversaries in Palestine (who had been followers of the Antiochene christology), suggested to the emperor the condemnation of the Nestorian writings known later as the *Three Chapters.* This led to the convocation of the Fifth Ecumenical Council (II Constantinopolitan) in 553; A. Guillaumont, *Les 'Kephalaia Gnostica' d'Évagre le Pontique et l'histoire de l'origénisme chez les Grecs et chez les Syriens,* Paris 1962, p. 128-159; Gray, *Defense,* p. 61-73.

[518] By the condemnation of the writings of these strongly diphysite theologians, Justinian (who had condemned them already in an edict of 543/44, from the sections of which comes the term *Three Chapters*) expected—in vain—to placate the Monophysites, who had regarded the Council of Chalcedon as a victory for Nestorianism, and to win them over into the imperial church.

[519] See n. 481.

[520] Vigilius arrived in the capital in 547 rather against his will, and stayed there for 8 years. In 548 in a separate document (*Iudicatum*), he too condemned the Nestorian writings in question. Since this evoked many protests in the West, he changed his mind and revoked it, claiming that only an ecumenical council could have authority to make a judgement (as the question implied the altering of Chalcedonian pronouncements). During the council he stayed on the Asiatic shore refusing to participate and also subsequently to subscribe to the anathemas against the *Three Chapters.* He yielded however in 554 and was allowed to return to Rome, but died on the way.

patriarchs met now together, and all the other bishops and metropolitans. The council settled also many (other matters). It was not accepted by everybody, yet it was called—for the lack of (a proper) name which it did not have—the Fifth Council. It is (only) briefly that we have made known these things about it.

On the great gathering of archimandrites and other Eastern monks together with them, which took place in the capital after the death of the empress, resting in peace, in the year 874 of Alexander (A.D. 562/3).

So after the death of the (rightly) believing empress Theodora,[521] who had cared for and supported the party of the believers—she had given them accommodation, hidden them and fed them—Justinian's advisors gathered and said:

"Now, now that the empress, who is among the saints, has died, seeing that it was because she was mindful of those who do not agree with you that they were obstinate and took small account of you, (now) if you send (orders) and gather and bring them (to the capital), all of them [**p. 140**] will follow you and will accept the Council (of Chalcedon) because they have become afraid and weak."

When the emperor heard these (words) from his advisors, he became fervently convinced in his mind that it would undoubtedly be good for this to happen.

First he began to admonish our humble self, that is me, John of Asia, that through us he would send a message to gather all the monasteries of Syria, promising gifts and ordering many expenses (to be covered) for the cost of the journey, for the litter carriers, for other animals, and for everything which is useful for a journey. And when next in (his) orders he pressed us assiduously to depart and travel to the regions of Syria with great promises and numerous supplies, we began to tell him about these doubts (of ours) and (asked) for what purpose he intended to have people worthy of respect for their white hair harassed by sending (orders) that they should leave their monasteries, for (then) they would be troubled and hurt by the length of their (journey), especially as they were in different places of exile. And when he retorted opposing this (with) many (arguments), he heard again that we declined from (being) mediators and ministers in this matter. Apologizing, we said that we were afraid of murmurings and curses of the holy and perfect people

---

[521] Theodora died in 548.

such as those. Thus, disappointed with us because of our refusal and disobedience in this case, he dismissed us and let us depart.

He had another man brought who was eager (to do) it and sent him (on that mission). So (the monks) gathered and arrived in a great and numerous assembly of honourable old age, about 400 men, [p. 141] so that a great and spacious residence called (that) "of Isidore"[522] was given to them and they stayed in it. Upon their appearance most of the city flocked in order to be blessed by them.

Thus they entered before the emperor. He looked at them and was astonished at the sight of them. [He began to investigate (the truth) with them],[523] and realized that they were sound in their truth and mighty in word. (They were) not as (the advisers) had supposed, and he did not find them weak (as) they had been described to him. Thus for one entire year and more they came in and out, talking and disputing, and they neither submitted nor weakened. (Finally) they asked and were permitted (to go) and departed not having achieved anything either.

The year 875 (A.D. 564): on the 6th of the month of September at the third hour, when the Gospel was being read, there was a great, powerful and terrible earthquake. It was so powerful and violent that he who was reading the Gospel in the Great Church (in Constantinople) fell down. Many places were devastated by it. Half of the city of Cyzicus collapsed and other cities also (were damaged).[524]

The year 876 (A.D. 565): in the month of June there was again a great, mighty and violent earthquake and many cities were overthrown by it. Among them cities of Phoenicia, of Arabia and Palestine, that is[525] Berytus, Tripolis, Tyre, Sidon, Sarepta, Byblos, Antarados and other cities and villages together with their surrounding regions collapsed and were ruined. By (God's) wrath many souls [p. 142] because of (their) sins were buried in their houses, with their belongings.[526]

---

[522]A hospice (ξενῶν) built, according to Procopius (*Buildings* I, 2, 17), by Justinian and Theodora somewhere between Hagia Sophia and the Church of St. Irene; see also Janin, *Églises*, p. 572.

[523] Added after Land's text.

[524] An earthquake in 564 is otherwise unknown, and thus the lemma may be a repetition (probably drawn from another source and put under the wrong date) of the account of the earthquake of 543, also on 6 September; see above p. 73, lemma 854 & n. 342; cp. Stein, *Bas-Empire*, p. 827.

[525] In the ms. the expression 'that is' is placed before 'Arabia'.

[526] See above lemmata 864 & 870, pp. 115 & 119, and nn. 489 & 507; probably all three lemmata refer to the same earthquake of 551; Plassard, 'Crise séismique', p. 19.

The year 877 (A.D. 566): the holy Theodosius of Alexandria died on the 19th of July; he had lived in exile for 31 and a half years.

The year 879 (A.D. 568): there was a violent earthquake on the 14th of January in the night, at the dawn of Friday.[527] (It was) more violent than all the previous (earthquakes), so that both walls of the capital—the inner wall of Constantine and the outer of Theodosius—cracked and burst apart so that many large houses were ruined and became mounds over their inhabitants. The rest (of the houses) remained standing, but torn open and cracked, so that there was no building without some mark of collapse due to this earthquake. Also numerous churches were in this condition: many of them had collapsed to the ground, but some remained standing, damaged, making a terrible sight. In such a condition were those (edifices) not only in the city but in all its surroundings, together with numerous solid buildings and magnificent suburban mansions[528] of the nobles of the empire, especially in the quarter of Hebdomon[529] beyond the gate of the city, and the entire area on the sea-shore as far as the town called Rhegion.[530]

In the great catastrophe this Rhegion was totally thrown to the ground together with its wall and all its other edifices, so that one could not recognize that (once) there had been a city. Moreover, in the province of Thrace many churches and all their surroundings far and wide (collapsed). Also the great porphyry column of the emperor, [p. 143] which had stood in front of the palace in Hebdomon upon which his statue had stood, collapsed in this earthquake. By the force of the earthquake it was lifted up and turned upside down, and falling down it wedged itself eight feet into the ground.[531]

In this way cities, villages and innumerable houses were ruined and destroyed. Innumerable houses were covered over and many people

---

[527] The correct date of this earthquake is 14 December 557; cp. Malalas 488f/295f; Agathias V, 3; see also Grumel, *Chronologie*, p. 478; Downey, 'Earthquakes', p. 598, with references to parallel sources.

[528] The Syriac uses here the Greek loanword πραισίδια, from Latin *praesidium*.

[529] Hebdomon: a suburb of the capital; as the name ("the seventh") says, it was situated seven miles west of the central measuring-point in Constantinople (*milion*); see also: Janin, *Constantinople*, p. 408-411, and map 3 at the end of this volume.

[530] Rhegion: a suburb of the capital with a harbour, further to the west than Hebdomon; see also map 3.

[531] The remains of the column of Theodosius II (408–450), have been preserved, as is clear from the inscription attached, see R. Demangel, *Contribution à la topographie de l'Hebdomon*, (Recherches françaises en Turquie 3), Paris 1945, p. 33-43.

perished in this collapse. For many days thereafter they were dug out and extracted, many of them (still) alive.

An earthquake as violent and terrible as this had not occurred among all those previous ones. The earth shook and swayed hither and thither, as a tree under (the force of) winds, and was continuously shaken for twenty days and nights. The people who had been saved made heart-felt supplications and the cities which had survived were in continuous fast and prayer, begging lest they also perish by (God's) wrath, that is by the awfulness of a violent earthquake.[532] The merciful emperor, seized with sorrow, would not put the imperial crown on his head for thirty days, but when the holy feasts of Christmas and Epiphany arrived he came out from his palace without the crown and went so to the church in the sight of everybody.

The year 882 (A.D. 570/1): (the following) Chalcedonian patriarchs are famous: Anastasius of Antioch, Apollinarius of Alexandria, Vigilius of Rome, Eutychius of Constantinople, Macarius of Jerusalem.[533] (Macarius) was deposed by Eustochius,[534] but he returned later, deposed Eustochius, and sat in [p. 144] his (old) place again.[535]

Famous among the (followers) of the consubstantiality[536] are Paul, patriarch of Antioch,[537] Jacob of Pesilta,[538] and John of Amid.

The year 883 (A.D. 571/2): the deposition of Eutychius of Cons(tantino)ple took place;[539] John became (patriarch) in his stead.[540]

---

[532] Cp. Agathias V, 5, 4 for supplications in this context.

[533] Anastasius I: 559–570 & 593–598; Macarius II: Oct.-Dec. 552 and again 563/4–575. For the other patriarchs, see n. 481.

[534] Eustochius 552–563/4; ms. (in both places): 'wtkys, 'Eutychius'; for the correct name of the bishop, see Evagrius, IV, 37; Festugière's transl. p. 400.

[535] Macarius was deposed because of his Origenist views. Having condemned Origen and Origenism he was reinstated; the cause of Eustochius's deposition is not clear.

[536] Syr. bar 'ītūtā; consubstantiality of the Son 'with us' is probably meant here, the position accepted by Severans (and Chalcedonians), but rejected by more extreme Monophysites. [S. Brock]

[537] Paul the Black, see above n. 479.

[538] See above n. 419.

[539] The correct date is 565; Eutychius was deposed (and exiled) for being an opponent of the emperor's Julianist position, see the following lemma and Barker, Justinian, p. 190. On Eutychius, see Mary Whitby, 'Eutychius, Patriarch of Constantinople: an epic holy man', in Homo Viator: Classical essays for John Bramble, ed. M. Whitby, P. Hardy, M. Whitby, Bristol 1987, p. 297-308; Av. Cameron, 'Eustratius' Life of the Patriarch Eutychius and the Fifth Ecumenical Council', in KAΘHΓHTPI: Essays presented to Joan Hussey, 1988, p. 225-47; eadem, 'Models of the Past in the Late Sixth Century: The Life of the Patriarch Eutychius', in Reading the Past in Late Antiquity, ed. by G. Clarke, Rushcutters Bay (Australia) 1990, p. 205-223.

The year 884 (A.D. 572/3): the emperor erred and left the orthodox faith. He fell into the fanciful error of the Phantasiasts, into which also the miserable Julian had previously fallen. Perhaps it is not shameful to say (here) that he went much beyond (Julian), saying:
"The body of our Lord is not corruptible, neither did it originate from a corruptible (one), namely because also the body of the Virgin Mary, who gave him birth, was not corruptible or capable of suffering either." And that, "Whoever says that the body of our Lord, or that of the Blessed Mary, was passible or corruptible falls in error".

And so he started composing documents and sent (an edict) to all the patriarchs demanding that they gather every bishop under their sway so that every one (of them) should subscribe to the edict he had composed. He gave a strict order that whoever would not subscribe and agree should be mercilessly sent off into exile. While his threat was severe and harsh his end approached rapidly and both he and his threat perished, together with his heresy.[541]

The year 885 (A.D. 574): one day in the month of May a great and terrible spear of fire appeared in the northern quarter (of the sky). Its beginning, that is its lower end, sprang from a star, and it was very long. First, it was seen to be rising towards the middle of night, but subsequently, in the (following) evening, it appeared to bow its head towards the east [p. 145] and gradually it became straight and stood upright, like a great lance. Later, towards the morning, it bent again and leant toward the western quarter. For two or three months it thus rose and was visible all the time. Then it turned and appeared again in the southern quarter, but on the death of the emperor Justinian it disappeared and was seen no more.[542]

We brought these things into the record of commemorated events for (our) successors in order that, by reading (it), they might reflect over their final consummation.

---

[540] John III Scholasticus, 565–577.

[541] On the emperor's aphthartodocetism, see F. Loofs, 'Die "Ketzerei" Justinians', in *Harnack-Ehrung: Beiträge zur Kirchengeschichte ... Adolf von Harnack ... dargebracht*, Leipzig 1921, p. 232-248; Barker, *Justinian*, p. 189-191; M. van Esbroeck, 'The Aphthartodocetic Edict of Justinian I and its Armenian Background', *Studia Patristica*: Proceedings of the Twelfth International Conference on Patristic Studies, Oxford 1995 (forthcoming).

[542] Grumel, *Chronologie*, p. 470 (year 565 ?); Schove, *Eclipses*, p. 292 (year 574).

The year 885 (A.D. 573/4): the emperor Justinian died[543] and Justinian,[544] the son of his sister, began to reign.

The year 889 (A.D. 577/8): Mar Jacob of Pesilta died and Mar John bi(shop) of Amid; in his stead came the holy Mar Cyriacus. In Edessa, instead of Mar Jacob, Mar Severus came, and instead of Paul of Antioch, the holy Mar Peter.[545]

---

[543] Justinian died on 15 November 565.

[544] I.e. Justin II, 565–578.

[545] For Jacob of Pesilta, titular metropolitan of Edessa, see n. 419 the Amidene bishops: C. Karalewsky, 'Amid', *DHGE* 2 (1914), col. 1240; notwithstanding PD's statement that Severus succeeded Jacob Baradaeus as the bishop of Edessa, the former was a Chalcedonian, d. 603 (Segal, *Edessa*, p. 114); Paul: see n. 479 Peter of Callinicus: 581–591.

GENERAL INDEX

References are to the pages of this volume, either to text or notes without distinction.

Abbreviations: b. - bishop; e. - emperor; k. - king; p. - patriarch; m. - monk, mon. - monastery;

Aaron, b. of Arsamosata 6, 20
Abarne (Çermak), warm springs of 3f
Abraham, b. of Anzitene 44
Abraham (Abram, Abraha, Ella Abreha), k. of Himyar 63, 99
Abraham, son of Euphrasius, priest 53
Abraham Bar Kaili, b. of Amid 29, 32, 34f, 37, 39, 103
Acacian schism 17
Acacius, p. of Antioch 2
Acacius, p. of Constantinople 1
Acts of Pilate 8
Adad, see Andug
Addai, *sāʿōrā*, of the Mon. of Pardaisa 44
Adulis, see Auzalis
Africa 50, 82
Agapetus, p. of Rome 98
Agathias 73, 115, 118, 126
Agathodoros, b. of Isba 20
agentes in rebus 30
Ahudemmeh, catholicos in Persia 99
Akhsenaia, see Philoxenus of Mabbug
Akoimetai, monks 8
Aksundon 50
Aleppo 22, 53
Alexander the Great xxx
Alexander, b. of Abila 19
Alexander, b. of Khonokhora 20
Alexandria xxvi, xxix, 1f, 16f, 19, 32, 52, 64, 77, 80, 92f, 98, 100, 102, 108f, 11, 121f
Amantius, *praepositus s. cubibuli* 18f
Amantius, *stratelates* 114
Amid xxf, xxvi, 5, 7, 19, 29-33, 37-39, 102-104, 106f, 111
    church Beth Shurla 32
Amidenes 27, 32
Anastasius, e. xvf, 2f, 5, 7, 12f, 15–17, 48, 700
Anastasius, p. of Antioch 127

Axumites 50

Baalbek (Heliopolis) 116f
Babylonia 6
Banū Ghassān, see Ghassanids
Bar Hebraeus xix
Bar Kaili, see Abraham Bar Kaili
Bar Sahde, b. in Persia 100
Bar Sauma, b. of Nisibis 12
Bar Sauma, archimandrite 12
Basil, p. of Antioch 2
Batnae 27
Baysar 63
Belisarius 30, 82
Berytus 5, 118-121, 125
Beth Ar(a)baye 29, 99
Beth Aramaye 6
Beth Shur(l)a 32
Bible, Old Testament:
  Gen *41,18-21* 84
  Ex *10,20* 120; *15,5* 120
  Num *16,30.33* 66; *20,17* 14
  2 Kings *18,4* 14; *23,4* 14; *23,14* 14; *23,19* 14
  Job *5,13* 97
  Ps *36,6* 87; *107,27* 79, 97; *119,137* 90
  Prov *8,13* 98
  Is *1,28* 80; *6,13* 82; *24, 3f* 81; *24,6* 75, 81; *24,19f* 82; *29,14* 97; *51,17.22* 96
  Jer *9,1* 85, 102; *9,12* 107; *9,17* 76; *9,21* 76; *11,20* 26; *14,7* 90; *17,10* 26; *18,11* 35; *20,12* 26; *22,19* 71, 93, 96; *50,41* 82
  Lam *2,11* 75
  Ezek *21,3* 76
  Dan *1,12.16* 15; *3,10-23* 39; *4,24* 41
  Hos *14,10* 107
  Joel *1,9* 75; *1,13* 75
  Hab *3,12* 90
Bible, New Testament:
  Mt *10,32* 60; *11,15* 107; *13,9* 107; *16,24* 28; *18,7* 21; *19,21* 115; *16,41* 107
  Mk *8,34* 28

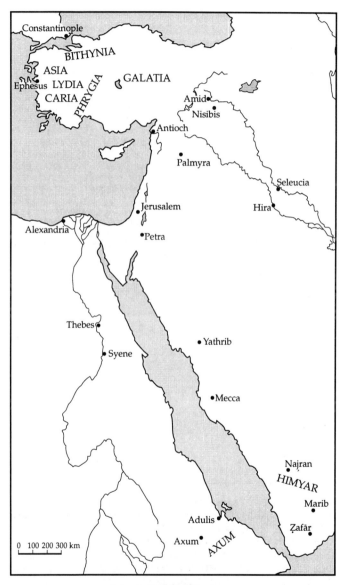

Constantinople

BITHYNIA

ASIA
Ephesus LYDIA
CARIA

PHRYGIA

GALATIA

Amid
Nisibis

Antioch

Palmyra

Seleucia

Jerusalem

Hira

Alexandria

Petra

Thebes

Syene

Yathrib

Mecca

Najran

HIMYAR

Marib

Adulis

Zafār

Axum

AXUM

0 100 200 300 km

Map 1: The Near East

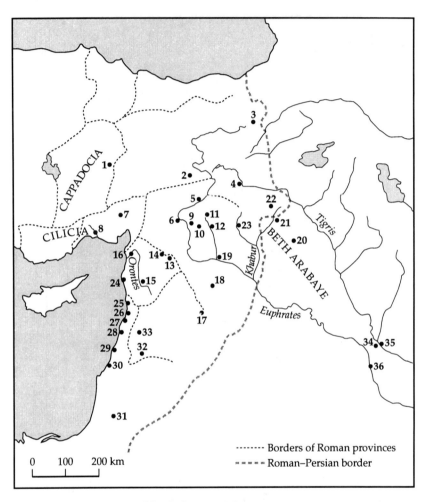

Map 2: Syria and Mesopotamia
1: CAESAREA; **2**: MELITENE; **3**: THEODOSIOPOLIS; **4**: AMID; **5**: SAMOSATA;
6: ZEUGMA; **7**: ANAZARBOS; **8**: TARSUS; **9**: BIRTHA; **10**: BATNAE; **11**:
EDESSA; **12**: HARRAN; **13**: GABBULA; **14**: ALEPPO; **15**: APAMAEA; **16**:
ANTIOCH; **17**: PALMYRA; **18**: SERGIOPOLIS; **19**: CALLINICUS; **20**: SINJAR; **21**:
NISIBIS; **22**: DARA; **23**: RESHAINA; **24**: LAODICEA; **25**: ANTARADOS; **26**:
TRIPOLIS; **27**: BYBLOS; **28**: BERYTUS; **29**: SIDON; **30**: TYRE; **31**: JERUSALEM;
32: DAMASCUS; **33**: BAALBEK; **34**: SELEUCIA; **35**: CTESIPHON; **36**: HIRA

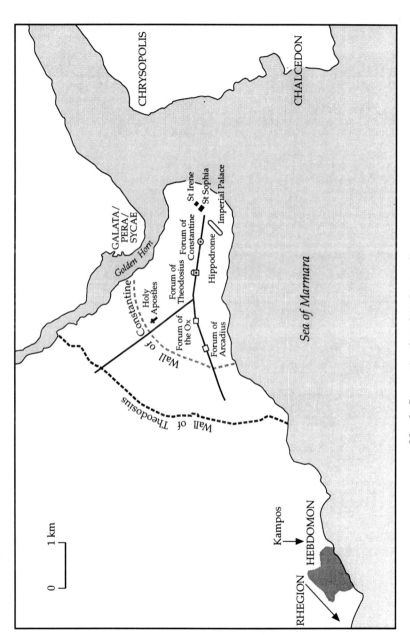

Map 3: Constantinople and its Surroundings

TRANSLATED TEXTS FOR HISTORIANS
Published Titles

Gregory of Tours: Life of the Fathers
Translated with an introduction by EDWARD JAMES
Volume 1: 176pp., 2nd edition 1991, ISBN 0 85323 327 6

The Emperor Julian: Panegyric and Polemic
Claudius Mamertinus, John Chrysostom, Ephrem the Syrian
edited by SAMUEL N. C. LIEU
Volume 2: 153pp., 2nd edition 1989, ISBN 0 85323 376 4

Pacatus: Panegyric to the Emperor Theodosius
Translated with an introduction by C. E. V. NIXON
Volume 3: 122pp., 1987, ISBN 0 85323 076 5

Gregory of Tours: Glory of the Martyrs
Translated with an introduction by RAYMOND VAN DAM
Volume 4: 150pp., 1988, ISBN 0 85323 236 9

Gregory of Tours: Glory of the Confessors
Translated with an introduction by RAYMOND VAN DAM
Volume 5: 127pp., 1988, ISBN 0 85323 226 1

The Book of Pontiffs (*Liber Pontificalis* to AD 715)
Translated with an introduction by RAYMOND DAVIS
Volume 6: 175pp., 1989, ISBN 0 85323 216 4

Chronicon Paschale 284–628 AD
Translated with notes and introduction by
MICHAEL WHITBY AND MARY WHITBY
Volume 7: 280pp., 1989, ISBN 0 85323 096 X

Iamblichus: On the Pythagorean Life
Translated with notes and introduction by GILLIAN CLARK
Volume 8: 144pp., 1989, ISBN 0 85323 326 8

Conquerors and Chroniclers of Early-Medieval Spain
Translated with notes and introduction by KENNETH BAXTER WOLF
Volume 9: 176pp., 1991, ISBN 0 85323 047 1

Victor of Vita: History of the Vandal Persecution
Translated with notes and introduction by JOHN MOORHEAD
Volume 10: 112pp., 1992, ISBN 0 85323 426 4

The Goths in the Fourth Century
by PETER HEATHER AND JOHN MATTHEWS
Volume 11: 224pp., 1992, ISBN 0 85323 426 4

Cassiodorus: *Variae*
Translated with notes and introduction by S. J. B. BARNISH
Volume 12: 260pp., 1992, ISBN 0 85323 436 1

The Lives of the Eighth-Century Popes (*Liber Pontificalis*)
Translated with an introduction and commentary by RAYMOND DAVIS
Volume 13: 288pp., 1992, ISBN 0 85323 018 8

Eutropius: Breviarium
Translated with an introduction and commentary by H. W. BIRD
Volume 14: 248pp., 1993, ISBN 0 85323 208 3

The Seventh Century in the West-Syrian Chronicles
Introduced, translated and annotated by ANDREW PALMER
including two Seventh-century Syriac apocalyptic texts
Introduced, translated and annotated by SEBASTIAN BROCK
with added annotation and an historical introduction by ROBERT HOYLAND
Volume 15: 368pp., 1993, ISBN 0 85323 238 5

Vegetius: Epitome of Military Science
Translated with notes and introduction by N. P. MILNER
Volume 16: 208pp., 2nd edition 1996, ISBN 0 85323 910 X

Aurelius Victor: De Caesaribus
Translated with an introduction and commentary by H. W. BIRD
Volume 17: 264pp., 1994, ISBN 0-85323-218-0

Bede: On the Tabernacle
Translated with notes and introduction by ARTHUR G. HOLDER
Volume 19: 176pp., 1994, ISBN 0-85323-368-3

The Lives of the Ninth-Century Popes (*Liber Pontificalis*)
Translated with an introduction and commentary by RAYMOND DAVIS
Volume 20: 360pp., 1995, ISBN 0-85323-479-5

Bede: On the Temple
Translated with notes by SEÁN CONNOLLY,
introduction by JENNIFER O'REILLY
Volume 21: 192pp., 1995, ISBN 0-85323-049-8

Pseudo-Dionysius of Tel-Mahre: *Chronicle*, Part III
Translated with notes and introduction by WITOLD WITAKOWSKI
Volume 22: 192pp., 1995, ISBN 0-85323-760-3

Venantius Fortunatus: Personal and Political Poems
Translated with notes and introduction by JUDITH GEORGE
Volume 23: 192pp., 1995, ISBN 0-85323-179-6

Donatist Martyr Stories: The Church in Conflict in Roman North Africa
Translated with notes and introduction by MAUREEN A. TILLEY
Volume 24: 144pp., 1996, ISBN 0 85323 931 2

For full details of Translated Texts for Historians, including prices and or'
information, please write to the following:
All countries, except the USA and Canada: Liverpool University Press.
Abercromby Square, Liverpool, L69 3BX, UK (*Tel* 0151-794 2233, F^
USA and Canada: University of Pennsylvania Press, Blockley H
Philadelphia, PA 19104-6097, USA (*Tel* (215) 898-6264, *Fax* (.